2,000 YEARS OF
SPIRITUAL WARFARE

**Recorded Accounts Of Demonic Activity
From The 1st To The 21st Centuries**

Daniel R. Jennings, M.Sc.

SEAN
MULTIMEDIA

2000 Years Of Spiritual Warfare: Recorded Accounts Of Demonic Activity From The 1ˢᵗ To The 21ˢᵗ Centuries

Copyright © 2016 by Daniel R. Jennings

Jennings, Daniel, R. 1977-
    2000 Years Of Spiritual Warfare: Recorded Accounts Of Demonic Activity From The 1ˢᵗ To The 21ˢᵗ Centuries.

ISBN-10: 1505579015
ISBN-13: 978-1505579017

Unless otherwise noted, Scripture quotations are from the King James Version, either modernized by the author or in their original form, or from the World English Bible and sometimes are a combination of the two.

οτι ουκ αδυνατησει παρα του θεου παν ρημα

Lucas I.XXXVII

TABLE OF CONTENTS

Introduction

"For we wrestle not against flesh and blood, but against principalities, against powers, against the rulers of the darkness of this world, against spiritual wickedness in high places."

-Paul, Ephesians 6:12

Man, from earliest times, has understood the world from a dualistic point of view. There is the visible and tangible world that is detected by sight, sound, hearing, smell and touch. But then man has curiously always believed in an invisible world that was at times detectable by these five senses, but usually operated undetected and hidden from mankind. This dualistic belief has historically been held by all people in all places at all times. Hence, we find descriptions of it in ancient Sumerian, Egyptian, Babylonian, Assyrian, Greek, Roman, Aztec, Mayan and Chinese literature dating back to the beginning of human writing.

Since the time of the Renaissance many have dismissed the idea of an invisible world relegating it to the level of naïve superstition. The incidents that were once thought to have been caused by unseen spirits began to be explained away by more "rational" and scientific explanations. As a result a belief in and desire to understand the role that invisible spiritual beings play in our world is greatly diminishing. Even Seminaries have begun to teach that spiritual warfare has no place or purpose in modern ministry. The Bible says "faith comes by hearing (Rom 10:17)" and so whatever we hear influences what we believe. If we hear that demons do not exist, it will influence us to believe that they do not. On the contrary, if we hear (and read) stories of how Christians have experienced unclean spirits throughout history it will build up our faith in the invisible world. That is the purpose of this book. This book attempts to collect various recorded incidents in which it is believed that the *invisible world* momentarily became *visible* demonstrating that demons do exist and influence humanity.

While in the research phase of this book I was able to find an ample supply of material available on this subject. Making it my goal to compile recorded incidents in which humans experienced an interaction with wicked spiritual forces I felt early on that it was best to set some parameters.

First, while there seemed to be a multitude of recorded events I have tried, for the most part, to include only those stories which were either eyewitness accounts or in which the author interviewed an eyewitness. Anything beyond this has a tendency to become exaggerated.

Secondly, though there have been many spiritual warfare cases recorded by those who did not embrace the Christian faith, it was decided that this book would only focus on those cases which involved Christians as this author has seen no evidence to suggest that any other philosophy or practice has been able to exercise the power over unclean spirits that those who have embraced the message of Christ have.

Thirdly, that being the case, I have focused most of the narratives listed to being taken from the time of Jesus up until the present, the only exception being that references will be made to the few Old Testament passages which refer to demonic activity. However, it must be noted that God's people in the Old Testament were generally not given power over demons as they are in the New Testament era (Mt 10:8, Mk 16:17). Except for those given a special anointing in the Old Testament (such as Moses and Elijah) God's people as a whole have only been given power over demons for roughly the last 2,000 years. Hence, the title of this work is *2000 Years Of Spiritual Warfare*.

With that being said I now present to you recorded accounts of demonic activity from the 1st to the 21st centuries.

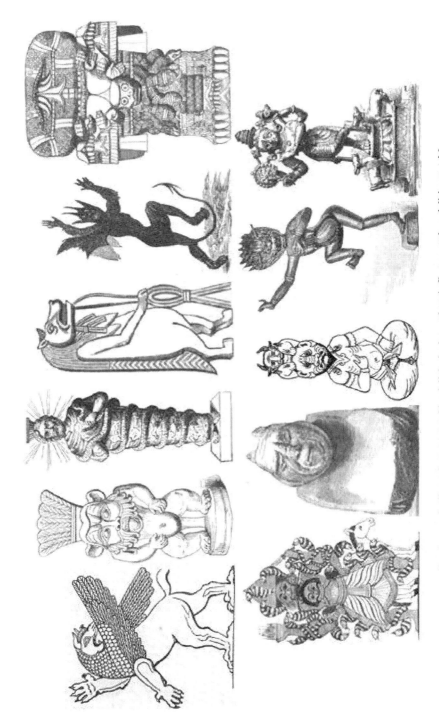

All cultures believe in a race of invisible beings that influence the visible world

3

Accounts From The Scriptures
(Up To The 1st Century)

Accounts Of Demonic Activity Causing Physical Illnesses

Behold, there was a woman who had a spirit of infirmity eighteen years, and she was bent over, and could in no way straighten herself up. When Jesus saw her, he called her, and said to her, "Woman, you are freed from your infirmity." He laid his hands on her, and immediately she stood up straight, and glorified God. And the ruler of the synagogue answered with indignation, because that Jesus had healed on the Sabbath day...Therefore the Lord answered him..."Ought not this woman, being a daughter of Abraham, **whom Satan had bound eighteen long years, be freed from this bondage** on the Sabbath day?" (*Luke 13:11-16*)

As they went out, behold, a mute man who was demon[1] possessed was brought to him. When the demon was cast out, the mute man

---

[1] Much confusion exists as to what exactly a "demon" is. The Greek word for demon (*daimon*) is believed to have been derived from *daiesthai* which means to distribute. The Greek writers used *daimon* to refer both to a god and also to lesser beings that were on a level above humans but below a god. According to the Septuagint translation of Deuteronomy 32:8 when God "divided the nations...he set the bounds of the nations according to the number of the angels of God." This has been interpreted to mean that each nation is assigned angels to oversee it (see Da 10:13). It is believed that these angels, instead of administering justice and righteously looking over the humans that they had been entrusted to take care of, abused, neglected, incited fear into their subjects, and ultimately ended up encouraging them to worship them as gods (De 32:17, Gn 6:1-4). Some believe that Psalm 82:1-8 is describing the judgment of God upon these angels where it is pronounced by God that as punishment they will be sentenced to death (Ps 82:7). Peter and Jude inform us that these angels were imprisoned in hell (2Pe 2:4; Jd 1:6-7). According to James 2:26 death is the separation of the spirit from the body. It would seem that the judgment of these angels was to have their bodies locked up in hell while their spirits were free to roam the earth, wherein they seek another body to possess (Mt 12:43-45).

This description fits perfectly with the Greek usage of the word *daimon* to refer to gods (i.e. the angels who incited mankind to worship them as gods) and to spiritual beings on a level below a god (i.e. an angel). The etymology of *daimon* being traced back to a word meaning to distribute seems to be an apparent reference to God's distributing of the nations to these angelic beings.

The punishment of the angels placed over the nations should not be confused with the casting to the earth of Satan (Re 12:7-13) which appears to have been a separate event. It is unclear whether Satan should be referred to as a

4

spoke. The multitudes marveled, saying, "Nothing like this has ever been seen in Israel!" (*Matthew 9:32-33*)

Then one possessed by a demon, blind and mute, was brought to him and he healed him, so that the blind and mute man both spoke and saw. (*Matthew 12:22*)

He was casting out a demon, and it was mute. It happened, when the demon had gone out, the mute man spoke; and the multitudes marveled. (*Luke 11:14*)

One of the multitude answered, "Teacher, I brought to you my son, who has a mute spirit; and wherever it seizes him, it throws him down, and he foams at the mouth, and grinds his teeth, and wastes away. I asked your disciples to cast it out, and they weren't able." He answered him, "Unbelieving generation, how long shall I be with you? How long shall I bear with you? Bring him to me." They brought him to him, and when he saw him, immediately the spirit convulsed him, and he fell on the ground, wallowing and foaming at the mouth. He asked his father, "How long has it been since this has come to him?" He said, "From childhood.[2] Often it has cast him both into the fire and into the water, to destroy him.[3] But if you can do anything, have compassion on us, and help us." Jesus said to him, "If you can believe, all things are possible to him who believes." Immediately the father of the child cried out with tears, "I believe. Help my unbelief!" When Jesus saw that a multitude came running together, he rebuked the unclean spirit, saying to him, "You mute and deaf spirit, I command you, come out of him, and never enter him again!" Having cried out, and convulsed greatly, it came out of him. The boy became like one dead; so much that most of them said, "He is dead." But Jesus took him by the hand, and raised him up; and he arose. When he had come into the house, his disciples asked him privately, "Why couldn't we

---

"demon" in the sense that he is now a disembodied spirit but because of his close association with them (Mk 3:21-27, Lk 10:17-20, 11:14-22) I have included references to him in this section. Much would depend upon when his fall took place, when he was cast out of heaven and what kind of discipline he received at that time. There seems to be a variety of opinions on this subject.

[2] Note that even children can be demonized.

[3] Note the intent of the spirit to injure and apparently bring about the death of the individual either through third degree burning or drowning.

cast it out?" He said to them, "This kind can come out by nothing, except by prayer and fasting."[4] (*Mark 9:17-29*)[5]

Again there was a day when the sons of God came to present themselves before the Lord, and Satan came also among them to present himself before the Lord. And the Lord said unto Satan, "From where did you come?" And Satan answered the Lord, and said, "From going to and fro in the earth, and from walking up and down in it." And the Lord said unto Satan, "Have you considered my servant Job, that there is none like him in the earth, a perfect and an upright man, one that feareth God, and eschews evil? And still he holds fast his integrity, although you moved me against him, to destroy him without cause." And Satan answered the Lord, and said, Skin for skin, yea, all that a man has will he give for his life. But put forth your hand now, and touch his bone and his flesh, and he will curse you to your face." And the Lord said unto Satan, "Behold, he is in your hand; but save his life." So Satan went forth from the presence of the Lord, and smote Job with sore boils from the sole of his foot unto his crown. And he took him a potsherd to scrape himself withal; and he sat down among the ashes. (*Job 2:1-8*)

Christ Heals The Gadarene Demoniac

---

[4] This point needs to be emphasized. The church has forgotten the need to (as evidenced above) and Jesus' instruction that after his ascension his disciples will fast (Mk 2:18-20). Mysteriously, many of the newer translations have opted to leave out the clause on fasting, translating this verse as "*This kind can come out only by prayer*".

[5] Compare the parallel accounts in Matthew 17:14-21 and Luke 9:37-42.

Accounts Of Demonic Activity Causing
Insanity, Mental Illness, Anxiety And Erratic Behavior

They arrived at the country of the Gadarenes, which is opposite Galilee. When Jesus stepped ashore, a certain man out of the city who had demons for a long time met him. He wore no clothes, and didn't live in a house, but in the tombs. When he saw Jesus, he cried out, and fell down before him, and with a loud voice said, "What do I have to do with you, Jesus, you Son of the Most High God? I beg you, don't torment me!"[6] For Jesus was commanding the unclean spirit to come out of the man. For the unclean spirit had often seized the man. He was kept under guard, and bound with chains and fetters. Breaking the bands apart, he was driven by the demon into the desert. Jesus asked him, "What is your name?" He said, "Legion," for many demons had entered into him.[7] They begged him that he would not command them to go into the abyss.[8] Now there was there a herd of many pigs feeding on the mountain, and they begged him that he would allow them to enter into those. He allowed them. The demons came out from the man, and entered into the pigs, and the herd rushed down the steep bank into the lake, and were drowned. When those who fed them saw what had happened, they fled, and told it in the city and in the country. People went out to see what had happened. They came to Jesus, and found the man from whom the demons had gone out, sitting at Jesus' feet, clothed and in his right mind; and they were afraid. Those who saw it told them how he who had been possessed by demons was healed. All the people of the surrounding country of the Gadarenes asked him to depart from them, for they were very much afraid. He entered into the boat, and returned. But the man

---

[6] An example of clairvoyant (psychic) powers--This individual does not appear to have ever had any previous contact with Jesus in order to have been able to recognize him, yet somehow, he knew who he was. The next sentence indicates the true source of the knowledge.

[7] A legion was a Roman military formation which could consist of anywhere from 4,200 to 6,000 men.

[8] Apparently the place referred to in 2Peter 2:4 where it is noted that "if God spared not the angels that sinned, but cast them down to hell, and delivered them into chains of darkness, to be reserved unto judgment..." which would equate "abyss" with hell. It is the same Greek word used to refer to the "bottomless" pit in Revelation 9:1-11 which seems to indicate a releasing of demons from their subterranean prison and the place where Satan is cast during the millennium (Re 20:1-3).

from whom the demons had gone out begged him that he might go with him, but Jesus sent him away, saying, "Return to your house, and declare what great things God has done for you." He went his way, proclaiming throughout the whole city what great things Jesus had done for him.[9] (*Luke 8:26-39*)

Now Yahweh's Spirit departed from Saul, and an evil spirit from Yahweh troubled him. Saul's servants said to him, "See now, an evil spirit from God troubles you. Let our lord now command your servants who are in front of you to seek out a man who is a skillful player on the harp. Then when the evil spirit from God is on you, he will play with his hand, and you will be well." Saul said to his servants, "Provide me now a man who can play well, and bring him to me." Then one of the young men answered, and said, "Behold, I have seen a son of Jesse the Bethlehemite who is skillful in playing, a mighty man of valor, a man of war, prudent in speech, and a handsome person; and Yahweh is with him." Therefore Saul sent messengers to Jesse, and said, "Send me David your son, who is with the sheep." Jesse took a donkey loaded with bread, and a container of wine, and a young goat, and sent them by David his son to Saul. David came to Saul, and stood before him. He loved him greatly; and he became his armor bearer. Saul sent to Jesse, saying, "Please let David stand before me; for he has found favor in my sight." When the spirit from God was on Saul, David took the harp, and played with his hand; so Saul was refreshed, and was well, and the evil spirit departed from him.[10] (*1Samuel 16:14-23*)

As they came, when David returned from the slaughter of the Philistine, the women came out of all the cities of Israel, singing

---

[9] Compare the parallel accounts in Matthew 8:28-34 and Mark 5:1-20.

[10] A number of things can be learned from this passage. First, the passage does not clearly state how the evil spirit troubled Saul but it seems to be implied that it was some kind of mental trouble (anxiety). Secondly, notice that God uses evil spirits as a discipline which demonstrates that anything a demon does is only with the permission of God. As the servants correctly pointed out, it was "an evil spirit **from** God..." demonstrating that God uses the evil spirits to accomplish His purposes in the earth. The idea that Satan and demons are just out running free, doing whatever they please is a gross misconception based on a misunderstanding of the sovereignty of God in all of the earth's affairs. Thirdly, notice the power of Christian music to dispel demons.

8

and dancing, to meet king Saul, with tambourines, with joy, and with instruments of music. The women sang to one another as they played, and said, "Saul has slain his thousands, and David his ten thousands." Saul was very angry, and this saying displeased him. He said, "They have ascribed to David ten thousands, and to me they have ascribed only thousands. What can he have more but the kingdom?" Saul watched David from that day and forward. On the next day, an evil spirit from God came mightily on Saul, and he prophesied in the middle of the house.[11] David played with his hand, as he did day by day. Saul had his spear in his hand; and Saul threw the spear, for he said, "I will pin David even to the wall!" David escaped from his presence twice. Saul was afraid of David, because Yahweh was with him, and had departed from Saul.[12] (*1Samuel 18:6-12*)

An evil spirit from Yahweh was on Saul, as he sat in his house with his spear in his hand; and David was playing with his hand. Saul sought to pin David to the wall with the spear; but he slipped away out of Saul's presence, and he stuck the spear into the wall. David fled, and escaped that night. Saul sent messengers to David's house, to watch him, and to kill him in the morning. Michal, David's wife, told him, saying, "If you don't save your life tonight, tomorrow you will be killed." So Michal let David down through the window. He went away, fled, and escaped. (*1Samuel 19:9-12*)

---

[11] Notice that demons can give people the ability to prophesy, a clear warning that we must test all prophecies and never forget that the source of a prophetic word may not be the Holy Spirit (1Th 5:20-21, 1Jn 4:1). Also, take note that Saul had at one time had the real Spirit of God but lost Him (1Sam 16:14) and, therefore, it must be remembered that just because a person has given a legitimate prophecy in the past this is no guarantee that all subsequent prophecies will be from God.

[12] Note how the evil spirit motivated Saul to act erratically based upon his fears. In my observation the world is filled with people who are behaving erratically and sinful because of fears (such as an unhealthy fear of germs or the fear of losing their job which leads them to sabotage their co-workers) and this fear often becomes so controlling that these people are diagnosed as having mental illness. Fear like this comes from Satan, not the Holy Spirit (Ro 8:15) and for people who are experiencing this, the solution is more spiritual than psychiatric.

Saul Afflicted By An Evil Spirit

Accounts Of Demonic Activity Giving
People Clairvoyant And Prophetic Abilities

In the synagogue there was a man who had a spirit of an unclean demon,[13] and he cried out with a loud voice, saying, "Ah! what have we to do with you, Jesus of Nazareth? Have you come to destroy us? I know you who you are: the Holy One of God!"[14] Jesus rebuked him, saying, "Be silent, and come out of him!"

---

[13] People are often confused as to the difference between a "spirit" and a "demon". As explained in a previous footnote, the "spirits" are the disembodied spirits of the angels who sinned against God in the overseeing of the nations that were entrusted to them. Their punishment was to experience death (i.e. the separation of their spirit from their bodies). The wage of sin is death for everyone, whether they are men or angels (Ro 6:23). Since they are really one and the same (demons and spirits) these two words are sometimes used interchangeably (compare Mt 15:22 with Mk 7:25).

To this we might add a few points on the Greek word for "spirit". The Greek word in the New Testament translated as "spirit" is *pneuma* and it carries with it the idea of wind or breath, implying that unclean spirits have the same consistency as air (i.e. not solid but rather gaseous and able to change their shape or move through cracks and crevices).

[14] As in the case of the Gadarene demoniac this individual appears to possess knowledge of Jesus' identity that he otherwise would not have known.

10

When the demon had thrown him down in their midst, he came out of him, having done him no harm.[15] (*Luke 4:33-35*)

It happened, as we were going to prayer, that a certain girl having a spirit of divination met us, who brought her masters much gain by fortune telling. Following Paul and us, she cried out, "These men are servants of the Most High God, who proclaim to us the way of salvation!"[16] She was doing this for many days. But Paul, becoming greatly annoyed, turned and said to the spirit, "I command you in the name of Jesus Christ to come out of her!" It came out that very hour. (*Acts 16:16-18*)

On the next day, an evil spirit from God came mightily on Saul, and he prophesied in the middle of the house. (*1Samuel 18:10*)

Then the king of Israel gathered the prophets together, about four hundred men, and said to them, "Should I go against Ramoth Gilead to battle, or should I refrain?"

They said, "Go up; for the Lord will deliver it into the hand of the king."

But Jehoshaphat said, "Isn't there here a prophet of Yahweh, that we may inquire of him?"

The king of Israel said to Jehoshaphat, "There is yet one man by whom we may inquire of Yahweh, Micaiah the son of Imlah; but I hate him, for he does not prophesy good concerning me, but evil."[17]

Jehoshaphat said, "Don't let the king say so."

Then the king of Israel called an officer, and said, "Quickly get Micaiah the son of Imlah."

Now the king of Israel and Jehoshaphat the king of Judah were sitting each on his throne, arrayed in their robes, in an open place at the entrance of the gate of Samaria; and all the prophets

---

[15] I would also like to draw attention to the fact that this individual was "**in** the synagogue". How often are demoniacally inspired or controlled individuals found *inside* of the church, even in places of leadership?

[16] Notice that this again demonstrates that people who are demon possessed will prophesy the truth about Christ and that just possessing a prophetic gift is no indicator that the gift is legitimate.

[17] In this narrative Micaiah is shown to be the only true prophet out of the roughly 400, demonstrating that the true prophets are generally always outnumbered by the false ones.

were prophesying before them. Zedekiah the son of Chenaanah made himself horns of iron, and said, "Yahweh says, 'With these you will push the Syrians, until they are consumed.'" All the prophets prophesied so, saying, "Go up to Ramoth Gilead, and prosper; for Yahweh will deliver it into the hand of the king."[18]

The messenger who went to call Micaiah spoke to him, saying, "See now, the prophets declare good to the king with one mouth. Please let your word be like the word of one of them, and speak good."

Micaiah said, "As Yahweh lives, what Yahweh says to me, that I will speak."

When he had come to the king, the king said to him, "Micaiah, shall we go to Ramoth Gilead to battle, or shall we forbear?"

He answered him, "Go up and prosper; and Yahweh will deliver it into the hand of the king." The king said to him, "How many times do I have to adjure you that you speak to me nothing but the truth in Yahweh's name?"

He said, "I saw all Israel scattered on the mountains, as sheep that have no shepherd. Yahweh said, 'These have no master. Let them each return to his house in peace.'"

The king of Israel said to Jehoshaphat, "Didn't I tell you that he would not prophesy good concerning me, but evil?"

Micaiah said, "Therefore hear Yahweh's word. I saw Yahweh sitting on his throne, and all the army of heaven standing by him on his right hand and on his left. Yahweh said, 'Who will entice Ahab, that he may go up and fall at Ramoth Gilead?' One said one thing; and another said another.

A spirit came out and stood before Yahweh, and said, 'I will entice him.'

Yahweh said to him, 'How?'

He said, 'I will go out and will be **a lying spirit in the mouth of all his prophets**.'

He said, 'You will entice him, and will also prevail. Go out and do so.' Now therefore, behold, **Yahweh has put a lying spirit in the mouth of all these your prophets**; and Yahweh has spoken evil concerning you."

---

[18] Take notice that false prophets, again, are shown to be speaking in the name of the one true God and ascribing power and authority to Him.

12

Then Zedekiah the son of Chenaanah came near, and struck Micaiah on the cheek, and said, "Which way did Yahweh's Spirit go from me to speak to you?"

Micaiah said, "Behold, you will see on that day, when you go into an inner room to hide yourself."

The king of Israel said, "Take Micaiah, and carry him back to Amon the governor of the city, and to Joash the king's son. Say, 'Thus says the king, 'Put this fellow in the prison, and feed him with bread of affliction and with water of affliction, until I come in peace.'"

Micaiah said, "If you return at all in peace, Yahweh has not spoken by me." He said, "Listen, all you people!"[19] (*1Kings 22:6-28*)

Now concerning spiritual things, brothers, I don't want you to be ignorant. You know that when you were Gentiles, you were led away to those mute idols, however you might be led. Therefore I make known to you that no man speaking by God's Spirit says, "Jesus is accursed." No one can say, "Jesus is Lord," but by the Holy Spirit.[20] (*1Corinthians 12:1-3*)

---

[19] Notice what is happening in this example. God desired to punish the wicked king Ahab and lead him to his destruction in battle. He did so by allowing an unclean spirit to prophesy through the false prophets that victory would be the king's if he went to battle. Ahab died in the battle (1Ki 22:34-38). This lesson shows us several things. First, not all persons claiming to have prophetic gifts are genuinely motivated by the Holy Spirit. Sometimes they are telling people things to lead them to destruction as God's discipline on them. These false prophets genuinely believe that they are speaking by God's Spirit. This is why Zedekiah was so angry with Micaiah (1Ki 22:24)—he had had a legitimate supernatural experience and was offended at Micaiah's assertion that it was not real. In truth, it was a real experience, just not one with the Holy Spirit but because of his own sinfulness God allowed him to be deceived. (This should motivate us to examine our own hearts lest we fall into a similar judgment). Secondly, note that God controls these false prophetic utterances and uses them to accomplish His will in the earth.

[20] Apparently an individual in the Corinthian church had come under the influence of an outside spiritual force, which he assumed to be the Holy Spirit, and was led to curse Jesus. This is really in line with the experiences above of Saul (1Sa 18:10) and Zedekiah (1Ki 22:6-28; 2Ch 18:1-34), who both spoke under the influence of an evil spirit. In Zedekiah's case it is certain from the text that he believed he was prophesying under the influence of the Holy Spirit. It leads one to wonder, how many of today's self-proclaimed prophets are prophesying under the influence of an evil spirit completely unaware that it is

Accounts Of Demons Giving
People The Ability To Work Miracles

For the mystery of lawlessness already works. Only there is one who restrains now, until he is taken out of the way. Then the lawless one[21] will be revealed, whom the Lord will kill with the breath of his mouth, and destroy by the manifestation of his coming; even he whose coming is according to the working of Satan with all power and signs and lying wonders, and with all deception of wickedness for those who are being lost, because they didn't receive the love of the truth, that they might be saved. Because of this, God sends them a delusion, that they should believe a lie; that they all might be judged who didn't believe the truth, but had pleasure in unrighteousness.[22] *(2Thessalonians 2:7-12)*

I saw coming out of the mouth of the dragon, and out of the mouth of the beast, and out of the mouth of the false prophet, **three unclean spirits, something like frogs; for they are spirits of demons, performing signs**; which go out to the kings of the whole inhabited earth, to gather them together for the war of that great day of God, the Almighty.[23]

---

not the Holy Spirit.

[21] Generally understood to be the Antichrist.

[22] This verse illustrates another principle of how God, in His sovereignty, uses the demons to achieve his purposes in the world. In this instance, Paul tells us that the Antichrist will come with demonically inspired miracles through the working of Satan but he also ends the passage by explaining that God is doing this to bring a "delusion" upon those "who [already] didn't believe the truth, but had pleasure in unrighteousness". This is what Paul talks about in Romans 1:18-32 where he refers to people who have already rejected God being given over to a "reprobate mind" wherein they actually begin thinking that the wrong thing is the right thing as a judgment from God upon them for their sinfulness (see Ps 81:10-12). In the case of the Antichrist, the people who follow him will have already rejected God and as a judgment God will allow Satan to empower the Antichrist so that he seems divine in order to further bring people who have already rejected God towards their damnation.

[23] In this instance, God is shown sovereignly using the demons to lead those who have already rejected God to their doom at Armageddon. The demons are allowed to perform miracles which persuade the already wicked kings to head to a battle which they can never win as judgment for their having already rejected God's will for their lives. This is really no different than what happened with Ahab in the last section and serves as one more strong warning to be cautious of

14

"Behold, I come like a thief. Blessed is he who watches, and keeps his clothes, so that he doesn't walk naked, and they see his shame." He gathered them together into the place which is called in Hebrew, Armageddon...I saw the heaven opened, and behold, a white horse, and he who sat on it is called Faithful and True. In righteousness he judges and makes war. His eyes are a flame of fire, and on his head are many crowns. He has names written and a name written which no one knows but he himself. He is clothed in a garment sprinkled with blood. His name is called "The Word of God." The armies which are in heaven followed him on white horses, clothed in white, pure, fine linen. Out of his mouth proceeds a sharp, double-edged sword, that with it he should strike the nations. He will rule them with an iron rod. He treads the wine press of the fierceness of the wrath of God, the Almighty. He has on his garment and on his thigh a name written, "KING OF KINGS, AND LORD OF LORDS."

I saw an angel standing in the sun. He cried with a loud voice, saying to all the birds that fly in the sky, "Come! Be gathered together to the great supper of God, that you may eat the flesh of kings, the flesh of captains, the flesh of mighty men, and the flesh of horses and of those who sit on them, and the flesh of all men, both free and slave, small and great." I saw the beast, and the kings of the earth, and their armies, gathered together to make war against him who sat on the horse, and against his army. The beast was taken, and with him the false prophet who worked the signs in his sight, with which he deceived those who had received the mark of the beast and those who worshiped his image. These two were thrown alive into the lake of fire that burns with sulfur. The rest were killed with the sword of him who sat on the horse, the sword which came out of his mouth. All the birds were filled with their flesh. (*Revelation 16:13-16, 19:11-21*)

I saw another beast coming up out of the earth.[24] He had two horns like a lamb, and he spoke like a dragon. He exercises all the authority of the first beast in his presence. He makes the earth and those who dwell in it to worship the first beast, whose fatal wound was healed. **He performs great signs, even making fire come**

---

those who claim to have miracle working powers.

[24] Understood by many to be a false prophet who will be used by God to entice those who have rejected Him to place their faith in the Antichrist.

down out of the sky to the earth in the sight of people. He deceives them who dwell on the earth because of the signs he was granted to do in front of the beast; saying to those who dwell on the earth, that they should make an image to the beast who had the sword wound and lived. It was given to him to give breath to it, to the image of the beast, that the image of the beast should both speak, and cause as many as wouldn't worship the image of the beast to be killed. (*Revelation 13:11-15*)

Moses Confronting The Magicians Of Pharaoh

16

Moses and Aaron went in to Pharaoh, and they did so, as Yahweh had commanded: and Aaron cast down his rod before Pharaoh and before his servants, and it became a serpent. Then Pharaoh also called for the wise men and the sorcerers. They also, **the magicians of Egypt, did the same thing with their enchantments**. For they each cast down their rods, and they became serpents: but Aaron's rod swallowed up their rods. (*Exodus 7:10-12*)

Yahweh said to Moses, "Tell Aaron, 'Take your rod, and stretch out your hand over the waters of Egypt, over their rivers, over their streams, and over their pools, and over all their ponds of water, that they may become blood...'"

Moses and Aaron did so, as Yahweh commanded; and he lifted up the rod, and struck the waters that were in the river, in the sight of Pharaoh, and in the sight of his servants; and all the waters that were in the river were turned to blood. The fish that were in the river died; and the river became foul, and the Egyptians couldn't drink water from the river; and the blood was throughout all the land of Egypt. **The magicians of Egypt did the same thing with their enchantments**; and Pharaoh's heart was hardened, and he didn't listen to them; as Yahweh had spoken.[25] (*Exodus 7:19-22*)

Yahweh spoke to Moses, Go in to Pharaoh, and tell him, "This is what Yahweh says, 'Let my people go, that they may serve me. If you refuse to let them go, behold, I will plague all your borders with frogs...'" Yahweh said to Moses, "Tell Aaron, 'Stretch out your hand with your rod over the rivers, over the streams, and over the pools, and cause frogs to come up on the land of Egypt.'" Aaron stretched out his hand over the waters of Egypt; and the frogs came up, and covered the land of Egypt. **The magicians did the same thing with their enchantments**, and brought up frogs on the land of Egypt.[26] (*Exodus 8:1-7*)

---

[25] In this can be seen the aforementioned principle of being given over to a reprobate mind. Pharaoh's heart was already sinful and, to fulfil His plan, God allowed him to become even more hardened by witnessing the demonically inspired miracles of his false magicians.

[26] It has been suggested that Pharaoh's magicians used simple sleight of hand or illusions to give the impression that they worked magic. While this is certainly

Accounts Of Demonic Activity
Affecting Christian Leaders And Ministry Efforts

By reason of the exceeding greatness of the revelations, that I should not be exalted excessively, there was given to me a thorn in the flesh, a messenger of Satan to torment me,[27] that I should not be exalted excessively. Concerning this thing, I begged the Lord three times that it might depart from me. He has said to me, "My grace is sufficient for you, for my power is made perfect in weakness." Most gladly therefore I will rather glory in my weaknesses, that the power of Christ may rest on me. Therefore I take pleasure in weaknesses, in injuries, in necessities, in persecutions, in distresses, for Christ's sake. For when I am weak, then am I strong.[28] (*2Corinthians 12:7-10*)

But we, brothers, being bereaved of you for a short season, in presence, not in heart, tried even harder to see your face with great desire, because we wanted to come to you—indeed, I, Paul, once and again—but Satan hindered us.[29] (*1Thessalonians 2:17-18*)

Accounts of Demonic Activity
Causing The Testing Of One's Faith

---

possible (and often the case with false prophets) if they did indeed know of a method to control animals, such as the frogs, they were aware of a technique that no modern veterinarian is aware of and were able to do something that no one living today knows how to do, leading me to conclude that there was a supernatural element to some of their enchantments.

[27] The Greek word for "messenger" here is *angelos*, a word elsewhere translated as "angel" giving rise to the belief that this incident involved some form of direct spiritual contact with an angel from Satan.

[28] Various opinions exist as to just what exactly the "thorn" was. Two things are clear, however: The thorn was Satanic, yet not beyond the sovereign control of God. As we have seen in other Scriptures, God was using the unclean spirit in Paul's life to accomplish His will (in this case, to keep Paul humble). God's saints can rest assured that Satan is never allowed to do anything to them that God does not allow for their own good (Ro 8:28). On a related note, it would seem that some Satanic attacks are sent with the intent that they will be short experiences, designed to encourage us to pray more fervently and are sent for the purpose of motivating us to more prayer.

[29] We are not told why God allowed Satan to hinder Paul's efforts but we can trust that it was completely under the control of God and used to accomplish His greater plan and purpose as Paul himself tells us that God guides and works out everything in the universe according to His will (Ep 1:11).

There was a man in the land of Uz, whose name was Job. That man was blameless and upright, and one who feared God, and turned away from evil. There were born to him seven sons and three daughters. His possessions also were seven thousand sheep, three thousand camels, five hundred yoke of oxen, five hundred female donkeys, and a very great household; so that this man was the greatest of all the children of the east. His sons went and held a feast in the house of each one on his birthday; and they sent and called for their three sisters to eat and to drink with them. It was so, when the days of their feasting had run their course, that Job sent and sanctified them, and rose up early in the morning, and offered burnt offerings according to the number of them all. For Job said, "It may be that my sons have sinned, and renounced God in their hearts." Job did so continually.

Now on the day when God's sons came to present themselves before Yahweh, Satan also came among them. Yahweh said to Satan, "Where have you come from?"

Then Satan answered Yahweh, and said, "From going back and forth in the earth, and from walking up and down in it."

Yahweh said to Satan, "Have you considered my servant, Job? For there is no one like him in the earth, a blameless and an upright man, one who fears God, and turns away from evil."

Then Satan answered Yahweh, and said, "Does Job fear God for nothing? Haven't you made a hedge around him, and around his house, and around all that he has, on every side? You have blessed the work of his hands, and his substance is increased in the land. But stretch out your hand now, and touch all that he has, and he will renounce you to your face."

Yahweh said to Satan, "Behold, all that he has is in your power. Only on himself don't stretch out your hand."[30]

So Satan went out from the presence of Yahweh. It fell on a day when his sons and his daughters were eating and drinking wine in their oldest brother's house, that there came a messenger to Job, and said, "The oxen were plowing, and the donkeys feeding beside them, and the Sabeans attacked, and took them away. Yes, they have killed the servants with the edge of the sword, and I alone have escaped to tell you."

---

[30] Notice how that Satan was completely bound by the will of God and could do nothing to Job without God's permission.

While he was still speaking, there also came another, and said, "The fire of God has fallen from the sky, and has burned up the sheep and the servants, and consumed them, and I alone have escaped to tell you."

While he was still speaking, there came also another, and said, "The Chaldeans made three bands, and swept down on the camels, and have taken them away, yes, and killed the servants with the edge of the sword; and I alone have escaped to tell you."

While he was still speaking, there came also another, and said, "Your sons and your daughters were eating and drinking wine in their oldest brother's house, and behold, there came a great wind from the wilderness, and struck the four corners of the house, and it fell on the young men, and they are dead. I alone have escaped to tell you."

Then Job arose, and tore his robe, and shaved his head, and fell down on the ground, and worshiped. He said, "Naked I came out of my mother's womb, and naked shall I return there. Yahweh gave, and Yahweh has taken away. Blessed be Yahweh's name." In all this, Job didn't sin, nor charge God with wrongdoing. (*Job 1:1-22*)

The Lord said, "Simon, Simon, behold, Satan asked to have all of you, that he might sift you as wheat, but I prayed for you, that your faith wouldn't fail. You, when once you have turned again, establish your brothers."

He said to him, "Lord, I am ready to go with you both to prison and to death!"

He said, "I tell you, Peter, the rooster will by no means crow today until you deny that you know me three times."

...He came out, and went, as his custom was, to the Mount of Olives. His disciples also followed him. When he was at the place, he said to them, "Pray that you don't enter into temptation."

He was withdrawn from them about a stone's throw, and he knelt down and prayed, saying, "Father, if you are willing, remove this cup from me. Nevertheless, not my will, but yours, be done."

An angel from heaven appeared to him, strengthening him. Being in agony he prayed more earnestly. His sweat became like great drops of blood falling down on the ground.

When he rose up from his prayer, he came to the disciples, and found them sleeping because of grief, and said to them, "Why do you sleep? Rise and pray that you may not enter into temptation."

While he was still speaking, behold, a multitude, and he who was called Judas, one of the twelve, was leading them. He came near to Jesus to kiss him. But Jesus said to him, "Judas, do you betray the Son of Man with a kiss?"

When those who were around him saw what was about to happen, they said to him, "Lord, shall we strike with the sword?" A certain one of them struck the servant of the high priest, and cut off his right ear.

But Jesus answered, "Let me at least do this"—and he touched his ear, and healed him. Jesus said to the chief priests, captains of the temple, and elders, who had come against him, "Have you come out as against a robber, with swords and clubs? When I was with you in the temple daily, you didn't stretch out your hands against me. But this is your hour, and the power of darkness."

They seized him, and led him away, and brought him into the high priest's house...all the disciples forsook him, and fled...But Peter followed from a distance. When they had kindled a fire in the middle of the courtyard, and had sat down together, Peter sat among them. A certain servant girl saw him as he sat in the light, and looking intently at him, said, "This man also was with him."

He denied Jesus, saying, "Woman, I don't know him."

After a little while someone else saw him, and said, "You also are one of them!"

But Peter answered, "Man, I am not!"

After about one hour passed, another confidently affirmed, saying, "Truly this man also was with him, for he is a Galilean!"

But Peter said, "Man, I don't know what you are talking about!" Immediately, while he was still speaking, a rooster crowed. The Lord turned, and looked at Peter. Then Peter remembered the Lord's word, how he said to him, "Before the rooster crows you will deny me three times." He went out, and wept bitterly.[31] (*Luke 22:31-62, Matthew 26:56*)

---

[31] This story often focuses on Peter as the object of testing by Satan (in the same way Job was tested) but notice at the beginning that Jesus said it was a test for all of them ("Satan asked to have all of you"). Jesus encouraged them to pray as they got closer to the time of testing but they were more interested in sleeping

Peter Denying Jesus As He Was Being Tested By Satan

Accounts Of Demons Inciting War
And Bringing Discipline For Wickedness

Abimelech the son of Jerubbaal went to Shechem to his mother's brothers, and spoke with them, and with all the family of the house of his mother's father, saying, "Please speak in the ears of all the men of Shechem, 'Is it better for you that all the sons of Jerubbaal, who are seventy persons, rule over you, or that one rule over you?' Remember also that I am your bone and your flesh."

His mother's brothers spoke of him in the ears of all the men of Shechem all these words. Their hearts inclined to follow Abimelech; for they said, "He is our brother." They gave him

than praying. All of the disciples failed the test (because they all ran and abandoned Jesus), which is why Jesus encouraged Peter to establish his brothers after he repented of his own failed testing. Like with Job and the Apostles, Satan appears to be allowed to test all Christians to see if they are genuine in what they are professing (see Re 12:9-10).

22

seventy pieces of silver out of the house of Baal Berith, with which Abimelech hired vain and light fellows, who followed him. He went to his father's house at Ophrah, and killed his brothers the sons of Jerubbaal, being seventy persons, on one stone: but Jotham the youngest son of Jerubbaal was left; for he hid himself. All the men of Shechem assembled themselves together, and all the house of Millo, and went and made Abimelech king, by the oak of the pillar that was in Shechem...

Abimelech was prince over Israel three years. **Then God sent an evil spirit between Abimelech and the men of Shechem**; and the men of Shechem dealt treacherously with Abimelech, that the violence done to the seventy sons of Jerubbaal might come, and that their blood might be laid on Abimelech their brother, who killed them, and on the men of Shechem, who strengthened his hands to kill his brothers. The men of Shechem set an ambush for him on the tops of the mountains, and they robbed all who came along that way by them, and Abimelech was told about it. Gaal the son of Ebed came with his brothers, and went over to Shechem; and the men of Shechem put their trust in him. They went out into the field, harvested their vineyards, trod the grapes, celebrated, and went into the house of their god, and ate and drank, and cursed Abimelech. Gaal the son of Ebed said, "Who is Abimelech, and who is Shechem, that we should serve him? Isn't he the son of Jerubbaal? Isn't Zebul his officer? Serve the men of Hamor the father of Shechem, but why should we serve him? I wish that this people were under my hand! Then I would remove Abimelech." He said to Abimelech, "Increase your army, and come out!"

When Zebul the ruler of the city heard the words of Gaal the son of Ebed, his anger burned. He sent messengers to Abimelech craftily, saying, "Behold, Gaal the son of Ebed and his brothers have come to Shechem; and behold, they incite the city against you....Abimelech rose up, and all the people who were with him, by night, and they laid wait against Shechem in four companies...Gaal went out before the men of Shechem, and fought with Abimelech. Abimelech chased him, and he fled before him, and many fell wounded, even to the entrance of the gate. Abimelech lived at Arumah; and Zebul drove out Gaal and his brothers, that they should not dwell in Shechem...Abimelech fought against the city all that day; and he took the city, and killed the people in it. He beat down the city, and sowed it with salt.

When all the men of the tower of Shechem heard of it, they entered into the stronghold of the house of Elberith. Abimelech was told that all the men of the tower of Shechem were gathered together. Abimelech went up to Mount Zalmon, he and all the people who were with him; and Abimelech took an ax in his hand, and cut down a bough from the trees, and took it up, and laid it on his shoulder. Then he said to the people who were with him, "What you have seen me do, make haste, and do as I have done!" All the people likewise each cut down his bough, and followed Abimelech, and put them at the base of the stronghold, and set the stronghold on fire on them; so that all the people of the tower of Shechem died also, about a thousand men and women. Then Abimelech went to Thebez, and encamped against Thebez, and took it. But there was a strong tower within the city, and all the men and women of the city fled there, and shut themselves in, and went up to the roof of the tower. Abimelech came to the tower, and fought against it, and came near to the door of the tower to burn it with fire. A certain woman cast an upper millstone on Abimelech's head, and broke his skull.

Then he called hastily to the young man his armor bearer, and said to him, "Draw your sword, and kill me, that men not say of me, 'A woman killed him.' His young man thrust him through, and he died."

When the men of Israel saw that Abimelech was dead, they each departed to his place. **Thus God repaid the wickedness of Abimelech, which he did to his father, in killing his seventy brothers; and God repaid all the wickedness of the men of Shechem on their heads; and the curse of Jotham the son of Jerubbaal came on them.**[32] (*Judges 9:1-56*)

Accounts Of Satan Motivating Or Tempting People To Sin
Jesus, full of the Holy Spirit, returned from the Jordan, and was led by the Spirit into the wilderness for forty days, being tempted by the devil. He ate nothing in those days. Afterward, when they were completed, he was hungry. The devil said to him, "If you are the

---

[32] Several things stand out in this narrative. First, notice how that demons were used by God in this instance to bring discipline to Abimelech for his wickedness. Secondly, note how that wars can be started by demons. Thirdly, notice that it is God who is in control and using the demons to bring it about to fulfill His will. Satan did not make the decision to do this, God did.

24

Son of God, command this stone to become bread."[33] Jesus answered him, saying, "It is written, 'Man shall not live by bread alone, but by every word of God.'"[34] The devil, leading him up on a high mountain, showed him all the kingdoms of the world in a moment of time.[35] The devil said to him, "I will give you all this authority, and their glory, for it has been delivered to me; and I give it to whomever I want. If you therefore will worship before me, it will all be yours."[36] Jesus answered him, "Get behind me Satan! For it is written, 'You shall worship the Lord your God, and you shall serve him only.'"[37] He led him to Jerusalem, and set him on the pinnacle of the temple, and said to him, "If you are the Son of God, cast yourself down from here, for it is written, 'He will put his angels in charge of you, to guard you;' and, 'On their hands they will bear you up, lest perhaps you dash your foot against a stone.'"[38] Jesus answering, said to him, "It has been said, 'You shall not tempt the Lord your God.'"[39] When the devil had completed every temptation, he departed from him until another time.[40] (*Luke 4:1-13*)

---

[33] The implication seems to be that this was a temptation to give up the fast. Note Satan's use of Jesus' obvious weakness in this attack.

[34] De 8:3

[35] Note Satan's ability to give visions.

[36] There is some question as to whether Satan's boast of being able to give the kingdoms of the world "to whomever I want" was truthful. Jesus told Pilate that "You could have no power at all against me, except it were given to you from above" (Jn 19:11) and Paul indicated that "there is no [civil] authority except from God, and those who exist are ordained by God...[the civil authority] is a servant of God to you for good...he is a servant of God..." (Ro 13:1-4). According to Jesus "the devil...is a liar (Jn 8:44)". It is sadly often the case that persons believe Satan's lie that if they would sin it would turn out for their best, only to experience the exact opposite.

[37] An abbreviated combination of verses such as Exodus 34:14, Deuteronomy 6:13, and 10:20.

[38] Ps 91:11-12. Note Satan's twisting of the Bible in order to entice Jesus into sin. It has often been the case that persons who want to sin will find a "Scriptural justification" for their behavior, supplied with what they were looking for by Satan himself.

[39] De 6:16

[40] Notice Jesus' strategy for handling temptation. When faced with temptation Jesus always referred back to the Scriptures to see what God said an individual should do in that situation and then He did it.

The chief priests and the scribes sought how they might put him (Jesus) to death, for they feared the people. **Satan entered into Judas**, who was surnamed Iscariot, who was numbered with the twelve. He went away, and talked with the chief priests and captains about how he might deliver him to them. They were glad, and agreed to give him money. He consented, and sought an opportunity to deliver him to them in the absence of the multitude. (*Luke 22:2-6*)

Now before the feast of the Passover, Jesus, knowing that his time had come that he would depart from this world to the Father, having loved his own who were in the world, he loved them to the end. During supper, **the devil having already put into the heart of Judas Iscariot**, Simon's son, to betray him, Jesus...was troubled in spirit, and testified, "Most certainly I tell you that one of you will betray me....It is he to whom I will give this piece of bread when I have dipped it." So when he had dipped the piece of bread, he gave it to Judas, the son of Simon Iscariot. After the piece of bread, then **Satan entered into him**. Then Jesus said to him, "What you do, do quickly."[41] (*John 13:1-27*)

The multitude of those who believed were of one heart and soul. Not one of them claimed that anything of the things which he

---

[41] The question has been raised as to Judas' ability to resist the temptation to betray the Lord with some holding that he was a mere puppet unable to resist his place as an agent in the cause of Jesus' death and others holding that he acted of his own volition. We have the promise from Scripture that God "will have all men to be saved, and to come unto the knowledge of the truth (1Ti 2:4)" and "The Lord...is longsuffering toward us, not willing that any should perish, but that all should come to repentance (2Pe 3:9)." These statements include Judas. However, Judas opened the door for demon possession by stealing from the disciples' treasury (Jn 12:4-6). The sin in his life opened the way for him to come under the judgment of God that He exercises through the agency of unclean spirits. This should serve as a stern warning to all to repent and forsake all of their sins, lest they experience this kind of judgment. Sin opens the door for oppression and possession. Judas did not have to follow the course that he chose but choosing sin is like a snowball effect. The more one chooses it the further into darkness it drags one as it opens the door for Satan to have more and more control over the individual. Notice also that God used the judgment against Judas to bring about His plan of having Jesus crucified for the sins of the world, further evidence that God uses the unclean spirits to accomplish His will. Note also that Judas' eventual suicide (Mt 27:3-10, Ac 1:16-19) is a behavior characteristic of a person demon possessed.

possessed was his own, but they had all things in common...neither was there among them any who lacked, for as many as were owners of lands or houses sold them, and brought the proceeds of the things that were sold, and laid them at the apostles' feet, and distribution was made to each, according as anyone had need...But a certain man named Ananias, with Sapphira, his wife, sold a possession, and kept back part of the price, his wife also being aware of it, and brought a certain part, and laid it at the apostles' feet. But Peter said, "Ananias, **why has Satan filled your heart to lie to the Holy Spirit**, and to keep back part of the price of the land? While you kept it, didn't it remain your own? After it was sold, wasn't it in your power? How is it that you have conceived this thing in your heart? You haven't lied to men, but to God." Ananias, hearing these words, fell down and died. Great fear came on all who heard these things. (*Acts 4:32-5:5*)

Yahweh God formed man from the dust of the ground, and breathed into his nostrils the breath of life; and man became a living soul. Yahweh God planted a garden eastward, in Eden, and there he put the man whom he had formed. Out of the ground Yahweh God made every tree to grow that is pleasant to the sight, and good for food, including the tree of life in the middle of the garden and the tree of the knowledge of good and evil...Yahweh God took the man, and put him into the garden of Eden to cultivate and keep it. Yahweh God commanded the man, saying, "You may freely eat of every tree of the garden; but you shall not eat of the tree of the knowledge of good and evil; for in the day that you eat of it, you will surely die."...

Now the serpent was more subtle than any animal of the field which Yahweh God had made. He said to the woman, "Has God really said, 'You shall not eat of any tree of the garden'?"

The woman said to the serpent, "We may eat fruit from the trees of the garden, but not the fruit of the tree which is in the middle of the garden. God has said, 'You shall not eat of it. You shall not touch it, lest you die.'"

The serpent said to the woman, "You won't really die, for God knows that in the day you eat it, your eyes will be opened, and you will be like God, knowing good and evil."

When the woman saw that the tree was good for food, and that it was a delight to the eyes, and that the tree was to be desired to make one wise, she took some of its fruit, and ate; and she gave some to her husband with her, and he ate it, too. Their eyes were opened, and they both knew that they were naked. They sewed fig leaves together, and made coverings for themselves.[42] (*Genesis 2:7-17; 3:1-7*)

Ananias' Temptation

Satan stood up against Israel, and moved David to take a census of Israel. David said to Joab and to the princes of the people, "Go, count Israel from Beersheba even to Dan; and bring me word, that I may know how many there are."

Joab said, "May Yahweh make his people a hundred times as many as they are. But, my lord the king, aren't they all my

---

[42] In this instance Satan is seen working through the snake (Re 12:9). Notice how that Satan twisted God's words to deceive Eve.

lord's servants? Why does my lord require this thing? Why will he be a cause of guilt to Israel?"

Nevertheless the king's word prevailed against Joab. Therefore Joab departed, and went throughout all Israel, then came to Jerusalem. Joab gave up the sum of the census of the people to David. All those of Israel were one million one hundred thousand men who drew a sword; and in Judah were four hundred seventy thousand men who drew a sword. But he didn't count Levi and Benjamin among them; for the king's word was abominable to Joab.

God was displeased with this thing; therefore he struck Israel.[43] (*1Chronicles 21:1-7*)

Accounts Of Unclean Spirits Giving False Teachings

But the Spirit says expressly that in later times some will fall away from the faith, paying attention to **seducing spirits** and doctrines of demons, through the hypocrisy of men who speak lies, branded in their own conscience as with a hot iron... (*1Timothy 4:1-2*)

'Now a thing was secretly brought to me. My ear received a whisper of it. In thoughts from the visions of the night, when deep sleep falls on men, fear came on me, and trembling, which made all my bones shake. **Then a spirit passed before my face**. The hair of my flesh stood up. It stood still, but I couldn't discern its appearance. A form was before my eyes. Silence, then I heard a voice, saying, 'Shall mortal man be more just than God? Shall a man be more pure than his Maker? Behold, he puts no trust in his servants. He charges his angels with error. How much more, those who dwell in houses of clay, whose foundation is in the dust, who are crushed before the moth! Between morning and evening they are destroyed. They perish forever without any regarding it. Isn't their tent cord plucked up within them? They die, and that without wisdom.'[44] (*Job 4:12-21*)

---

[43] The sin in this instance was that David was ascribing his victory to the power of the people, rather than the power of God from whom all victory really comes.

[44] In this case, Job's friend Eliphaz the Temanite relates how a spirit appeared to him at night and taught him a doctrine. The only problem is that later in the book God specifically rebukes Eliphaz, telling him that he has not spoken correctly about Him: "It came about after the LORD had spoken these words to Job, that the LORD said to Eliphaz the Temanite, 'My wrath is kindled against you and against your two friends, because you have not spoken of Me what is

Accounts Of Individuals Forming
Relationships With Unclean Spirits

Now Samuel was dead, and all Israel had mourned for him, and buried him in Ramah, even in his own city. Saul had sent away those who had familiar spirits and the wizards out of the land. The Philistines gathered themselves together, and came and encamped in Shunem; and Saul gathered all Israel together, and they encamped in Gilboa. When Saul saw the army of the Philistines, he was afraid, and his heart trembled greatly. When Saul inquired of Yahweh, Yahweh didn't answer him by dreams, by Urim, or by prophets. Then Saul said to his servants, "Seek for me a woman who has a **familiar spirit**,[45] that I may go to her, and inquire of her."

His servants said to him, "Behold, there is a woman who has a familiar spirit at Endor."

Saul disguised himself and put on other clothing, and went, he and two men with him, and they came to the woman by night. Then he said, "Please consult for me by the familiar spirit, and bring me up whomever I shall name to you."

The woman said to him, "Behold, you know what Saul has done, how he has cut off those who have familiar spirits, and the wizards, out of the land. Why then do you lay a snare for my life, to cause me to die?"

Saul swore to her by Yahweh, saying, "As Yahweh lives, no punishment will happen to you for this thing."

Then the woman said, "Whom shall I bring up to you?"

He said, "Bring Samuel up for me."

When the woman saw Samuel, she cried with a loud voice; and the woman spoke to Saul, saying, "Why have you deceived me? For you are Saul!"

The king said to her, "Don't be afraid! What do you see?"

---

right as My servant Job has' (Job 42:7NASB)." This illustrates two principles. First, demons can be seen on occasion (Eliphaz said that he saw him). Secondly, we must base our beliefs on Scripture, not supernatural encounters.

[45] A familiar spirit is an unclean spirit that a person has formed a relationship with (i.e. one that they have become "familiar" with). Forming such a relationship was strictly forbidden by the Law of Moses (Le 19:31, 20:6, 20:27, De 18:10-12).

The woman said to Saul, "I see a god coming up out of the earth."

He said to her, "What does he look like?"

She said, "An old man comes up. He is covered with a robe." Saul perceived that it was Samuel, and he bowed with his face to the ground, and showed respect.

Samuel said to Saul, "Why have you disturbed me, to bring me up?"

Saul answered, "I am very distressed; for the Philistines make war against me, and God has departed from me, and answers me no more, by prophets, or by dreams. Therefore I have called you, that you may make known to me what I shall do."

Samuel said, "Why then do you ask me, since Yahweh has departed from you and has become your adversary? Yahweh has done to you as he spoke by me. Yahweh has torn the kingdom out of your hand, and given it to your neighbor, even to David. Because you didn't obey Yahweh's voice, and didn't execute his fierce wrath on Amalek, therefore Yahweh has done this thing to you today. Moreover Yahweh will deliver Israel also with you into the hand of the Philistines; and tomorrow you and your sons will be with me. Yahweh will deliver the army of Israel also into the hand of the Philistines."

Then Saul fell immediately his full length on the earth, and was terrified, because of Samuel's words...

Now the Philistines fought against Israel, and the men of Israel fled from before the Philistines, and fell down slain on Mount Gilboa. The Philistines followed hard after Saul and after his sons; and the Philistines killed Jonathan, Abinadab, and Malchishua, the sons of Saul. The battle went hard against Saul, and the archers overtook him; and he was distressed by reason of the archers. Then Saul said to his armor bearer, "Draw your sword, and thrust me through with it, lest these uncircumcised come and abuse me."

But his armor bearer would not; for he was terrified. Therefore Saul took his sword, and fell on it...So Saul died for his trespass which he committed against Yahweh, because of Yahweh's word, which he didn't keep; and also **because he asked counsel of one who had a familiar spirit**, to inquire, and didn't inquire of Yahweh. Therefore he killed him, and turned the kingdom over to David the son of Jesse. (*1Samuel 28:3-20, 1Chronicles 10:1-4, 13-14*)

Saul Approaches The Witch Of Endor

Manasseh was twelve years old when he began to reign, and he reigned fifty-five years in Jerusalem. His mother's name was Hephzibah. He did that which was evil in Yahweh's sight, after the abominations of the nations whom Yahweh cast out before the children of Israel. For he built again the high places which Hezekiah his father had destroyed; and he raised up altars for Baal, and made an Asherah, as Ahab king of Israel did, and worshiped all the army of the sky, and served them. He built altars in Yahweh's house, of which Yahweh said, "I will put my name in Jerusalem." He built altars for all the army of the sky in the two courts of Yahweh's house. He made his son to pass through the fire, practiced sorcery, used enchantments, and **dealt with those who had familiar spirits**, and with wizards. He did much evil in Yahweh's sight, to provoke him to anger. (*2Kings 21:1-6*)

Josiah was eight years old when he began to reign, and he reigned thirty-one years in Jerusalem. His mother's name was Jedidah the daughter of Adaiah of Bozkath. He did that which was right in Yahweh's eyes, and walked in all the way of David his father, and didn't turn away to the right hand or to the left...Moreover **Josiah removed those who had familiar spirits**, the wizards, and the teraphim, and the idols, and all the abominations that were seen in the land of Judah and in Jerusalem, that he might confirm the words of the law which were written in the book that Hilkiah the priest found in Yahweh's house. There was no king like him before him, who turned to Yahweh with all his heart, and with all his soul, and with all his might, according to all the law of Moses; and there was none like him who arose after him. (*2Kings 22:1-2, 23:24-25*)

Accounts Of People Injuring
Themselves Under The Influence Of Evil Spirits

They came to the other side of the sea, into the country of the Gadarenes. When he had come out of the boat, immediately a man with an unclean spirit met him out of the tombs. He lived in the tombs. Nobody could bind him any more, not even with chains, because he had been often bound with fetters and chains, and the chains had been torn apart by him, and the fetters broken in pieces. Nobody had the strength to tame him. Always, night and day, in the tombs and in the mountains, he was crying out, and **cutting himself** with stones. (*Mark 5:1-5*)

After many days, Yahweh's word came to Elijah, in the third year, saying, "Go, show yourself to Ahab; and I will send rain on the earth."

Elijah went to show himself to Ahab...When Ahab saw Elijah, Ahab said to him, "Is that you, you troubler of Israel?"

He answered, "I have not troubled Israel; but you, and your father's house, in that you have forsaken Yahweh's commandments, and you have followed the Baals. Now therefore send, and gather to me all Israel to Mount Carmel, and four hundred fifty of the prophets of Baal, and four hundred of the prophets of the Asherah, who eat at Jezebel's table."

So Ahab sent to all the children of Israel, and gathered the prophets together to Mount Carmel. Elijah came near to all the people, and said, "How long will you waver between the two sides? If Yahweh is God, follow him; but if Baal, then follow him."

The people didn't say a word.

Then Elijah said to the people, "I, even I only, am left as a prophet of Yahweh; but Baal's prophets are four hundred fifty men. Let them therefore give us two bulls; and let them choose one bull for themselves, and cut it in pieces, and lay it on the wood, and put no fire under; and I will dress the other bull, and lay it on the wood, and put no fire under it. You call on the name of your god, and I will call on Yahweh's name. The God who answers by fire, let him be God."

All the people answered, "What you say is good."

Elijah said to the prophets of Baal, "Choose one bull for yourselves, and dress it first; for you are many; and call on the name of your god, but put no fire under it."

They took the bull which was given them, and they dressed it, and called on the name of Baal from morning even until noon, saying, "Baal, hear us!" But there was no voice, and nobody answered. They leaped about the altar which was made. At noon, Elijah mocked them, and said, "Cry aloud; for he is a god. Either he is deep in thought, or he has gone somewhere, or he is on a journey, or perhaps he sleeps and must be awakened."

They cried aloud, and **cut themselves in their way with knives and lances, until the blood gushed out on them**.[46] When midday was past, they prophesied until the time of the evening offering; but there was no voice, no answer, and nobody paid attention.

At the time of the evening offering, Elijah the prophet came near, and said, "Yahweh, the God of Abraham, of Isaac, and of Israel, let it be known today that you are God in Israel, and that I am your servant, and that I have done all these things at your word. Hear me, Yahweh, hear me, that this people may know that you, Yahweh, are God, and that you have turned their heart back again."

Then Yahweh's fire fell, and consumed the burnt offering, the wood, the stones, and the dust, and licked up the water that was in the trench. When all the people saw it, they fell on their faces.

---

[46] It is believed by some that they were led to cut themselves by the unclean spirits that they were worshiping. Under normal circumstances, people do not hurt themselves (Ep 5:29).

They said, "Yahweh, he is God! Yahweh, he is God!" (*1Kings 18:1-2, 17-39*)

One of the multitude answered, "Teacher, I brought to you my son, who has a mute spirit; and wherever it seizes him, it throws him down, and he foams at the mouth, and grinds his teeth, and wastes away...**Often it has cast him both into the fire and into the water, to destroy him**. (*Mark 9:17-22*)

The chief priests and the scribes sought how they might put him (Jesus) to death, for they feared the people. **Satan entered into Judas**, who was surnamed Iscariot, who was numbered with the twelve. He went away, and talked with the chief priests and captains about how he might deliver him to them. They were glad, and agreed to give him money. He consented, and sought an opportunity to deliver him to them in the absence of the multitude...Then Judas, who betrayed him, when he saw that Jesus was condemned, felt remorse, and brought back the thirty pieces of silver to the chief priests and elders, saying, "I have sinned in that I betrayed innocent blood." But they said, "What is that to us? You see to it." He threw down the pieces of silver in the sanctuary, and departed. **He went away and hanged himself**. (*Matthew 27:3-5, Luke 22:2-6*)

Accounts Of Unclean Spirits
Motivating People To Hurt Others

But some of the itinerant Jews, exorcists, took on themselves to invoke over those who had the evil spirits the name of the Lord Jesus, saying, "We adjure you by Jesus whom Paul preaches." There were seven sons of one Sceva, a Jewish chief priest, who did this. The evil spirit answered, "Jesus I know, and Paul I know, but who are you?" The man in whom the evil spirit was leaped on them, and overpowered them, and prevailed against them, so that they fled out of that house naked and wounded. This became known to all, both Jews and Greeks, who lived at Ephesus. Fear fell on them all, and the name of the Lord Jesus was magnified. (*Acts 19:13-17*)

Accounts Of Unclean Spirits Influencing Animals

Now there was a herd of many pigs feeding far away from them. The demons begged him, saying, "If you cast us out, permit us to go away into the herd of pigs." He said to them, "Go!" They came out, and went into the herd of pigs: and behold, the whole herd of pigs rushed down the cliff into the sea, and died in the water. (*Matthew 8:30-32*)

Aaron stretched out his hand over the waters of Egypt; and the frogs came up, and covered the land of Egypt. **The magicians did the same** thing with their enchantments, **and brought up frogs on the land** of Egypt.[47] (*Exodus 8:6-7*)

**Pharaoh's Magicians Were
Able To Influence The Frogs In Egypt**

Accounts Of Possession With No Specific Details Given
Jesus went about in all Galilee...The report about him went out into all Syria. They brought to him all who were sick, afflicted with various diseases and torments, possessed with demons, epileptics, and paralytics; and he healed them. (*Matthew 4:23-24*)

---

[47] Compare also the influence of Satan upon the snake in the garden of Eden (Ge 3:1-15).

When evening came, they brought to him many possessed with demons. He cast out the spirits with a word, and healed all who were sick... (*Matthew 8:16*)

For a woman, whose little daughter had an unclean spirit, having heard of him (Jesus), came and fell down at his feet. Now the woman was a Greek, a Syrophoenician by race. She begged him that he would cast the demon out of her daughter. But Jesus said to her, "Let the children be filled first, for it is not appropriate to take the children's bread and throw it to the dogs." But she answered him, "Yes, Lord. Yet even the dogs under the table eat the children's crumbs." He said to her, "For this saying, go your way. The demon has gone out of your daughter." She went away to her house, and found the child having been laid on the bed, with the demon gone out.[48] (*Mark 7:25-30*)

At evening, when the sun had set, they brought to him all who were sick, and those who were possessed by demons. All the city was gathered together at the door. He healed many who were sick with various diseases, and cast out many demons. He didn't allow the demons to speak, because they knew him. (*Mark 1:32-34*)

He (Jesus) went into their synagogues throughout all Galilee, preaching and casting out demons. (*Mark 1:39*)

He called to himself the twelve, and began to send them out two by two; and he gave them authority over the unclean spirits...They went out and preached that people should repent. They cast out many demons, and anointed many with oil who were sick, and healed them. (*Mark 6:7-13*)

Now when Jesus had risen early on the first day of the week, he appeared first to Mary Magdalene, from whom he had cast out seven demons. (*Mark 16:9*)

When the sun was setting, all those who had any sick with various diseases brought them to him; and he laid his hands on every one of them, and healed them. Demons also came out from many,

---

[48] Compare the parallel account in Matthew 15:22-28.

crying out, and saying, "You are the Christ, the Son of God!" Rebuking them, he didn't allow them to speak, because they knew that he was the Christ.[49] (*Luke 4:40-41*)

It happened soon afterwards, that he (Jesus) went about through cities and villages, preaching and bringing the good news of the Kingdom of God. With him were the twelve, and certain women who had been healed of evil spirits and infirmities: Mary who was called Magdalene, from whom seven demons had gone out; and Joanna, the wife of Chuzas, Herod's steward; Susanna; and many others; who served him from their possessions. (*Luke 8:1-3*)

The unclean spirits, whenever they saw him (Jesus), fell down before him, and cried, "You are the Son of God!"[50] (*Mark 3:11*)

He came down with them, and stood on a level place, with a crowd of his disciples, and a great number of the people from all Judea and Jerusalem, and the sea coast of Tyre and Sidon, who came to hear him and to be healed of their diseases; as well as those who were troubled by unclean spirits, and they were being healed. (*Luke 6:17-18*)

In that hour he cured many of diseases and plagues and evil spirits; and to many who were blind he gave sight.[51] (*Luke 7:21*)

Multitudes also came together from the cities around Jerusalem, bringing sick people, and those who were tormented by unclean spirits: and they were all healed. (*Acts 5:16*)

Philip went down to the city of Samaria, and proclaimed to them the Christ. The multitudes listened with one accord to the things that were spoken by Philip, when they heard and saw the signs which he did. For unclean spirits came out of many of those who

---

[49] Note how that even demons will acknowledge the Messiahship and Sonship of Jesus.

[50] This seems to indicate that unclean spirits can sometimes be seen. Otherwise, how could Mark have known that they "fell down" before him unless they had been actually seen doing so? Does this explain some sightings of "ghosts"?

[51] This lets us know that while demons can cause illnesses, not all illnesses are demonic.

38

had them. They came out, crying with a loud voice. Many who had been paralyzed and lame were healed. (*Acts 8:5-7*)

And God did special miracles by the hands of Paul: So that handkerchiefs or aprons from his body were brought unto the sick, and the diseases departed from them, and the evil spirits went out of them. (*Acts 19:11-12*)[52]

Summary Of Old And New
Testament Accounts Of Demonic Activity

1. Origin And Physical Characteristics Of The Demons
    A. The term demon and unclean spirit can be used interchangeably (Mt 15:22, Mk 7:25).

    B. Demons are the spirits of the angels who did not administer their authority over the nations according to God's commands. As a punishment, their spirits were separated from their bodies. Their bodies were imprisoned in hell and they were forced to serve God as bodiless spirits (Gn 6:1-4, De 32:8LXX, Ps 82:1-8, 2Ch 18:20-22, 2Pe 2:4, Jd 1:6-7, Mt 12:43-45).

    C. The Greek word for "spirit" carries with it the idea of wind or breath, implying that unclean spirits have the same consistency as air (i.e. not solid but rather gaseous and able to change their shape or move through cracks and crevices) (Mt 12:43, Jn 3:8).

    D. Unclean spirits can sometimes be seen (Jo 4:12-21, Mk 3:11).

2. Demons Are Completely Under God's Control
    A. Unclean spirits cannot affect a human without God's permission (Jo 1:8-12, 2:4-6, Mt 10:29).

---

[52] It is important to note that in the above instances one of the reasons that these individuals had been allowed to be overtaken by these unclean spirits was so that they could be delivered in front of others to demonstrate the authority and power of Jesus. This is one reason that God allows people be afflicted by evil spirits, so that they may be delivered as a testimony to persuade others to believe in Christ. All the more impetus for us to be open, as the Lord leads us, to praying for the deliverance of those whom we encounter that are in bondage to Satan.

B. Evil spirits are used by God to discipline people (Jg 9:1-56, 1Sa 16:14-23, 18:6-12, 19:9-12, 1Ki 22:6-28, Re 16:13-16, 19:11-21).

3. God Sometimes Decides To Allow Demons To Affect People Mentally And Physically

A. Demons can affect people physically to include causing illnesses (Jo 2:1-8, Mt 9:32-33, 12:22, Lk 13:11-16) but not all physical illness is demonic in origin (Mt 4:23-24, 8:16, Mk 1:32-34, Lk 6:17-18).

B. Demons can control a person's tongue (Mt 9:32-33, 12:22, Mk 9:17, Lk 11:14).

C. Demons can affect what a person sees (Mt 9:32-33) to include giving them visions (Lk 4:5).

D. Demons can affect what a person hears (Mk 9:25).

E. Demons can cause a person to fall to the ground (Mk 9:18, Lk 4:33-35).

F. Demons can cause a person to experience convulsions or trembling in their body (Mk 9:26).

G. Unclean spirits will sometimes lead people to injure themselves (1Ki 18:28, Mt 27:3-5, Mk 5:5, 9:17-22).

H. People can have multiple demons inside of them (Lk 8:1-3, 8:26-39, Mk 16:9).

I. Demons can cause insanity, mental illness, anxiety and erratic behavior (Lk 8:26-39, 1Sa 16:14-23, 18:6-12).

4. God Has Provided Methods For Dealing With Demons When They Affect People

A. Faith, prayer, fasting and persistence are keys to seeing people delivered of unclean spirits (Mk 9:28-29, 7:25-30).

B. Music can lessen the effects of unclean spirits on a person (1Sa 16:23).

C. Those who do not worship Christ do not have power over unclean spirits when they affect others (Ac 19:13-17).

D. Demons may cause physical effects to occur in the bodies of a possessed person when they are cast out of them (Mk 9:26, Lk 4:35, Ac 8:5-7).

5. Demons Are Allowed To Encourage People To Sin To Test Them

A. Demons encourage, or tempt, people to sin (Ge 2:7-17; 3:1-7, 1Ch 21:1-7, Lk 4:1-13, Lk 22:2-6, Jn 13:1-27, Ac 4:32-5:5).
B. These times of temptation may occur when a person is physically weak (Lk 4:1-2).
C. Unclean spirits are allowed to put God's people into circumstances that will test whether they are a real Christian or not (Jo 1:1-2:10, Lk 22:31-62).
D. Quoting Scripture is one method for dealing with demonic times of testing (Lk 4:1-13).
E. During these times of testing, unclean spirits may be given authority by God over certain areas of the person's life to include causing financial loss, loss of loved ones and health problems (Jo 1:1-22, 2:1-7).
F. During these times of testing Christians are encouraged to pray (Lk 22:31, 39-40).

6. Demons May Be Used In The Life Of A Believer By God To Accomplish His Purposes
A. Unclean spirits may be used by God in the life of a believer to keep them humble (2Co 12:7-10).
B. With God's permission, unclean spirits can affect ministry efforts (1Th 2:17-18).

7. Demonic Influence In Relationships
A. Demons can cause division between people (Jg 9:23).
B. Unclean spirits motivate people to hurt others (1Sa 18:6-12, 19:9-12, Ac 19:13-17).

8. Demonic Influence In The Church
A. Some people who are found amongst God's people have formed relationships with unclean spirits and use them to either make money, seek supernatural knowledge or guidance (1Sa 28:3-20, 1Ch 10:1-4, 13-14, 2Ki 21:1-6, 22:1-2, 23:24-25).
B. Demons can give people knowledge about spiritual things they ordinarily would not have (Mk 1:23-24, Lk 4:33-35, 8:26-39, Ac 16:16-18).
C. Demons can give people the ability to prophesy (1Sa 18:10, 1Ki 22:6-28, 2Ch 18:1-34).

D. God will allow an unclean spirit to inspire a false prophet to prophesy in order to discipline His people (1Ki 22:6-28).
E. God allows unclean spirits to perform miracles in false prophets as a judgment against those who have rejected Him to lead them to destruction (2Th 2:7-12, Re 16:13-16, 19:11-21).
F. False prophets genuinely believe that they are being inspired by the Holy Spirit (1Ki 22:23-24, 2Ch 18:22-23, 1Co 12:1-3).
G. Falsely inspired prophets speak in the name of the Lord (1Ki 22:6-28, 2Ch 18:1-34).
H. People speaking under the influence of a demon may acknowledge that Jesus is the Messiah and the Son of God (Mk 3:11, Lk 4:40-41).
I. False prophets may be led to say things that are completely contrary to the Christian faith (1Co 12:1-3).
J. Demons can give people the ability to perform miracles that look just like the miracles of the Holy Spirit (Ex 7:10-12, 7:19-22, 8:1-7, 2Th 2:7-12, Re 13:11-15, 16:13-16).
K. People in leadership in the church may be influenced by Satan (Lk 22:2-6, Jn 13:1-27).
L. People with unclean spirits can be present when God's people meet for fellowship, worship and teaching (Mk 1:23).
M. Unclean spirits encourage people to embrace false teachings (Jo 4:12-21, 1Ti 4:1-2).

9. Demonic Influence In Nature
A. Demons can control weather phenomena (Jo 1:1-22).
B. Unclean spirits can influence animals (Ge 3:1-4, Ex 8:6-7, Mt 8:30-32).

10. Demonic Influence In Politics
A. Demons are used by God to incite wars according to His plans (Jg 9:1-56, Re 16:13-16, 19:11-21).

Accounts From Early Christian Literature
(2nd-5th Centuries)

Justin Martyr

BIO: [d. ca.165AD] *A Gentile who converted to Christianity after failing to find satisfaction from his studies in philosophy. Impressed by Christian martyrs, he was eventually led to accept Christ after an elderly Christian taught him about the Hebrew prophets. He was martyred during the reign of Marcus Aurelius.*

For every demon, when exorcised in the name of this very Son of God — (who is the First-born of every creature, who became man by the Virgin, who suffered, and was crucified under Pontius Pilate by your nation, who died, who rose from the dead, and ascended into heaven) — is overcome and subdued. (*Dialogue With Trypho, Ch. 85*)

And now you can learn from what is under your own observation. For countless demoniacs throughout the whole world, and in your city, many of our Christian men exorcising them in the name of Jesus Christ (who was crucified under Pontius Pilate) have healed and do heal, rendering helpless and driving the possessing devils out of the men, though they could not be cured by all the other exorcists, and those who used incantations and drugs. (*Second Apology, Ch. 6*)

And now we, who believe on our Lord Jesus, who was crucified under Pontius Pilate, when we exorcise all demons and evil spirits, have them subjected to us.[53] (*Dialogue With Trypho, Ch. 76*)

Theophilus

BIO: [115?-c.182AD] *A bishop of Antioch and a dedicated fighter against heresy. He was one of the earliest commentators upon the Gospels, perhaps the first, and he seems to have been the earliest Christian historian of the Church of the Old Testament.*

---

[53] Note the extreme level of authority that the early church exercised over demonic entities.

...but [the Greco-Roman authors, poets and philosophers,] being inspired by demons and puffed up by them, they spoke at their instance whatever they said. For indeed the poets, — Homer, to wit, and Hesiod, being, as they say, inspired by the Muses, — spoke from a deceptive fancy, and not with a pure but an erring spirit. And this, indeed, clearly appears from the fact, that even to this day the possessed are sometimes exorcised in the name of the living and true God; and these spirits of error themselves confess that they are demons who also formerly inspired these writers. (*The Apology of Theophilus to Autolycus, 2:8*)

Irenaeus

BIO: [c.125-c.202AD] *A bishop of Lyons, in modern day France, who is remembered as being a strong apologist against heretical teachings.*

He shall also judge false prophets, who... acting in some other way under the influence of a wicked spirit, pretend to utter prophecies, while all the time they lie against God.[54] (*Against Heresies, 4:33:6*)

And there is none other name of the Lord given under heaven whereby men are saved, save that of God, which is Jesus Christ the Son of God, to which also the demons are subject and evil spirits and all apostate energies, by the invocation of the name of Jesus Christ, crucified under Pontius Pilate.[55] (*Proof Of The Apostolic Preaching, 96*)

Hippolytus of Rome

BIO: [170-236AD] *A disciple of Irenaeus and author of numerous Christian works covering such subjects as exegesis, apology, dogma, moral, discipline, history and geography.*

Before bringing new people to hear the Word they shall first be brought before the teachers at the house, before all of the other

---

[54] This is apparently a reference to something happening in his time that he was aware of.
[55] Note that it was just an accepted matter of fact amongst the Christians of the early Church that the demons would and did submit unto them.

people come in...If someone is there who has a demon, a person like this shall not hear the Word of the teacher until they are purified.[56] (*Apostolic Tradition, 15:1,8*)

Minucius Felix
BIO: [fl. 210AD] *One of the earliest Christian apologists.*

A great many, even some of your own people, know all those things that the demons themselves confess concerning themselves, as often as they are driven by us from bodies by the torments of our words and by the fires of our prayers. Saturn himself, and Serapis, and Jupiter, and whatever demons you worship, overcome by pain, speak out what they are; and assuredly they do not lie to their own discredit, especially when any of you are standing by. Since they themselves are the witnesses that they are demons, believe them when they confess the truth of themselves; for when abjured by the only and true God, unwillingly the wretched beings shudder in their bodies,[57] and either at once leap forth, or vanish by degrees, as the faith of the sufferer assists or the grace of the healer inspires. Thus they fly from Christians when near at hand, whom at a distance they harassed by your means in their assemblies. And thus, introduced into the minds of the ignorant, they secretly sow there a hatred of us by means of fear. For it is natural both to hate one whom you fear, and to injure one whom you have feared, if you can. Thus they take possession of the minds and obstruct the hearts, that men may begin to hate us before they know us; lest, if known, they should either imitate us, or not be able to condemn us.[58] (*The Octavius of Minucius Felix, Ch. 27*)

Tertullian

BIO: [c.160-225AD] *A North African Christian leader whose ministry efforts influenced men such as Augustine of Hippo and Jerome.*

Why may not those who go into the temptations of the show[59] become accessible also to evil

---

[56] This is interesting in that it seems to indicate that in some of the early churches, before persons were allowed to hear the sermon they would be delivered from any demons that they had. This leaves many questions

45

spirits? We have the case of the woman — the Lord Himself is witness — who went to the theater, and came back possessed. In the outcasting, accordingly, when the unclean creature was upbraided with having dared to attack a believer, he firmly replied, "And in truth I did it most righteously, for I found her in my domain."...How many other undoubted proofs we have had in the case of persons who, by keeping company with the devil in the shows, have fallen from the Lord![60] (*The Shows, Ch. 26*)

Let a person be brought before your tribunals, who is plainly under demoniacal possession. The wicked spirit, bidden to speak by a follower of Christ, will as readily make the truthful confession that he is a demon, as elsewhere he has falsely asserted that he is a god. (*Apology, Ch. 23*)

For God, Creator of the universe, has no need of odors or of blood.[61] These things are the food of devils. But we not only reject those wicked spirits: we overcome them; we daily hold them up to contempt; we exorcise them from their victims, as multitudes can testify. (*To Scapula, Ch. 2*)

---

unanswered. Was this procedure only used in the cases where it was without any doubt that the person was demonized (i.e. an individual behaving like the Gadarene demoniac)? Were all persons examined to see if they had demons before they were allowed to attend a church service? How widespread was this practice? Could there have been the fear of a demoniac interfering with the service, perhaps based upon a previous experience, that led to this practice? We will note here that there is some disagreement as to whether Hippolytus of Rome was the actual author of this work or if another, now unknown, Christian wrote it. Regardless of the author, this document describes an interesting practice of spiritual warfare that was present, at least in some capacity, in the early church.

[57] This appears to be a reference to trembling in the demonized individual, which was caused by the demons trembling in fear at the mentioning of the name of God. Compare James 2:19 where it notes that "the devils also believe, and tremble."

[58] Note that Minucius felt that the demons feared the early Christians because of the power that they had over them. Today, it seems to be just the opposite, with Christians fearing demons and avoiding confrontation with them.

[59] The public shows, such as events at a theater.

[60] This should make Christians think twice before attending a movie theater or other questionable entertainment venue.

[61] Pagan rituals.

For what more delightful than to have God the Father and our Lord at peace with us, than revelation of the truth, than confession of our errors, than pardon of the innumerable sins of our past life?...What nobler than to tread under foot the gods of the nations — to exorcise evil spirits — to perform cures — to seek divine revealings — to live to God?[62] (*The Shows, Ch. 29*)

The clerk of one of them[63] who was liable to be thrown upon the ground by an evil spirit, was set free from his affliction; as was also the relative of another, and the little boy of a third. How many men of rank (to say nothing of common people) have been delivered from devils, and healed of diseases! (*To Scapula, Ch. 4*)

In disguise, however, of these souls [of dead people], demons operate, especially such as used to dwell in them when they were in life, and who had driven them, in fact, to the fate which had at last carried them off [to death]. For, as we have already suggested, there is hardly a human being who is unattended by a demon[64]...This imposture of the evil spirit lying concealed in the persons of the dead, we are able, if I am not mistaken, to prove by actual facts, when in cases of exorcism (the evil spirit) affirms himself sometimes to be one of the relatives of the person possessed by him, sometimes a gladiator or a *bestiarius*,[65] and sometimes even a god; always making it one of his chief cares to extinguish the very truth which we are proclaiming, that men may not readily believe that all souls remove to Hades, and that they may overthrow faith in the resurrection and the judgment.[66] And yet for all that, the demon, after trying to circumvent the bystanders, is vanquished by the pressure of divine grace, and sorely against his will confesses all the truth. (*A Treatise On The Soul, Ch. 57*)

---

[62] The early Christians seem to have rejoiced in their authority to cast out demons, readily embracing the challenge to destroy the works of the devil.

[63] An advocate.

[64] Tertullian here is suggesting that the demon that becomes attached to an unbelieving person will pretend to be that person's ghost after they die. This would make sense in light of how ghosts often seem to know the history of the person they are claiming to be.

[65] An athlete (or prisoner) who was sent into the arena to combat wild beasts.

[66] Sound advice directed towards all attempts at contacting the spirits of deceased persons (spiritualism, necromancy, etc.).

Or, if you will, let there be produced [in the presence of a Christian] one of the "god-possessed", as they are supposed, who, inhaling at the altar, conceive divinity from the fumes, who are delivered of it by retching, who vent it forth in agonies of gasping. Let that same [goddess, the] Virgin Caelestis herself, the rain-promiser, let [the god] Aesculapius discoverer of medicines, ready to prolong the life of Socordius, and Tenatius, and Asclepiodotus, now in the last extremity, if they would not confess, in their fear of lying to a Christian, that they were demons, then and there shed the blood of that most impudent follower of Christ[67]...Do you say that it is done by magic, or some trick of that sort? You will not say anything of the sort, if you have been allowed the use of your ears and eyes. For what argument can you bring against a thing that is exhibited to the eye in its naked reality? If, on the one hand, they are really gods, why do they pretend to be demons [by saying that they are when Christians exorcise them]? Is it from fear of us? In that case your divinity is put in subjection to Christians; and you surely can never ascribe deity to that which is under authority of man, nay (if it adds aught to the disgrace) of its very enemies. (*Apology, Ch. 23*)

Origen

BIO: [c.185-254] *A third century theologian and head of the catechetical school of Alexandria. He is believed to have composed as many as six thousand works, though most of them are now lost.*

And the name of Jesus can still remove distractions from the minds of men, and expel demons, and also take away diseases; and produce a marvelous meekness of spirit and complete change of character, and a humanity, and goodness, and gentleness in those individuals who

---

[67] This was addressed to a secular, governmental authority. The reference to "shedding of blood" is Tertullian's encouragement to the secular authorities to perform an execution against those who say that they are Christians but cannot cast out a demon, because the failure to be able to cast out a demon was proof that they were not really a Christian. Obviously this is extreme and unbalanced on Tertullian's part but it goes to show the confidence he had that any true Christian could exercise power over the demons. How many churchgoers would there be left if his recommendation were carried out today?

do not pretend to be Christians just for the sake of survival or the supply of any human needs,[68] but who have honestly accepted the doctrine concerning God and Christ, and the judgment to come. (*Against Celsus, 1:67*)

...there are still preserved among Christians traces of that Holy Spirit which appeared in the form of a dove.[69] They expel evil spirits, and perform many cures, and foresee certain events, according to the will of the Logos.[70] (*Against Celsus, 1:46*)

...those demons which many Christians cast out of persons possessed with them? And this, we may observe, they do without the use of any curious arts of magic, or incantations, but merely by prayer and simple adjurations[71] which the plainest person can use. Because for the most part it is unlettered persons who perform this work; thus making known the grace which is in the word of Christ, and the despicable weakness of demons, which, in order to be overcome and driven out of the bodies and souls of men, do not require the power and wisdom of those who are mighty in argument, and most learned in matters of faith.[72] (*Against Celsus, 7:4*)

Lastly, many Greek writers have been of opinion that the art of poetry cannot exist without madness; whence also it is several times related in their histories, that those whom they call poets were suddenly filled with a kind of spirit of madness. And what are we to say also of those whom they call diviners, from whom, by the working of those demons who have the mastery over them,

---

[68] A reference to the early church's emphasis on ministry to the poor and needy (Ac 20:35, Ro 15:26, Ga 2:10, 1Ti 5:3, 16, Ja 1:27).

[69] Mt 3:16

[70] *Logos* is the Greek word for "Word" and is a reference to Jesus.

[71] An adjuration would be something similar to the command Paul gave to the spirit influencing the psychic girl in Acts 16:16-18 when he said "I command you in the name of Jesus Christ to come out of her!"

[72] As noted here, it was demonstrated in the early church that the most uneducated person who committed their life and heart to the cause of Christ were given authority and power over demons. Authority over demonic power is God's gracious gift to every Christian from the doctoral level scholar to the layperson who never learned to read. Notice that Origen points out that it was usually the uneducated that were witnessed exercising authority over these demons.

answers are given in carefully constructed verses? Those persons, too, whom they term Magi or Malevolent, frequently, by invoking demons over boys of tender years, have made them repeat poetical compositions which were the admiration and amazement of all. Now these effects we are to suppose are brought about in the following manner: Just as holy and immaculate souls, after devoting themselves to God with all affection and purity, and after preserving themselves free from all contagion of evil spirits, and after being purified by lengthened abstinence, and filled with holy and religious training, assume by this means a portion of divinity, and earn the grace of prophecy, and other divine gifts; so also are we to suppose that those who place themselves in the way of the opposing powers, (i.e., who purposely admire and adopt their manner of life and habits) receive their inspiration, and become partakers of their wisdom and doctrine. And the result of this is that they are filled with the working of those spirits to whose service they have subjected themselves.[73] (*First Principles, 3:3:3*)

For it is not by incantations that Christians seem to prevail (over evil spirits), but by the name of Jesus, accompanied by the announcement of the narratives which relate to Him; for the repetition of these has frequently been the means of driving demons out of men, especially when those who repeated them did so in a sound and genuinely believing spirit.[74] Such power, indeed, does the name of Jesus possess over evil spirits, that there have been instances where it was effectual, when it was pronounced even by bad men, which Jesus Himself taught (would be the case), when He said: "Many shall say to Me in that day, In Thy name we have cast out devils, and done many wonderful works."[75] (*Against Celsus, 1:6*)

---

[73] Origen here notes that there is a method for experiencing inspiration under the influence of an unclean spirit and that those who seek this experience in the way that the heathens do will end up experiencing it. I have noticed even in Christian churches that many similar pagan practices have begun to creep in and that these same churches seem to be at the forefront of claiming to have supernatural experiences. It is wise (and Biblical) to test all spirits (1Jn 4:1) and to discard any practices leading to mystical experiences that cannot be sanctioned by the Scriptures.

[74] That is, by just reading or repeating the stories from the Gospels in a spirit of faith God has used that to drive out the demonic spirit.

[75] Mt 7:22

But let us also attend to this, "This kind does not go out except by prayer and fasting,"[76] in order that if at any time it is necessary that we should be engaged in the healing of one suffering from such a disorder, we may not adjure, nor put questions,[77] nor speak to the impure spirit as if it heard, but devoting ourselves to prayer and fasting, may be successful as we pray for the sufferer, and by our own fasting may thrust out the unclean spirit from him. (*Commentary On The Gospel Of Matthew, 13:7*)

Dionysius of Alexandria

BIO: [c.190-c.265] *One of the heads of the catechetical school at Alexandria and eventually bishop of that city. He is often referred to as "The Great".*

For among the emperors who preceded him (Valerian), there was not one who exhibited so kindly and favorable a disposition toward them (the Christians) as he did; yea, even those [emperors] who were said to have become Christians openly did not receive them with that extreme friendliness and graciousness with which he received them at the beginning of his reign; and his whole house was filled then with the pious, and it was itself a very church of God. But the master and president of the Magi of Egypt prevailed on him to abandon that course, urging him to slay and persecute those pure and holy men (i.e. the Christians) as adversaries and obstacles to their accursed and abominable incantations. For there are, indeed, and there were men who, by their simple presence, and by merely showing themselves, and by simply breathing and uttering some words, have been able to dissipate the artifices of wicked demons. (*Epistle 11: To Hermammon, Sec. 2*)

---

[76] Mt 17:21. Note Origen's inclusion of the fasting clause in his quotation of this verse around 246AD.

[77] Christians are often tempted when attempting to cast out a demon to engage the spirit in a question and answer session. This should be avoided for at least two reasons. Satan is a liar (Jn 8:44) and, therefore, any information that he gives cannot be trusted as reliable. Secondly, demons may take advantage of this to speak hurtful things (i.e. reminders of extremely hurtful or embarrassing past events) against those attempting to cast them out in an attempt to distract them from what they are doing. There is no Scriptural example of any person questioning a demon as they were being cast out.

**Reproduction Of A 5th Century
Depiction Of An Exorcism**

Cyprian

BIO: [200?-258] *A bishop of Carthage who ministered during a time of government sanctioned persecution.*

Another,[78] who was in the baths, (for this was wanting to her crime and to her misfortunes, that she even went at once to the baths,[79] when she had lost the grace of the laver of life[80]); there, unclean as she was, was seized by an unclean spirit, and tore with her teeth the tongue with which she had either impiously eaten or spoken.[81] After the wicked food had been taken, the madness of the mouth was armed to its own destruction. She herself was her own

---

[78] This is in reference to a Christian who was given the choice by the government to engage in some sort of pagan ritual or suffer punishment. They chose to renounce their faith by engaging in the ritual.

[79] The public bathhouses were known for being places of immoral behavior, and therefore, not the kind of environment that Christians should place themselves in.

[80] The expression "laver of life" is a reference to baptism.

[81] The reference to eating or speaking is a reference to the pagan ritual that she performed, either eating an animal that was sacrificed or verbally renouncing her faith.

executioner, nor did she long continue to live afterwards: tortured with strong pains of the belly and bowels, she expired. (*On The Lapsed, 24*)

How many there are daily who do not repent nor make confession of the consciousness of their crime, who are filled with unclean spirits [as a punishment]![82] (*On The Lapsed, 26*)

You should be ashamed to worship those whom you yourself defend; you should be ashamed to hope for protection from those whom you yourself protect. Oh, would you but hear and see them when they are adjured by us, and tortured with spiritual scourges, and are ejected from the possessed bodies with tortures of words, when howling and groaning at the voice of man and the power of God, feeling the stripes and blows, they confess the judgment to come![83] Come and acknowledge that what we say is true; and since you say that you thus worship gods, believe even those whom you worship. Or if you will even believe yourself, he — i.e., the demon—who has now possessed your breast, who has now darkened your mind with the night of ignorance, shall speak concerning yourself in your hearing. You will see that we are entreated by those whom you entreat, that we are feared by those whom you fear, whom you adore. You will see that under our hands they stand bound, and tremble as captives, whom you look up to and venerate as lords: assuredly even thus you might be confounded in those errors of yours, when you see and hear your gods, at once upon our interrogation betraying what they are, and even in your presence unable to conceal those deceits and trickeries of theirs. (*An Address To Demetrianus, 14-15*)

Firmilian

---

[82] This should give all Christians an extra incentive to not give in to temptation. Judas came under Satan's power due to his sinfulness. Geraldine Taylor, daughter-in-law of James Hudson Taylor, founder of the China Inland Mission, noted how of those cases of demon possession which had come under her personal observation "nearly all were said to have begun in some fit of anger or grief, lasting perhaps for days (*Pastor Hsi of North China, Ch. 10, p.109*)." See Ephesians 4:26 in connection with Taylor's observations.

[83] Note, again, the authority and power that the early Christians exercised over demonic powers.

BIO: [d. ca. 269] *The bishop of Caesarea in Cappadocia and a former student of Origen.*

But I wish to relate to you some facts concerning a circumstance which occurred among us, pertaining to this very matter. About twenty-two years ago, in the times after the Emperor Alexander...a severe persecution arose against us of the Christian name...the faithful being set in this state of disturbance, and fleeing here and there for fear of the persecution, and leaving their country and passing over into other regions...there arose among us on a sudden a certain woman, who in a state of ecstasy announced herself as a prophetess, and acted as if filled with the Holy Ghost. And she was so moved by the impulse of the principal demons, that for a long time she both made anxious and deceived the brotherhood, accomplishing certain wonderful and portentous things, and promised that she would cause the earth to be shaken. Not that the power of the demon was so great that he could prevail to shake the earth, or to disturb the elements; but that sometimes a wicked spirit, prescient, and perceiving that there will be an earthquake, pretends that he will do what he sees will happen. By these lies and boastings he had so subdued the minds of individuals, that they obeyed him and followed wherever he commanded and led.[84] He would also make that woman walk in the keen winter with bare feet over frozen snow, and not to be troubled or hurt in any degree by that walking. Moreover, she would say that she was hurrying to Judea and to Jerusalem, pretending as if she had come from there.[85] Here also she deceived one of the presbyters, a countryman, and another, a deacon, so that they had intercourse with that same woman, which was shortly afterwards detected.[86] For on a sudden there appeared unto her one of the exorcists,[87] a man approved and

---

[84] This incident demonstrates the dangers of false prophets in the church who claim to speak and act under the inspiration of the Holy Spirit—*people begin to follow them instead of the real Holy Spirit and end up being led away from God's will ultimately.*

[85] Note this false prophetess uses both demonically inspired special ability as well as deceit in order to take advantage of the people.

[86] Mt 7:15-20

[87] This term has been replaced in modern Protestant churches by expressions such as "Deliverance Minister", etc. but the older term was exorcist. It was an official position in the early church. In the third century Cornelius noted that there were fifty-two exorcists in the church at Rome alone (*Cornelius To Fabius*

always of good conversation in respect of religious discipline; who, encouraged by the exhortation also of very many brothers who were themselves strong and praiseworthy in the faith, raised himself up against that wicked spirit to overcome it; which moreover, by its subtle fallacy, had predicted this a little while before, that a certain adverse and unbelieving tempter would come.[88] Yet that exorcist, inspired by God's grace, bravely resisted, and showed that that which was before thought holy, was indeed a most wicked spirit. But that woman, who previously by wiles and deceitfulness of the demon was attempting many things for the deceiving of the faithful, among other things by which she had deceived many, also had frequently dared this; to pretend that with an invocation not to be contemned she sanctified bread and celebrated, the Eucharist, and to offer sacrifice to the Lord, not without the sacrament of the accustomed utterance; and also to baptize many, making use of the usual and lawful words of interrogation, that nothing might seem to be different from the ecclesiastical rule. (*Letter 74:10, in the collected letters of Cyprian of Carthage*)

Cornelius I

BIO: [d. ca. 252] *Cornelius was the 20th successor after Peter to the office of bishop of Rome, serving as bishop for two years before being martyred. He is remembered chiefly for his dispute with Novatian over the bishopric of Rome.*

Permit us to say further: On account of what works or conduct had he (Novatian) the assurance to contend for the episcopate? Was it that he had been brought up in the Church from the beginning, and had endured many conflicts in her behalf, and had passed through many and great dangers for religion? Truly this is not the fact. But Satan, who entered and dwelt in him for a long time, became the occasion of his believing. Being delivered by the exorcists, he fell into a severe sickness; and as he seemed about to die, he received baptism by pouring, on the bed where he lay; if indeed we can say that such a one did receive it. And when he was healed of his sickness he did not receive the other things which it is necessary to

---

of Antioch, in *Eusebius of Caesarea's Ecclesiastical History, 6:43:11*)

[88] Reminiscent of certain modern day "prophets" who refer to their detractors as unbelievers.

have according to the canon of the Church, even the being sealed by the bishop. And as he did not receive this, how could he receive the Holy Spirit? (*Epistle to Fabius of Antioch* in *Eusebius of Caesarea's Ecclesiastical History 6:43*)

Though Persecuted By Roman Emperors, Such As Valerian Above, The Early Christians Flourished In Spiritual Warfare

Lactantius

BIO: [c. 250-c. 325] *A fourth century Christian writer and Latin tutor for the Roman Emperor Flavius Constantine's son.*

...demons...fear the righteous, that is, the worshippers of God, adjured by whose name they depart from the bodies of the possessed: for, being lashed by their words as though by scourges, they not only confess themselves to be demons, but even utter their own names — those which are adored in the temples — which they generally do in the presence of their own worshippers; not, it is plain, to the disgrace of religion, but to the disgrace of their own

56

honor, because they cannot speak falsely to God, by whom they are adjured, nor to the righteous, by whose voice they are tortured. Therefore oftentimes having uttered the greatest howlings, they cry out that they are beaten, and are on fire, and that they are just on the point of coming forth: so much power has the knowledge of God, and righteousness! (*The Divine Institutes, 2:16*)

...the unclean spirits of demons, having received permission, throw themselves into the bodies of many;[89] and when these have afterwards been driven out, they who have been healed cling to the [Christian] religion, the power of which they have experienced. (*The Divine Institutes, 5:23*)

For in that He extended His hands on the cross, He plainly stretched out His wings towards the east and the west, under which all nations from either side of the world might assemble and repose. But of what great weight this sign is, and what power it has, is evident, since all the host of demons is expelled and put to flight by this sign. And as He Himself before His passion put to confusion demons by His word and command, so now, by the name and sign of the same passion, unclean spirits, having insinuated themselves into the bodies of men, are driven out, when racked and tormented, and confessing themselves to be demons, they yield themselves to God, who harasses them. What therefore can the Greeks expect from their superstitions and with their wisdom, when they see that their gods, whom they do not deny to be demons also,[90] are subdued by men through the cross? (*The Epitome Of The Divine Institutes, 51*)

Diocletian, as being of a fearful nature, was a searcher into the future, and during his stay in the East he began to slay victims, that from their livers he might obtain a prediction of events; and while he sacrificed, some attendants of his, who were Christians, stood

---

[89] It is important to keep in mind that all demonic activity only occurs by God's permission to accomplish his purposes (Jb 1:1-2:13, Ep 1:11). This was noted several times in the previous chapter. The popular concept that Satan and his demonic forces are running wild and uncontrolled to create havoc is simply not Scriptural.

[90] Lactantius is here referring to how the Greeks used the word for demon interchangeably for a god as well, as was explained in a previous footnote. See also 1Corinthians 10:20-21.

by, and they put the immortal sign [of the cross] on their foreheads. At this the demons were chased away, and the holy rites interrupted. The fortune tellers trembled, unable to investigate the wonted marks on the entrails of the victims. They frequently repeated the sacrifices, as if the former had been unsuccessful; but the victims, slain from time to time, afforded no tokens for divination. At length Tages, the chief of the fortune tellers, either from guess or from his own observation, said, "There are profane persons here, who obstruct the rites." Then Diocletian, in furious passion, ordered not only all who were assisting at the holy ceremonies, but also all who resided within the palace, to sacrifice, and, in case of their refusal, to be scourged. And further, by letters to the commanding officers, he directed that all soldiers should be forced to the same wicked behavior, under pain of being dismissed from the service. (*Of The Manner In Which The Persecutors Died, 10*)

Behold, someone excited by the impulse of the demon is out of his senses, raves, is mad: let us lead him into the temple of the excellent and mighty Jupiter [to procure a healing]; or since Jupiter knows not how to cure men, into the lane of Aesculapius or Apollo. Let the priest of either, in the name of his God, command the wicked spirit to come out of the man: that can in no way happen. What, then, is the power of the gods, if the demons are not subject to their control? But, in truth, the same demons, when adjured by the name of the true God, immediately flee. What reason is there why they should fear Christ, but not fear Jupiter, unless that they whom the multitude esteem to be gods are also demons? Lastly, if there should be placed in the midst one who is evidently suffering from an attack of a demon, and the priest of the Delphian Apollo, they will both in the same way dread the name of God; and Apollo will as quickly depart from his priest as the spirit of the demon from the man; and his god being adjured and put to flight, the priest will be for ever silent. Therefore the demons, whom they acknowledge to be accursed things, are the same as the gods to whom they offer supplications. If they imagine that we are unworthy of belief, let them believe Homer, who associated the supreme Jupiter with the demons; and also other poets and philosophers, who speak of the same beings at one time as demons, and at another time as gods, — of which names one is true, and the other false. For those most wicked spirits, when they are adjured, then confess that they are demons; when they are worshipped, then they falsely say that they are gods; in order that they may lead men into errors, and call them away from the knowledge of the true God, by which alone eternal death can be escaped. They are the same who, for the sake of overthrowing man, have founded various systems of worship for themselves through different regions, — under false and assumed names, however, that they might deceive.[91] For because they were unable by themselves to aspire to divinity, they took to themselves the names of powerful kings, under whose titles they might claim for themselves divine honors;[92] which error may be dispelled, and brought to the light of truth. For if anyone desires to inquire further into the matter, let him assemble those who are skilled in calling forth spirits from the dead. Let them call forth Jupiter, Neptune, Vulcan, Mercury, Apollo, and Saturnus the father of all. All will answer from the lower regions; and being questioned they will speak, and confess respecting themselves and God. After these things let them call up Christ; He will not be present, He will not appear, for He was not more than two days in the lower regions.[93] What proof can be brought forward more certain than this? (*The Divine Institutes, 4:27*)

Eusebius of Caesarea

BIO: [c. 260-c. 340?] *A bishop of Caesarea and acquaintance of Roman Emperor Flavius Constantine. He is remembered chiefly for writing a history of the church from before the time of Christ up until his time.*

Who else than He, with an invisible and yet powerful hand, has driven from human society like wild animals that ever noxious and destructive tribe of evil spirits who of old had made all nations their prey, and by the motions of their images had practiced many a delusion among men? Who else, beside our Savior, by the invocation of his name, and by unfeigned prayer addressed through

---

[91] Lactantius is here referring to how all false gods are the creations of demons, attempting to divert worship away from God to themselves.
[92] A reference to the belief that a society's gods are based upon ancient human rulers whose legacies have taken on mythological characteristics over time to the point that they no longer resemble humans but divinities.
[93] Ro 10:7, Ep 4:9-10

him to the Supreme God, has given power to banish from the world the remnant of those wicked spirits to those who with genuine and sincere obedience pursue the course of life and conduct which he has himself prescribed? (*Oration In Praise Of Constantine, 16:9*)

Arnobius

BIO: [fl. 297-303] *A former rhetoric teacher in Africa who was led to embrace Christianity through dreams. Author of a work against idolatry.*

Was He one of us, who, after His body had been laid in the tomb, manifested Himself in open day to countless numbers of men[94]...whose name, when heard, puts to flight evil spirits, imposes silence on fortune tellers, prevents men from consulting the augurs,[95] causes the efforts of arrogant magicians to be frustrated, not by the dread of His name, as you allege, but by the free exercise of a greater power? (*Seven Books Against The Heathen, 1:46*)

Cyril of Jerusalem

BIO: [c.315-386] *A bishop of Jerusalem who was extensively involved in combating Arianism.*

Let us then not be ashamed of the Cross of our Savior, but rather glory in it. *For the word of the Cross is unto Jews a stumbling-block, and unto Gentiles foolishness,*[96] but to us salvation...If any disbelieve the power of the Crucified, let him ask the devils; if any believe not words, let him believe what he sees. Many have been crucified throughout the world, but by none of these are the devils scared; but when they see even the Sign of the Cross of Christ, who was crucified for us, they shudder. (*Catechetical Lecture, 13:3*)

Palladius

---

[94] 1Co 15:3-8
[95] A group of ancient Roman officials charged with observing and interpreting omens for guidance in public affairs.
[96] 1Co 1:23

BIO: [368-c.431] *A monk who became the bishop of Helenopolis in Bithynia. Known for writing an autobiographical and anecdotal history of some early Christian monks who lived in the Egyptian desert.*

Before my eyes a young lad was brought to him[97] possessed by an evil spirit. So, putting one hand on his head and the other on his heart, he prayed so much that he made him hang in midair. Then the boy swelled like a wineskin and festered so that he became a mass of erysipelas.[98] And having cried out suddenly, he produced water through all his senses, and calming down returned to his original size. So he anointed him with holy oil and handed him to his father, and having poured water upon him ordered that he should touch neither flesh nor wine for forty days. And so he healed him. (*The Lausiac History, 28:22*)

The stories about Posidonius the Theban are many...I lived with him at Bethlehem for one year...And this was the miracle he did in Bethlehem. A certain woman approaching her confinement had an unclean spirit and, when she was actually about to be delivered, she had difficult labor, the spirit tormenting her. The husband, therefore, since his wife was suffering from the demon, came and besought that holy man to come. So he stood up----we were present, having come at the same time to pray----and prayed, and after kneeling down for the second time he drove out the spirit. So he stood up and said to us: "Pray, for at this moment the unclean spirit is going out, and there should be a sign, that we may be convinced." So the demon on his way out of her threw down the whole wall of the precincts, foundations and all. Now the woman had been six years without speech. After the demon had gone out she gave birth to a child and spoke.[99] (*The Lausiac History, 36:1-5*)

You have heard from many the story of the blessed Innocent, the priest of the Mount of Olives, but none the less you will hear it also from us who lived with him for three years...Once a young man was brought to him before our eyes taken by a spirit and by

---

[97] That is, Macarius of Alexandria.
[98] A skin disorder characterized by a rash and swelling.
[99] Mt 9:32-33

paralysis, so that I, having seen him, wished publicly to repel the mother of the man who had been brought, since I despaired of his cure. Well, it happened in the meantime that the old man having come up saw her standing and weeping and lamenting over the unspeakable misfortune of her son. So the good old man wept and, moved with compassion, took the young man and entered into his oratory, which he had built with his own hands, and in which relics of John the Baptist were laid. And having prayed over him from the third hour to the ninth, he restored the young man to his mother cured that same day, having driven out both his paralysis and the demon. His paralysis was such that the boy, when he spat, spat on his own back, so twisted was he. (*The Lausiac History, 44:1-4*)

Sozomen

BIO: [c. 380-c. 447] *A native of Palestine who wrote a history of the Christian church covering the years 323-423AD.*

My grandfather was of pagan parentage; and, with his own family and that of Alaphion, had been the first to embrace Christianity in Bethelia, a populous town near Gaza, in which there are temples highly reverenced by the people of the country, on account of their antiquity and structural excellence. The most celebrated of these temples is the Pantheon...a word which signifies that the temple is the residence of all the gods. It is said that the above-mentioned families were converted through the instrumentality of the monk Hilarion. Alaphion, it appears, was possessed of a devil; and neither the pagans nor the Jews could, by any incantations and enchantments, deliver him from this affliction; but Hilarion, by simply calling on the name of Christ, expelled the demon, and Alaphion, with his whole family, immediately embraced Christianity. (*Church History, 5:15*)[100]

---

[100] For some of the entries for this chapter I modernized the 19th century English translations to make them easier to read.

Some Observations On
The Decline Of Demonic Activity

In 312AD a Roman soldier with aspirations of becoming emperor embraced the Christian religion after experiencing a supernatural dream and a vision of a cross in the sky with the accompanying instructions to "Conquer by this". Taking this vision to heart and decorating his army with a Christian symbol Flavius Constantine conquered the Roman Empire.[101] After becoming emperor he ended the persecution of Christians which had occurred some ten times since the first century.[102] This began a political campaign, which would be continued by most of Constantine's successors, of de-paganizing the Roman Empire and establishing in its place a Christian kingdom. Interestingly, after the conversion of Constantine and the ensuing favor which all but one of the emperors after him assigned to Christianity, demonic activity began to greatly decline in the Roman world. In fact, this decline is so marked that contemporary references to demonic activity in the Middle Ages almost disappear with most references to demonic activity written at that time being references to past events. Whereas before the embracing of Christianity by the Roman emperors, Christians talked about their personal, eyewitness encounters with demoniacs, Christians now found themselves having to refer to accounts of demon possession in the *past tense*. And Christians took note of this. As early as 318 Athanasius commented that "whereas formerly every place was full of the deceit of the oracles, and the oracles at Delphi and Dodona, and in Bœotia and Lycia and Libya and Egypt and those of the Cabiri, and the Pythoness, were held in repute by men's imagination, now, since Christ has begun to be preached everywhere, their madness also has ceased and there is none among them to divine any more. And whereas formerly demons used to deceive men's fancy, occupying springs or rivers, trees or stones, and thus imposed upon the simple by their juggleries; now, after the divine visitation of the Word, their deception has ceased.

---

[101] Eusebius of Caesarea's *Life of Constantine, 1:8, 28-31*
[102] Under emperors Nero (64AD), Domitian (81), Trajan (108), Antoninus (162), Severus (192), Maximinus (235), Decius (249), Valerian (257), Aurelian (274), and the Diocletian/Maximian (303) administrations.

For by the Sign of the Cross, though a man but use it, he drives out their deceits."[103] Eusebius of Caesarea, writing in the year 335, noted how that Jesus "with an invisible and yet potent hand, has driven from human society like savage beasts that ever noxious and destructive tribe of evil spirits who of old had made all nations their prey…our Savior…has given power to banish from the world the remnant of those wicked spirits."[104] Fifty years later Gregory of Nyssa would note

"For who is there that does not know that every part of the world was overspread with demoniacal delusion which mastered the life of man through the madness of idolatry; how this was the customary rule among all nations, to worship demons under the form of idols…all these things passed away like smoke into nothingness, the madness of their oracles and prophesyings ceased, the annual pomps and pollutions of their bloody hecatombs came to an end, while among most nations altars entirely disappeared, together with porches, precincts, and shrines, and all the ritual besides which was followed out by the attendant priest of those demons…So that in many of these places no memorial exists of these things having ever been. But, instead, throughout the whole world there have arisen in the name of Jesus temples and altars…"[105]

Numerous examples of demonic activity from the Middle Ages could be cited, but as mentioned above it is usually presented from the perspective of a past event from a generation or more earlier rather than an eyewitness account. In the process of being passed down orally, these stories appear to have become unbelievably exaggerated.[106]

---

[103] *On The Incarnation Of The Word*, Ch. 47:1-2
[104] *Oration In Praise Of Constantine, 16*
[105] *The Great Catechism, 18*
[106] I will refer the reader to such works as Athanasius' *Life of Antony*, Jerome's *Life of Saint Hilarion*, Sulpitus Severus' *On The Life of Saint Martin*, and Gregory the Great's *Dialogues* and encourage them to make their own decisions regarding the accuracy of these accounts. Of note, certain accounts recorded in the *Life of Antony* do seem very plausible and realistic, though there was much in it attributed to demonic activity that I found to be questionable. Many of the

However, in keeping with the theme of this book, that it would be a survey of recorded instances of demonic activity from the past 2,000 years, I have decided to include a few stories which do seem believable. I will leave it up to the reader to judge.

After Flavius Constantine Embraced Christianity
The Power Of Demons In The Roman Empire Seemed To Diminish

unbelievable references to demonic activity in the above works are probably traceable to real incidents which were simply morphed into unbelievable reports over time.

Accounts From The Middle Ages
(5th-16th Centuries)

Anonymous

BIO: [c. 493- early 500's] *The following account was recorded by a disciple of Daniel the Stylite, the man whom this narrative involves. Daniel the Stylite (c.410-c.490) was a monk who lived on top of a pillar near Constantinople. The author never identifies himself.*

Once he[107] heard some men speaking in Syrian saying that there was a church in that place that was inhabited by demons who would often cause ships to sink and had injured, and were still injuring, many of the people who passed by that location to the point that it was impossible for anyone to walk on that road in the evening and not even at noonday.[108]

While everyone continued complaining about the destructive power which lived in the place, the Divine Spirit came upon Daniel and he remembered that great man, Antony, the model of asceticism [and his disciple Paul]. His mind was led to reflect on their struggles against demons, the many temptations that they suffered from them and how they had gained the victory over them by the strength of Christ and were deemed worthy of great crowns.[109] At this point he asked a man who understood Syrian about the church and begged him to show him where it was.

When they reached the porch of the church, just like a brave soldier who would strip himself for battle before going out against an army of barbarians, so he, too, entered into the church reciting the words spoken by the prophet David in the Psalms: "The Lord is my light and my savior, whom shall I fear? The Lord is the defender of my life, of whom shall I be afraid?"[110] and the rest. And holding the undefeatable weapon of the Cross, he went around into each corner of the church kneeling down on one knee and then rising again and made prayers.

---

[107] That is, Daniel the Stylite.
[108] The text doesn't say that this was actually happening. It merely states that people were *saying* that it was happening.
[109] See Athanasius' *Life of Antony.*
[110] Ps 27:1

66

After dark they say that stones were thrown at him and that there was the sound of a crowd of people knocking and making an uproar;[111] but he continued in prayer. In this manner, he spent the first and second nights; but on the third night he was overcome with sleep, just like it might overtake any man bearing the weakness of the flesh. Immediately, many phantoms appeared[112] as of giant shapes, some of whom said, "Who led you to take possession of this place, poor wretch? Do you desire to die a miserable death? Come, let us drag him out and throw him into the water!"[113] Again, others were carrying, it seemed, large stones and stood at his head, apparently intending to crush it into pieces. Upon waking up,[114] the athlete of Christ again went around the corners of the church praying and singing and saying to the spirits, "Depart from here! If you do not, then you shall be devoured by flames by the strength of the Cross and in this manner be forced to flee". But they made an even greater racket and howled even louder. But he despised them and, not taking even the slightest notice of their racket, bolted the door of the church and left a small window through which he could converse with the people that came up to visit with him.

Meanwhile, his fame had spread abroad in those parts and you could see men and women streaming with their children up to see the holy man and to marvel at how the place that was previously so wild and impassable now lay in such a perfect calm, and that where demons had recently danced, there Christ was now glorified day and night because of the patience of the just man. (*The Life And Works Of Our Holy Father, St. Daniel The Stylite, Ch. 14-16*)[115]

---

[111] In the 17th century Increase Mather recorded the cases of Nicholas Desborough, William Morse and George Walton who experienced stones and other objects being mysteriously thrown inside and outside of their homes and attributed it to demonic activity (*Remarkable Providences, Ch.5*). Adam Clarke is recorded as having heard strange noises from a kitchen as if objects were being moved when no one was there (*An Account of the Infancy and Literary Life of Adam Clarke, Bk. 1, pp.76-77*). Samuel Wesley, father to Methodist movement founder John Wesley, himself witnessed strange noises in his home (discussed below).

[112] That is, in a dream.

[113] Compare Matthew 17:15.

[114] Notice how demons can speak to people in their dreams.

[115] The aforementioned phenomena at the Wesley home (detailed in chapter six) and my own experiences in a Nazarene Church have confirmed my belief that

Jonas of Bobbio

BIO: [c. 599-d. after 659] *A monk and biographer of several well known Christians. His biographical account of Columban, from which the excerpt below comes, was based upon his interviews with some of Columban's close friends. Columban was an abbot and missionary who was born in Ireland around 540 and died at Bobbio, Italy, in 640.*

From *Cavalo* he[116] went to the river *Chora* where he stayed in the house of a noble and pious lady, named Theudemanda, and healed twelve demoniacs who came to him. (*The Life of Saint Columban, Ch. 39*)

Then leaving Auxerre, Columban saw a youth possessed by a demon running swiftly toward him. This youth had run twenty miles with all his might. Seeing him, Columban waited until the man, wounded by the devil's art, should come. The latter fell at the feet of the man of God and was immediately cured by his prayers and visibly restored to health. (*The Life of Saint Columban, Ch. 40*)

While Columban remained there, a certain woman tormented by a demon came to him, together with her daughter who was also suffering from a severe disease. When he saw them, he prayed to the Lord for them; after they had been healed, he commanded them to return home. (*The Life of Saint Columban, Ch. 46*)

Caesar of Heisterbach

BIO: [1180-c.1249] *Prior in the monastery at Heisterbach. Author of a popular book on sermon illustrations.*

When our abbot was celebrating mass last year on the Mount of the Holy Savior near Aachen, a possessed woman was brought to him after the mass. When he had read the gospel lesson concerning the Ascension over her head and at these words, "They shall lay hands on the sick and they shall recover,"[117] had placed his hand upon her head, the devil gave such a terrible roar that we were all

---

evil spirits may "haunt" church buildings and properties.

[116] That is, Columban.

[117] Mk 16:18

terrified. Adjured to depart, he replied, "The Most High does not wish it yet."[118] When asked in what manner he entered, he did not reply nor did he permit the woman to reply. Afterward she confessed that when her husband in anger said, "Go to the devil!" she felt the latter enter through her ear.[119] Moreover that woman was from the province of Aachen and very well known. (*Distinctio 5, Ch. 11*)

**Daniel The Stylite Was Not
Afraid To Practice Spiritual Warfare**

---

[118] Take note of the reference to the sovereignty of God over the demons in this situation.

[119] Reminiscent of the murderer of John Lennon, Mark David Chapman's testimony that after his act of murder he asked Jesus to deliver him from the demon that controlled him and as it left he felt it come out of his mouth. Note, however, in the case above that this is merely her opinion as to how she became possessed. It may have been that, after her deliverance, she tried to think back as to when and how she had become demonized. Remembering her husband's words and that her ear itched at the same moment she assumed that this was the time and place of entry. It may or may not have been. She could have opened the door any number of ways.

Accounts From The Early Modern Era
(16th-18th Centuries)

Martin Luther

BIO: [1483-1546] *German monk whose stand against the Vatican played a large part in the Reformation of the church and creation of Protestantism.*

We cannot expel demons with certain ceremonies and words, as Jesus Christ, the prophets, and the apostles did. All we can do, is in the name of Jesus Christ, to pray the Lord God, of his infinite mercy, to deliver the possessed persons. And if our prayer is offered up in full faith, we are assured by Christ himself (John 16:23),[120] that it will be efficacious, and overcome all the devil's resistance. I might mention many instances of this. (*Table Talk, 629*)

There☐☐ at Arnstadt the pastor has driven a devil out of a young girl in a truly Christian way.☐ Regarding this event we say: may the will of God, who is still alive, be done, even though the devil should be sorry about this.☐ (*Letter To Katie, from Weimar, July 2, 1540*)

Increase Mather

BIO: [1639-1723] *President of Harvard College and the foremost minister of his day in Colonial America. He is reported to have spent sixteen hours a day studying.*

Very remarkable was that Providence wherein Ann Cole of Hartford in New-England was concerned. She was, and is

---

[120] "In that day you will not question Me about anything. Truly, truly, I say to

accounted, a person of real piety and integrity; nevertheless, in the year 1662, then living in her fathers house (who has likewise been esteemed a godly man), she was taken with very strange fits, wherein her tongue was improved by a daemon to express things which she herself knew nothing of; sometimes the discourse would hold for a considerable time; the general purpose of which was, that such and such persons (who were named in the discourse which passed from her) were consulting how they might carry on mischievous designs against her and several others, mentioning sundry wayes they should take for that end, particularly that they would afflict her body, spoil her name, &c. The general answer made amongst the daemons was, "She runs to the rock." This having continued some hours, the daemons said, "Let us confound her language, that she may tell no more tales." She uttered matters unintelligible.[121] And then the discourse passed into a Dutch tone (a Dutch family then lived in the town), and therein an account was given of some afflictions that had befallen divers; amongst others, what had befallen a woman that lived next neighbour to the Dutch family, whose arms had been strangely pinched in the night, declaring by whom and for what cause that course had been taken with her. The Reverend Mr. Stone (then teacher of the church in Hartford) being by, when the discourse hapned, declared that he thought it impossible for one not familiarly acquainted with the Dutch (which Ann Cole had not in the least been) should so exactly imitate the Dutch tone in the pronunciation of English. Several worthy persons (viz., Mr. John Whiting, Mr. Samuel Hooker, and Mr. Joseph Haines) wrote the intelligible sayings expressed by Ann Cole, whilest she was thus amazingly handled.

The event was, that one of the persons (whose name was Greensmith,[122] being a lewd and ignorant woman, and then in prison on suspicion for witchcraft) mentioned in the discourse as active in the mischief done and designed, was by the magistrate sent for; Mr. Whiting and Mr. Haines read what they had written, and the woman being astonished thereat, confessed those things to be true, and that she and other persons named in this preternatural discourse, had had familiarity with the devil.[123] Being asked

---

you, if you ask the Father for anything in My name, He will give it to you."

[121] Compare Luke 11:14.

[122] That is, Rebecca Greensmith.

[123] This teaches us that just because a person is able to pronounce the secret sins

71

whether she had made an express covenant with him, she answered, she had not, only as she promised to go with him when he called, which accordingly she had sundry times done, and that the devil told her that at Christmass they would have a merry meeting, and then the covenant between them should be subscribed.

The next day she was more particularly enquired of concerning her guilt respecting the crime she was accused with. She then acknowledged, that though when Mr. Haines began to read what he had taken down in writing, her rage was such that she could have torn him in pieces, and was as resolved as might be to deny her guilt (as she had done before), yet after he had read awhile, she was (to use her own expression) as if her flesh had been pulled from her bones, and so could not deny any longer: she likewise declared, that the devil first appeared to her in the form of a deer or fawn, skipping about her, wherewith she was not much affrighted, and that by degrees he became very familiar, and at last would talk with her; moreover, she said that the devil had frequently the carnal knowledge of her body;[124] and that the witches had meetings at a place not far from her house; and that some appeared in one shape, and others in another; and one came flying amongst them in the shape of a crow. Upon this confession, with other concurrent evidence, the woman was executed; so likewise was her husband, though he did not acknowledge himself guilty. Other persons accused in the discourse made their escape. Thus doth the devil use to serve his clients. After the suspected witches were either executed or fled, Ann Cole was restored to health, and has continued well for many years, approving herself a serious Christian.[125] (*Remarkable Providences Illustrative of the*

---

of others that this does not mean they are necessarily speaking under the influence of the Holy Spirit.

[124] Were these experiences via a vision or was it something that was actually seen and experienced? Note also that the devil became familiar with her by degrees. Satan's method of operation is usually to creep into people's lives slowly, gaining an inch here and an inch there until over time he has full possession of an individual.

[125] The executions of the Greensmiths took place in January 1662. This event took place some thirty years before the so-called "Salem Witchcraft Trials" in which nineteen persons were wrongfully executed for witchcraft and should not be confused with it. The above event should in no way be interpreted to mean that it is advisable to act upon information given by demons through the

Another thing which caused a noise in the countrey, and wherein Satan had undoubtedly a great influence, was that which hapned at Groton. There was a maid in that town (one Elizabeth Knap) who in the moneth of October, anno 1671, was taken after a very strange manner, sometimes weeping, sometimes laughing, sometimes roaring hideously, with violent motions and agitations of her body, crying out "Money, money," &c. In November following, her tongue for many hours together was drawn like a semicircle up to the roof of her mouth, not to be removed, though some tried with their fingers to do it. Six men were scarce able to hold her in some of her fits,[126] but she would skip about the house yelling and looking with a most frightful aspect.

December 17: Her tongue was drawn out of her mouth to an extraordinary length; and now a daemon began manifestly to speak in her. Many words were uttered wherein are the labial letters,[127] without any motion of her lips, which was a clear demonstration that the voice was not her own. Sometimes words were spoken seeming to proceed out of her throat, when her mouth was shut; sometimes with her mouth wide open, without the use of any of the organs of speech. The things then uttered by the devil were chiefly railings and revilings of Mr. Willard (who was at that time a worthy and faithful pastor to the church in Groton). Also the daemon belched forth most horrid and nefandous blasphemies, exalting himself above the Most High. After this she was taken speechless for some time.

One thing more is worthy of remark concerning this miserable creature. She cried out in some of her fits, that a woman (one of her neighbours) appeared to her, and was the cause of her affliction. The person thus accused was a very sincere, holy woman, who did hereupon, with the advice of friends, visit the poor wretch; and though she was in one of her fits, having her eyes shut, when the innocent person impeached by her came in, yet could she (so powerful were Satans operations upon her) declare

---

possessed. Had this advice been taken the "Salem Witchcraft Trials" tragedy would have never occurred. The following two narratives will demonstrate this more clearly.

[126] Compare Mark 5:3-4.

[127] Letters of the alphabet that can only be pronounced with the use of the lips.

who was there, and could tell the touch of that woman from any ones else.[128] But the gracious party, thus accused and abused by a malicious devil, prayed earnestly with and for the possessed creature; after which she confessed that Satan had deluded her, making her believe evil of her good neighbour without any cause. Nor did she after that complain of any apparition or disturbance from such an one. Yea, she said, that the devil had himself, in the likeness and shape of divers, tormented her, and then told her it was not he but they that did it.[129] (*Remarkable Providences Illustrative of the Earlier Days of American Colonisation, Ch.5*)

Cotton Mather

BIO: [1663-1728] *Son of Increase Mather and a leading figure in the Salem Witchcraft Trials of 1692, the results of which were nineteen innocent persons being wrongfully executed. What follows is Mather's account of a court trial in which a minister named George Burroughs was accused of practicing witchcraft, the basis of his charge being that certain persons claimed to have experienced him appearing to them in a ghostly form and claiming to be a witch. This was referred to as "Spectral Evidence" and was considered legal evidence that could be used to convict a person of witchcraft in colonial New England. Spectral evidence, however, was nothing more than a demon appearing in the form in a person, claiming to be them and confessing their practice of witchcraft in an attempt to destroy the reputation and life of that individual. Burroughs would be found guilty and executed on August 19, 1692.*[130]

---

[128] An example of psychic ability given through the aid of a demon.

[129] This story should serve as a warning against trusting information that a person who is demon possessed offers. If Knap's information had been accepted it could have led to the neighbor being accused of and executed for being a witch when she was totally innocent. Our next narrative will make this unsettlingly clear.

[130] In preparing this section I realized that Mather's 17th century English would be very hard to understand by many modern readers so I took the liberty of updating it in many places throughout this narrative. This is the only narrative in which I have chosen to do so. For those wishing to read the original, it can be

I. This George Burroughs[131] was indicted for practicing witchcraft, and in the prosecution of the charge against him, he was accused by five or six of the bewitched,[132] as the cause of their sufferings; he was accused by eight of the confessing witches, as being a principal leader at some of their Hellish meetings, and as one who had been given the promise of being a king in Satan's kingdom, now going to be established...about thirty testimonies were brought in against him; nor were these judged to be even half of what might have been considered as evidence for his conviction: however they were enough to fix the character of a witch upon him...

II. The court...heard the testimonies of several persons, who were most notoriously bewitched, and every day tortured by invisible hands, and these now all charged the Specters[133] of George Burroughs to have a share in their sufferings.[134] At the examination of the said George Burroughs the bewitched people were grievously harassed with supernatural troubles, which could not possibly be faked;[135] and they still ascribed it unto the efforts of George Burroughs to kill them.[136] And now upon his trial, one of the bewitched persons[137] testified, that in her sufferings, a little black haired man came to her, saying his name was Burroughs and

---

found easily on the internet and in many libraries.

[131] Throughout his narrative Mather referred to George Burroughs as G.B. For sake of reading ease I have replaced this with Burroughs' actual name.

[132] Persons claiming to have been affected by the magical influence of a witch.

[133] Ghostly apparitions who were said to have appeared to the bewitched, in the form of the accused. The appearance of the accused in a ghostly form was taken by the courts to be evidence of their guilt.

[134] The prosecution witnesses included individuals who had experienced some kind of supernatural appearance of Burroughs to them which had caused them suffering. More detail of these experiences will follow in the narrative.

[135] While at the trial, these witnesses experienced unusual phenomena (demonic attacks) while Burroughs was being questioned by the lawyers, which led the court to believe that Burroughs had entered into a pact with a familiar spirit and was using his relationship with the spirit to affect the witnesses.

[136] These persons truly believed that they were being supernaturally molested by Burroughs to the point that they were willing to express this knowing that their testimony could cause a man's execution.

[137] Ann Putnam, her testimony after the execution of Burroughs helped to confirm the demonic deception involved in the Salem witchcraft trials. Putnam was only twelve years old yet she would serve as a witness claiming that sixty two persons had afflicted her using witchcraft.

bidding her to take hold of a book which he showed unto her; and bragging that he was a conjurer, above the ordinary rank of witches; that he often persecuted her with the offer of that book, saying, she should be well, and need fear nobody, if she would but sign it; but he inflicted cruel pains and hurts upon her, because of her denying to do so. The testimonies of the other sufferers concurred with these;[138] and it was remarkable, that whereas biting was one of the ways which the witches used for the troubling of the sufferers, when they cried out that George Burroughs was biting them, the print of the teeth would be seen on the flesh of the complainers, and just such a set of teeth as George Burroughs' would then appear upon them, which could be distinguished from those of some other men's teeth.[139] Others of them testified, that in their torments, George Burroughs tempted them to go unto a Sacrament,[140] unto which they perceived him with a sound of a trumpet summoning other witches, who quickly after the sound would come from all quarters unto the meeting place. One of them falling into a kind of trance,[141] afterwards affirmed, that George Burroughs had carried her into a very high mountain, where he showed her mighty and glorious kingdoms, and said, he would give them all to her, if she would write in his book; but she told him, they were none of his to give; and refused the motions, enduring through much misery for that refusal.[142]

It cost the court a wonderful deal of trouble, to hear the testimonies of the sufferers; for when they were going to give in their depositions, they would for a long time be taken with fits, that made them incapable of saying anything.[143] The Chief Judge asked the prisoner, who he thought hindered these witnesses from giving

---

[138] Persons who were not spiritually discerning would be easily led astray to believe by these experiences that Burroughs was indeed the cause of their molestation. This should serve as a grim warning to all of us to exercise caution when dealing with any kind of supernatural experience.

[139] In this example of molestation bite marks matching the teeth of Burroughs would supernaturally appear upon the afflicted.

[140] A sacred assembly of witches.

[141] Notice that demons can cause people to fall into a trance.

[142] Compare Matthew 4:8-9.

[143] This public show of affliction only served to convince the court that Burroughs was working with the Devil. After all, it appeared that the witnesses were being restrained by a supernatural force from testifying against the defendant and this would only naturally cast suspicion upon him given that the charges were that he had entered into a pact with a demon.

their testimonies? and he answered, He supposed it was the Devil. That Honorable person[144] then replied, 'How come the Devil is so much against having any Testimony born against you?', which cast him into a very great confusion.

III. It has been a frequent thing for the Bewitched people to be entertained with apparitions of ghosts of murdered people, at the same time that the specters of the witches trouble them. These ghosts do always frighten those who see them more than all the other spectral representations; and when they show themselves, they cry out, of being murdered by the witchcraft or other violent actions of the persons who are then present in a specter form...Accordingly several of the bewitched had given in their testimony, that they had been troubled with the apparitions of two women, who said that they were George Burroughs' two wives,[145] and that he had been the cause of the death of them; and that the Magistrates must be told of it, before whom if Burroughs upon his trial denied it, they did not know but that they should appear again in the court. Now, George Burroughs had been infamous for the barbarous treatment of his two successive wives, all the country over.[146] Moreover, it was testified, the specter of George Burroughs...told them, he had killed (besides others) Mrs. Lawson and her daughter Ann...[147]

Well, George Burroughs being now upon his trial, one of the bewitched persons was cast into horror at the ghosts of Burroughs' two deceased wives then appearing before him, and crying for vengeance against him. Hereupon several of the bewitched persons were successively called in, who all not knowing what the former had seen and said, concurred in their horror of the apparition, which they affirmed that he had before him. But he, though much appalled, utterly denied that he discerned anything of it; nor was it any part of his conviction...Now, as there might have been testimonies enough of George Burroughs' aversion to prayer and the other ordinances of God, though by his profession he was singularly obliged thereunto;[148]

---

[144] The Chief Judge.

[145] Burroughs had been widowed twice.

[146] If this was true it might help to explain why God allowed Satan to attack Burroughs in this manner. Sin is an open door to demonic attack.

[147] Persons whom Burroughs had contact with in Salem-Village where he had previously been a minister.

so, there now came in against the prisoner the testimonies of several persons, who confessed of their own having been horrible witches, and ever since their confessions had been themselves terribly tortured by the devils and other witches, even like the other sufferers; and therein undergone the pains of many deaths for their confessions.

These now testified, that George Burroughs had been at witch-meetings with them; and that he was the person who had seduced and compelled them into the snares of witchcraft: That he promised them fine clothes, for doing it; that he brought puppets to them, and thorns to stick into those puppets, for the afflicting of other people;[149] and that he encouraged them, with the rest of the crew, to bewitch all Salem-Village, but to be sure to do it gradually, if they would succeed in what they did.[150]

When the Lancashire Witches were condemned,[151] I don't remember that there was any considerable further evidence, than that of the bewitched, and then that of some that confessed. We see so much already against George Burroughs but this being indeed not enough, there were other evidences that would give the evidence already produced credibility...[152]

It was testified, that keeping his two successive wives in a strange kind of slavery, he would when he came home from abroad pretend to tell the talk which any had with them;[153] that he has brought them to the point of death, by his harsh dealings with his wives, and then made the people about him to promise that in case death should happen, they would say nothing of it; that he used all means to make his wives write, sign, seal, and swear a covenant, never to reveal any of his secrets; that his wives had privately

---

[148] If this was true, it could also help to explain why God allowed Satan to attack Burroughs in this manner.

[149] Similar to a voodoo doll.

[150] Why would the court trust the testimony of a confessed witch? They could be manipulated by demons to give false testimony or they could be motivated to give false testimony with the hopes that they would get a lighter sentence.

[151] This occurred in 1612.

[152] These included supposed feats of strength that Burroughs had accomplished (which to a modern reader really do not appear at all to be supernatural) and the negative testimony of the brother of one of Burroughs wives, which, if Burroughs really was abusive towards his wife as was reported, one would expect to be negative.

[153] In a psychic way.

complained unto the neighbors about frightful apparitions of evil spirits,[154] with which their house was sometimes infested; and that many such things have been whispered among the neighborhood. There were also some other testimonies, relating to the death of people, whereby the consciences of an impartial jury were convinced that George Burroughs had bewitched the persons mentioned in the complaints...

VIII. Faltering, faulty, inconsistent, and contrary answers upon judicial and deliberate examination, are counted some unlucky symptoms of guilt, in all crimes, especially in witchcrafts. Now there never was a prisoner more eminent for them, than George Burroughs both at his examination and on his trial. His evasiveness, contradictions, and falsehoods, were very obvious: he had little to say, but that he had heard some things that he could not prove, reflecting upon the reputation of some of the witnesses. Only he gave in a paper to the jury; wherein, although he had many times before granted, not only that there are witches, but also that the present sufferings of the country are the effect of horrible witchcrafts, yet he now goes to prove, that there neither are, nor ever were witches, nor that having made a compact with the Devil, can send a devil to torment other people at a distance...

IX. The jury brought him in guilty: but when he came to die, he utterly denied the fact, whereof he had been thus convicted.[155] (*Wonders Of The Invisible World, The Tryal Of G.B. At A Court Of Oyer And Terminer, Held In Salem, 1692*)

Samuel Wesley & Family

BIO: [1666-1735] *Anglican rector of Epworth and the father of John Wesley, founder of the Methodist movement.*

From the first of December, my children and servants heard many strange noises, groans, knockings, &c., in every story, and most of the rooms of my house.

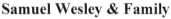

[154] Here Mather is showing his belief in evil spirits appearing as "apparitions". One is left to wonder why he did not assume that the "apparitions" of Burroughs' two deceased wives were not evil spirits in disguise for the purpose of leading people astray.

[155] When Burroughs was taken to the platform for his public hanging he recited

But I hearing nothing of it myself, they would not tell me for some time, because, according to the vulgar opinion, it if boded any ill to me, I could not hear it. When it increased, and the family could not easily conceal it, they told me of it.

My daughters, Susannah and Ann, were below stairs in the dining room; and heard, first at the doors, then over their heads, and the night after a knocking under their feet, though nobody was in the chambers or below them. The like they and my servants heard in both the kitchens, at the door against the partition, and over them. The maid-servant heard groans as of a dying man. My daughter Emilia, coming down stairs to draw up the clock and lock the doors at ten at night, as usual, heard under the staircase a sound among some bottles there, as if they had been all dashed to pieces; but when she looked, all was safe.

Something like the steps of a man was heard going up and down stairs, at all hours of the night, and vast rumblings below stairs, and in the garrets. My man, who lay in the garret, heard some one come slaring through the garret to his chamber, rattling

---

the Lord's Prayer in such a powerful way that it brought tears to some of the spectators. Fearing that the execution would be halted Cotton Mather rode up on a horse and declared to the people that the Devil has often been transformed into an angel of light which appeased the people to the point that the execution was able to continue (*The Witchcraft Delusion In New England, p.38-39*). A year later Mather's father, Increase, published a book in which he maintained that it should be recognized that demons could appear in the form of human beings in an attempt to destroy the lives of innocent persons (*Cases Of Conscience Concerning Evil Spirits Personating Men*). Fourteen years after the Salem Witchcraft Trials Ann Putnam, whose testimony of experiencing the "specter" of Burroughs was used to find him guilty, prepared a written apology which was read before her church congregation in which she stated, "I desire to be humbled before God for that sad and humbling providence...that I then being in my childhood should...be made an instrument for the accusing of several persons of a grievous crime whereby their lives were taken from them, whom now I have just grounds and good reason to believe they were innocent persons, and that it was a great *delusion of Satan* that deceived me in that sad time, whereby I justly fear I have been instrumental with others though ignorantly and unwittingly to bring upon myself and this land the guilt of innocent blood...what I did was ignorantly being *deluded by Satan*...for which cause I desire to lie in the dust and earnestly beg forgiveness of God and from all those unto whom I have given just cause of sorrow and offence, whose relations were taken away or accused (*The New England Historical and Genealogical Register, Vols. 12, 1858, p.246*)." May we never again rely on the testimony of demons when it comes to the fate of a man's life.

by his side, as if against his shoes, though he had none there; at other times walking up and down stairs, when all the house were in bed, and gobbling like a turkey-cock. Noises were heard in the nursery, and all the other chambers; knocking first at the feet of the bed and behind it; and a sound like that of dancing in a matted chamber, next to the nursery, when the door was locked, and nobody in it.

My wife would have persuaded them it was rats within doors, and some unlucky people knocking without; till at last we heard several loud knocks in our own chamber, on my side of the bed; but till, I think, the 21st at night, I heard nothing of it. That night I was waked a little before one by nine distinct very loud knocks, which seemed to be in the next room to ours, with a sort of a pause at every third stroke. I thought it might be somebody without the house; and having got a stout mastiff, hoped he would soon rid me of it.

The next night I heard six knocks, but not so loud as the former. I know not whether it was in the morning after Sunday the 23d, when about seven my daughter Emily called her mother into the nursery, and told her she might now hear the noises there. She went in, and heard it at the bedstead, then under the bed, then at the head of it. She knocked, and it answered her. She looked under the bed, and thought something ran from thence, but could not well tell of what shape, but thought it most like a badger.

The next night but one we were awaked about one by the noises, which were so violent, it was in vain to think of sleep while they continued. I rose, and my wife would rise with me. We went into every chamber, and down stairs; and generally as we went into one room we heard it in that behind us, though all the family had been in bed several hours. When we were going down stairs, and at the bottom of them, we heard, as Emily had done before, a clashing among the bottles, as if they had been broke all to pieces, and another sound distinct from it, as if a peck of money had been thrown down before us. The same, three of my daughters heard at another time.

We went through the hall into the kitchen, when our mastiff came whining to us, as he did always after the first night of its coming; for then he barked violently at it, but was silent afterward, and seemed more afraid than any of the children. We still heard it rattle and thunder in every room above or behind us, locked as well

81

as open, except my study, where as yet it never came. After two, we went to bed, and were pretty quiet the rest of the night.

Wednesday night, December 26, after or a little before ten, my daughter Emilia heard the signal of its beginning to play, with which she was perfectly acquainted; it was like the strong winding up of a jack. She called; and I went into the nursery, where it used to be most violent. The rest of the children were asleep. It began with knocking in the kitchen underneath, then seemed to be at the bed's feet, then under the bed, at last at the head of it. I went down stairs, and knocked with my stick against the joists of the kitchen. It answered me as often and as loud as I knocked; but then I knocked as I usually do at my door, 1—2 3 4 5 6—7; but this puzzled it, and it did not answer, or not in the same method; though the children heard it do the same exactly twice or thrice after.

I went up stairs, and found it still knocking hard, though with some respite, sometimes under the bed, sometimes at the bed's head. I observed my children that they were frighted in their sleep and trembled very much till it waked them. I stayed there alone, bid them go to sleep, and sat at the bed's feet by them, when the noise began again. I asked it what it was, and why it disturbed innocent children, and did not come to me in my study, if it had anything to say to me. Soon after it gave one knock on the outside of the house, (all the rest were within,) and knocked off for that night.

I went out of doors, sometimes alone, at others with company, and walked round the house, but could see or hear nothing. Several nights the latch of our lodging-chamber would be lifted up very often, when all were in bed. One night when the noise was great in the kitchen, and on a deal partition, and the door in the yard, the latch whereof was often lifted up, my daughter Emilia went and held it fast on the inside: but it was still lifted up, and the door pushed violently against her, though nothing was to be seen on the outside.

When we were at prayers, and came to the prayers for King George and the prince, it would make a great noise over our heads constantly, whence some of the family called it a Jacobite.[156] I

---

[156] A political movement that aimed to restore the Roman Catholic Stuart King James II of England and his heirs to the thrones of England, Scotland and Ireland. King George I was on the opposite side.

have been thrice pushed by an invisible power, once against the corner of my desk in the study, a second time against the door of the matted chamber, a third time against the right side of the frame of my study door, as I was going in.

I followed the noise into almost every room in the house, both by day and by night, with lights and without, and have sat alone for some time, and when I heard the noise, spoke to it to tell me what it was, but never heard any articulate voice, and only once or twice two or three feeble squeaks, a little louder than the chirping of a bird; but not like the noise of rats, which I have often heard.

I had designed Friday, December 28, to make a visit to a friend, Mr. Downs, at Normanby, and stay some days with him; but the noises were so boisterous on Thursday night that I did not care to leave my family. So I went to Mr. Hoole, of Haxey, and desired his company on Friday night. He came; and it began after ten, a little later than ordinary. The younger children were gone to bed, the rest of the family and Mr. Hoole were together in the matted chamber. I sent the servants down to fetch in some fuel, went with them, and stayed in the kitchen till they came in. When they were gone I heard loud noises against the doors and partition; and at length the usual signal, though somewhat after the time. I had never heard it before, but knew by the description my daughter had given me. It was much like the turning about of a windmill when the wind changes. When the servants returned, I went up to the company, who had heard the other noises below, but not the signal. We heard all the knocking as usual, from one chamber to another, but at its going off, like the rubbing of a beast against the wall. From that time till January 24th we were quiet.

Having received a letter from Samuel the day before relating to it, I read what I had written of it to my family; and this day, at morning prayer, the family heard the usual knocks at the prayer for the king. At night they were more distinct, both in the prayer for the king, and that for the prince; and one very loud knock at the *amen* was heard by my wife, and most of the children, at the inside of my bed. I heard nothing myself. After nine, Robert Brown, sitting alone by the fire in the back kitchen, something came out of the copper-hole like a rabbit, but less, and turned round five times very swiftly. Its ears lay flat upon its neck, and its little scut stood straight up. He ran after it with the tongs in his hands; but when he could find nothing, he was frighted, and went to the maid in the parlor.

On Friday, the 25th, having prayers at church, I shortened, as usual, those in the family at morning, omitting the confessions, absolution, and prayers for the king and prince. I observed, when this is done, there is no knocking. I therefore used them one morning for a trial; at the name of King George it began to knock, and did the same when I prayed for the prince. Two knocks I heard, but took no notice after prayers, till after all who were in the room, ten persons besides me, spoke of it, and said they heard it. No noise at all the rest of the prayers.

Sunday, January 27. Two soft strokes at the morning prayers for King George, above stairs.[157] (*Journal Of Samuel Wesley*)

John Wesley's Investigation Into The Matter
When I was very young, I heard several letters read, wrote to my elder brother by my father, giving an account of strange disturbances which were in his house at Epworth, in Lincolnshire.
1. When I went down thither, in the year 1720, I carefully inquired into the particulars. I spoke to each of the persons who were then in the house, and took down what each could testify of his or her own knowledge: The sum of which was this: —:
2. On December 2, 1716, while Robert Brown, my father's servant, was sitting with one of the maids, a little before ten at night, in the dining-room which opened into the garden, they both heard one knocking at the door. Robert rose and opened it, but could see nobody. Quickly it knocked again, and groaned. "It is Mr. Turpin," said Robert; "he has the stone, and uses to groan so." He opened the door again twice or thrice, the knocking being twice or thrice repeated. But still seeing nothing, and being a little startled, they rose and went up to bed.

When Robert came to the top of the garret-stairs, he saw a hand mill, which was at a little distance, whirled about very swiftly. When he related this, he said, "Nought vexed me, but that

---

[157] Four years after these events Samuel's son, John Wesley (founder of the Methodist movement), visited his parents home and conducted a thorough investigation into these events. What follows is his written report upon the occurrences.

it was empty. I thought, if it had but been full of malt, he might have ground his heart out for me."

When he was in bed, he heard as it were the gobbling of a turkey cock close to the bed-side; and soon after, the sound of one stumbling over his shoes and boots. But there were none there: He had left them below.

3. The next day, he and the maid related these things to the other maid, who laughed heartily, and said, "What a couple of fools are you! I defy anything to fright me." After churning in the evening, she put the butter in the tray, and had no sooner carried it into the dairy, than she heard a knocking on the shelf where several pantheons of milk stood, first above the shelf, then below. She took the candle, and searched both above and below; but, being able to find nothing, threw down butter, tray, and all, and ran away for life.

4. The next evening, between five and six o'clock, my sister Molly, then about twenty years of age, sitting in the dining-room, reading, heard as if it were the door that led into the hall open, and a person walking in that seemed to have on a silk nightgown, rustling and trailing along. It seemed to walk round her, then to the door, then round again; but she could see nothing. She thought, "It signifies nothing to run away; for whatever it is it can run faster than me." So she rose, put her book under her arm, and walked slowly away.

5. After supper, she was sitting with my sister Suky (about a year older than her) in one of the chambers, and telling her what had happened. She quite made light of it; telling her, "I wonder you are so easily frighted: I would fain see what would fright me." Presently a knocking began under the table. She took the candle and looked, but could find nothing. Then the iron casement began to clatter, and the lid of a warming-pan. Next the latch of the door moved up and down without ceasing. She started up, leaped into the bed without undressing, pulled the bedclothes over her head, and never ventured to look up till next morning.

6. A night or two after, my sister Hetty, a year younger than my sister Molly, was waiting as usual, between nine and ten, to take away my father's candle, when she heard one coming down the garret-stairs, walking slowly by her; then going down the best stairs, then up the back-stairs, and up the garret-stairs: And at every step it seemed the house shook from top to bottom. Just then

my father knocked. She went in, took his candle, and got to bed as fast as possible.

7. In the morning, she told this to my eldest sister; who told her, "You know I believe none of these things. Pray let me take away the candle tonight, and I will find out the trick." She accordingly took my sister Hetty's place, and had no sooner taken away the candle, than she heard a noise below. She hastened down stairs to the hall, where the noise was; but it was then in the kitchen. She ran into the kitchen, where it was drumming on the inside of the screen. When she went round, it was drumming on the outside, and so always on the side opposite to her. Then she heard a knocking at the back-kitchen door. She ran to it, unlocked it softly, and, when the knocking was repeated, suddenly opened it; but nothing was to be seen. As soon as she had shut it, the knocking began again. She opened it again, but could see nothing. When she went to shut the door, it was violently thrust against her. She let it fly open, but nothing appeared. She went again to shut it, and it was again thrust against her: But she set her knee and her shoulder to the door, forced it to, and turned the key. Then the knocking began again; but she let it go on, and went up to bed. However, from that time, she was thoroughly convinced that there was no imposture in the affair.

8. The next morning, my sister telling my mother what had happened, she said, "If I hear anything myself, I shall know how to judge."

Soon after, she begged her to come into the nursery. She did; and heard, in the corner of the room, as it were the violent rocking of a cradle: But no cradle had been there for some years. She was convinced it was preternatural, and earnestly prayed it might not disturb her in her own chamber, at the hours of retirement. And it never did.

She now thought it was proper to tell my father. But he was extremely angry, and said, "Suky, I am ashamed of you. These boys and girls fright one another; but you are a woman of sense, and should know better. Let me hear of it no more."

At six in the evening, he had family-prayers, as usual. When he began the prayer for the King, a knocking began all round the room; and a thundering knock attended the Amen. The same was heard from this time every morning and evening, while the prayer for the King was repeated.

As both my father and mother are now at rest, and incapable of being pained thereby, I think it my duty to furnish the serious reader with a key to this circumstance. The year before King William died, my father observed my mother did not say Amen to the prayer for the King. She said she could not; for she did not believe the Prince of Orange was King. He vowed he would never cohabit with her till she did. He then took his horse, and rode away; nor did she hear anything of him for a twelvemonth. He then came back, and lived with her as before. But I fear his vow was not forgotten before God.

9. Being informed that Mr. Hoole, the Vicar of Haxey, (an eminently pious and sensible man,) could give me some farther information, I walked over to him. He said, "Robert Brown came over to me, and told me your father desired my company. When I came, he gave me an account of all that had happened; particularly the knocking during family-prayer. But that evening (to my great satisfaction) we had no knocking at all: But between nine and ten, a servant came in, and said, 'Old Jeffries is coming;' (that was the name of one that died in the house;) 'for I hear the signal.' This, they informed me, was heard every night, about a quarter before ten. It was toward the top of the house, on the outside, at the northeast corner, resembling the loud creaking of a saw; or rather, that of a windmill, when the body of it is turned about, in order to shift the sails to the wind. We then heard a knocking over our heads; and Mr. Wesley, catching up a candle, said, 'Come, Sir; now you shall hear for yourself.' We went up stairs; he with much hope, and I (to say the truth) with much fear. When we came into the nursery, it was knocking in the next room; when we were there, it was knocking in the nursery. And there it continued to knock, though we came in; particularly at the head of the bed, (which was of wood,) in which Miss Hetty and two of her younger sisters lay. Mr. Wesley, observing that they were much affected, though asleep, sweating and trembling exceedingly, was very angry; and, pulling out a pistol, was going to fire at the place from whence the sound came. But I catched him by the arm, and said, 'Sir, you are convinced this is something preternatural. If so, you cannot hurt it; but you give it power to hurt you.' He then went close to the place, and said sternly, 'Thou deaf and dumb devil, why dost thou fright these children that cannot answer for themselves? Come to me in my study, that am a man.' Instantly it knocked his knock, (the

particular knock which he always used at the gate,) as if it would shiver the board in pieces; and we heard nothing more that night."

10. Till this time my father had never heard the least disturbance in his study. But the next evening, as he attempted to go into his study, (of which none had any key but himself,) when he opened the door, it was thrust back with such violence as had like to have thrown him down. However, he thrust the door open, and went in. Presently there was knocking, first on one side, then on the other; and, after a time, in the next room, wherein my sister Nancy was. He went into that room, and (the noise continuing) adjured it to speak; but in vain. He then said, "These spirits love darkness: Put out the candle, and perhaps it will speak." She did so: And he repeated his adjuration: But still there was only knocking, and no articulate sound. Upon this he said, "Nancy, two Christians are an overmatch for the devil. Go all of you down stairs: It may be, when I am alone, he will have courage to speak." When she was gone, a thought came in, and he said, "If thou art the spirit of my son Samuel, I pray, knock three knocks, and no more."[158] Immediately all was silence; and there was no more knocking at all that night.

11. I asked my sister Nancy, (then about fifteen years old,) whether she was not afraid, when my father used that adjuration. She answered, she was sadly afraid it would speak, when she put out the candle; but she was not at all afraid in the day-time, when it walked after her, as she swept the chambers, as it constantly did, and seemed to sweep after her: Only, she thought he might have done it for her, and saved her the trouble.

12. By this time, all my sisters were so accustomed to these noises, that they gave them little disturbance. A gentle tapping at their bed-head usually began between nine and ten at night. They then commonly said to each other, "Jeffrey is coming: It is time to go to sleep." And if they heard a noise in the day, and said to my youngest sister, "Hark, Kezzy, Jeffrey is knocking above," she would run up stairs, and pursue it from room to room, saying she desired no better diversion.

---

[158] Samuel, Jr. was Samuel Wesley's eldest son who was away at the time of the occurrences. In the days before telephones it could take considerable time to find out the wellbeing of loved ones who lived at a distance away. In the midst of their supernatural happenings, the family had begun to fear that the events meant that he had died.

13. A few nights after, my father and mother were just gone to bed, and the candle was not taken away, when they heard three blows, and a second and a third three, as it were with a large oaken staff, struck upon a chest which stood by the bedside. My father immediately arose, put on his night-gown, and, hearing great noises below, took the candle, and went down. My mother walked by his side. As they went down the broad stairs, they heard as if a vessel full of silver was poured upon my mother's breast, and ran jingling down to her feet. Quickly after, there was a sound, as if a large iron ball was thrown among many bottles under the stairs: But nothing was hurt. Soon after, our large mastiff dog came and ran to shelter himself between them. While the disturbances continued, he used to bark and leap, and snap on one side and the other; and that frequently before any person in the room heard any noise at all. But, after two or three days, he used to tremble and creep away before the noise began; and by this the family knew it was at hand: Nor did the observation ever fail.

A little before my father and mother came into the hall; it seemed as if a very large coal was violently thrown upon the floor, and dashed all in pieces: But nothing, was seen.

My father then cried out, "Suky, do you not hear? All the pewter is thrown about the kitchen:" But when they looked, all the pewter stood in its place. There then was a loud knocking at the back-door. My father opened it, but saw nothing. It was then at the fore-door. He opened that; but it was still lost labor. After opening first the one, then the other, several times, he turned, and went up to bed. But the noises were so violent all over the house, that he could not sleep till four in the morning.

14. Several gentlemen and Clergymen now earnestly advised my father to quit the house; but he constantly answered, "No; let the devil flee from me: I will never flee from the devil." But he wrote to my eldest brother at London to come down. He was preparing so to do, when another letter came, informing him the disturbances were over; after they had continued (the latter part of the time, day and night) from the second of December to the end of January.[159]

(An Account Of The Disturbances In My Father's House)

---

[159] Though it spans some nine pages, this is only a brief account of the occurrences. A wealth of material relating to this, including written accounts by several of the eyewitnesses, are included in Adam Clarke's *Memoirs Of The Wesley Family* (New York: Carlton and Porter: n.d.), pp. 201-237. Interestingly,

**David Brainerd Experienced Demonic
Activity As A Missionary To Native Americans**

Emilia, who appeared to be more disturbed by it than any of the other family members, indicated that she was still having experiences with it thirty four years later.

David Brainerd

BIO: [1718-1747] *A Colonial American missionary to the Indians in New York, Pennsylvania and New Jersey. His diary, published after his death by Jonathan Edwards, is considered a minor classic and was influential in spurring others into missionary work. In the following excerpts Brainerd relates the conversion of an Indian witch.*

Aug. 8. In the afternoon I preached to the Indians...afterwards, when I spoke to one and another more particularly, whom I perceived under much concern [for their personal salvation], the power of God seemed to descend upon the assembly *"like a mighty rushing wind"*[160]...Almost all persons of all ages were bowed down with concern together, and scarcely one was able to withstand the shock of this surprising operation...Another man advanced in years, who had been a murderer, a pawaw[161] or conjurer, and a notorious drunkard, was likewise brought now to cry for mercy with many tears...*Feb.* 1...In the evening chatechised in my usual method...One man considerably in years, who had been a remarkable drunkard, a conjurer and murderer, and was awakened some months before, was now brought to great extremity under his spiritual distress; so that he trembled for hours together, and apprehended himself just dropping into hell, without any power to rescue or relieve himself...*May.* 9...Baptized one man this day, the conjurer, murderer, &c. mentioned in my diary of Aug. 8, 1745, and Feb. 1, 1746, who appears to be such a remarkable instance of divine grace, that I cannot omit to give some brief account of him here...that which was the worst of all his conduct, was his *conjuration*. He was one of those who are sometimes called powaws, among the Indians; and, not withstanding his frequent attendance upon my preaching, he still followed his old charms and juggling tricks, "giving out that himself was some great one, and to him they gave heed,"[162] supposing him to be possessed of a great power. When I have instructed them respecting the miracle wrought by Christ in healing the sick, and mentioned them as evidence of his divine

---

[160] Ac 2:2
[161] Spelled various ways throughout this narrative by Brainerd.
[162] Ac 8:9-10

mission, and the truths of his doctrine; they have quickly observed the wonders of that kind, which this man had performed by his magic charms. Hence they had a high opinion of him and his superstitious notions; which seemed to be a fatal obstruction to some of them in regard to their receiving the Gospel. I have often though that it would be a great favour to the design of evangelizing these Indians, if God would take that wretch out of this world; for I had scarcely any hope of his ever becoming good. But God…has been pleased to take a much more desirable method with him…The first genuine concern for his soul, that ever appeared in him, was excited by seeing my Interpreter and his wife baptised at the Forks of Delaware, July 21, 1745. Which so prevailed upon him, that with the invitation of an Indian who was a friend to Christianity, he followed me down to Crossweeksung, in the beginning of August, following in order, to hear me preach…at which time he was more effectually awakened, and brought under great concern for his soul. And then he says, upon his "feeling the word of God in his heart," as he expresses it, his spirit of *conjuration* left him entirely, so that he has had no more power of that nature since, than any other man living. He also declares, that he does not now so much as know, how he used to charm and conjure, and that he could not now do any thing of that nature if he were ever so desirous of it. He continued under convictions of his sinful and perishing state, and a considerable degree of concern for his soul, all the fall and former part of the winter past…until at length he was brought into the acute anguish and utmost agony of soul, mentioned in my Journal of Feb. 1st…after this he was brought to the utmost calmness and composure of mind…although he had to his apprehensions scarcely any hope of salvation…While he was in this frame, he several times asked me "When I would preach again?" and seemed desirous to hear the word of God every day…After he had continued in this frame of mind more than a week, while I was discoursing publicly, he seemed to have a lively soul-refreshing view of the excellency of Christ and the way of salvation by him; which melted him into tears…Since then, he has appeared to be a humble, devout and affectionate Christian…In all respects, so far as I am capable of judging, he bears the marks of one "created anew in Christ Jesus to do good works."[163]

---

[163] Ep 2:10

His zeal for the cause of God was pleasing to me, when he was with me at the Forks of Delaware in February last. There being an old Indian at the place where I preached, who threatened to bewitch me, and my religious people who accompanied me there; this man presently challenged him to do his worst; telling him that himself had been as great a conjuror as he; and that not withstanding, as soon as he felt that word to his heart which these people loved, meaning the word of God, his power of conjuring immediately left him. "And so it would you," said he, "if you did but once feel it in your heart; and you have no power to hurt them, nor so much as to touch one of them." (*Memoirs of the Rev. David Brainerd, Entries for August 8, 1745, February 1, 1746, and May 9, 1746*)[164]

Though Many Native Americans Were Abused By The Europeans, Some Europeans Were Truly Motivated By A Sincere Desire To Help Rescue Them From The Power Of Satan. Here The Native American Princess Pocahontas Is Seen Accepting Christ.

---

[164] These entries are listed under Chapters 7 and 8. Brainerd's entry for May 9, 1746 details the lengthy period of conviction that the Indian conjurer went through on his way to ultimately finding peace through Christ. The reader is encouraged to read this entry in its entirety.

What further contributes to their[165] aversion to Christianity is, the influence which their *powaws* (*conjurers* or *diviners*) have upon them. These are the sort of persons who are supposed to have a power of *foretelling future events*, or *recovering the sick*, at least oftentimes, and of *charming, inchanting*, or *poisoning persons* to *death* by their *magic* divinations. Their spirit, in its various operations, seems to be a Satanical imitation of the spirit of prophecy with which the church in early ages was favoured. Some of these diviners are endowed with the spirit in infancy;-others in adult age.—It seems not to depend upon their own will, nor to be acquired by any endeavours of the person who is the subject of it, although it is supposed to be given to children sometimes in consequence of some means which the parents use with them for that purpose; one of which is to make the child swallow a small living frog, after having performed some superstitious rites and ceremonies upon it. They are not under the influence of this spirit always alike,—but it comes upon them at times. Those who are endowed with it, are accounted singularly favoured.

I have laboured to gain some acquaintance with this affair of their *conjuration*, and have for that end consulted and queried with the man mentioned in my Diary, May 9, who, since his conversion to Christianity, has endeavoured to give me the best intelligence he could of this matter. But it seems to be such a *mystery of iniquity*, that I cannot well understand it, and do not know oftentimes what ideas to affix to the terms he makes use of. So far as I can learn, he himself has not any clear notions of the thing, now his spirit of divination is gone from him.[166] However, the manner in which he says he obtained this spirit of divination was this; —he was admitted into the presence of a *great*[167] *man*,[168] who informed him, that he loved, pitied and desired to do him good.[169] It was not in this world that he saw the great man, but in a world *above* at a vast distance from this.[170] The great man, he says,

---

[165] The Native Americans.

[166] Notice in what follows how similarly this demonic entity presented himself to the character and nature of God and Jesus in this counterfeit experience of the Native American powaw.

[167] Gigantic.

[168] A counterfeit of God who appeared to Moses as a gigantic man (Ex 33:18-23).

[169] A counterfeit of the love of God (Jn 3:16, Ro 5:8).

was clothed in the day; yeah, with the brightest day he ever saw; a day of many years, yea, of everlasting continuance![171] This whole world, he says, was drawn upon him, so that *in* him, the earth, and all things in it, might be seen.[172] I asked him, if rocks, mountains, and seas were drawn upon, or appeared in him? He replied, that every thing that was beautiful and lovely in the earth was upon him, and might be seen by looking on him, as well as if one was on the earth to take a view of them there. By the side of the great man, he says, stood his *shadow* or spirit; for he used (*chichung,*) the word they commonly use to express the part of the man which survives the body, which word properly signifies a *shadow*.[173] This shadow, he says, was as lovely as the man himself,[174] and filled *all places*,[175] and was most agreeable as well as wonderful to him.— Here he says, he tarried some time, and was unspeakably entertained and delighted with a view of the great man, of his shadow or spirit, and of all things *in him*. What is most of all astonishing, he imagines all this to have passed before he was born. He never had been, he says, in this world at that time. What confirms him in the belief of this, is, that the great man told him, that he must come down to earth, be born of *such* a woman, meet with *such* and *such* things, and in particular, that he should once in his life be guilty of *murder*. At this he was displeased, and told the great man, he would never murder. But, the great man replied, "I have said it, and it shall be so." Which has accordingly happened.[176] At this time, he says, the great man asked him what he would choose in life. He replied, First to be a *hunter*, and afterwards to be a *powaw* or *diviner*. Whereupon the great man told him, he should

---

[170] A counterfeit of the heavens and the realm above the heavens where God resides (Ps 115:3, Mk 16:19, Ep 4:10).

[171] A counterfeit of God who lives in "unapproachable light" (2Sa 22:13, Ac 22:6, 1Ti 6:16, 1Jn 1:5).

[172] A counterfeit of God who is the maker, owner and preserver of all things (Ne 9:6, Ps 24:1, Ec 11:5, Ro 11:36, 1Co 8:6, Re 4:11).

[173] A counterfeit of the Holy Spirit who is the Spirit of both God the Father and of Jesus (Mt 10:20, 1Pe 1:11).

[174] A counterfeit of the Holy Spirit as to his being the literal Spirit of God.

[175] A counterfeit of the Holy Spirit of whom it is said "Where shall I go from your Spirit? Or where shall I flee from your presence? If I ascend up into heaven, you are there: if I make my bed in hell, behold, you are there (Ps 139:7-8)."

[176] A counterfeit of God who has the power to speak things into existence (He 11:3, Ge 1:1-26).

have what he desired,[177] and that his *shadow* should go along with him down to earth, and be with him for ever.[178] There was, he says, all this time no words spoken between them. The conference was not carried on by any human language, but they had a kind of mental intelligence of each others thoughts, dispositions, and proposals.[179] After this, he says, he saw the great man no more; but supposes he now came down to earth to be born, but the spirit or shadow of the great man still attended him, and ever after continued to appear to him in dreams and other ways,[180] until he felt the power of God's word upon his heart; since which it has entirely left him.

The spirit, he says, used sometimes to direct him in dreams to go to such a place and hunt, assuring him he should there meet with success, which accordingly proved so. When he had been there some time, the spirit would order him to another place. So that he had success in hunting, according to the great man's promise made to him at the time of his chusing this employment.[181]

There were some times when this spirit came upon him in a *special* manner, and he was full of what he saw in the great man.[182] Then, he says, he was *all light,* and not only *light* himself, but it was light all *around him,* so that he could see through men, and knew the thoughts of their hearts[183]…my interpreter tells me, that he heard one of them tell a certain Indian the secret thoughts of his

---

[177] A counterfeit of God who is concerned with his children's desires and gives to them in answer to their prayers (Jn 16:24, Ph 4:6-7, 1Pe 5:7).

[178] A counterfeit of the indwelling presence of the Holy Spirit whom Jesus promised would be with the Church forever (Jn 14:16, 2Co 1:22).

[179] Telepathy.

[180] A counterfeit of the ministry of the Holy Spirit as a real presence in the believer's life (Jn 14:16-18, Ph 2:1).

[181] A counterfeit of the Holy Spirit's leading in the believer's life (Mt 4:1, Ro 8:14).

[182] A counterfeit of the filling of the Holy Spirit (Ex 31:1-3, Lk 1:41-55, Ac 2:4, Ac 4:8-12, 31, 13:6-12).

[183] A counterfeit of the gift of prophecy (1Co 14:24-25). I believe that if one will honestly look at this scenario it will become alarmingly clear just how close a demon can make themselves resemble God the Father and the Holy Spirit. In this instance one need only insert Christian terms in place of Native American ones and there would be virtually no difference between this experience and a very Christian sounding one—*yet it would have all been a Satanic counterfeit!* How many supernatural experiences (visions, dreams, voices, spiritual gifts, etc.) have been accepted as legitimate simply because they *appeared* to be genuine (2Co 11:14)?

heart, which he had never divulged. The case was this, the Indian was bitten with a snake, and was in extreme pain with the bite. Whereupon the *diviner*, who was applied to for his recovery, told him, that at *such a time* he[184] had promised, that the next deer he killed, he would sacrifice it to some *great power*, but had broken his promise. Now, said he, that great power has ordered this snake to bite you for your neglect. The Indian confessed it was so, but said he had never told any body of it…The influence which these *powaws* have upon them, either through the esteem or fear they have of them, is no small hindrance to their embracing Christianity…When I have apprehended them afraid of embracing Christianity, lest they should be inchanted or poisoned, I have endeavoured to relieve their minds of this fear, by asking them, Why their *powaws* did not inchant and poison me, seeing they had as much reason to hate me for preaching to them, and desiring them to become Christians, as they could have to hate them in case they should actually become such? That they might have an evidence of the power and goodness of God engaged for the protections of Christians, I ventured to bid a challenge to all their *powaws* and *great powers* to do their worst on me first of all, and thus laboured to tread down their influence. (*Memoirs of the Rev. David Brainerd, Ch.10, Sec.3* under the section entitled *Difficulties Attending The Christianizing Of The Indians-First Difficulty, The Rooted Aversion To Christianity That Generally Prevails Among Them*)

John Wesley

BIO: [1703-1791] *An Anglican priest whose ministry efforts resulted in the formation of the Methodist denomination.*

I rode over to Jonathan Booth's, at Woodseats, whose daughter had been ill in a very uncommon manner. The account her parents gave of it was as follows: — About the middle of December, 1752, ELIZABETH BOOTH, junior, near ten years old, began to

---

[184] The Indian bitten by the snake.

complain of a pain in her breast, which continued three days: On the fourth day, in a moment, without any provocation, she began to be in a vehement rage, reviling her mother, and throwing at the maid what came next to hand. This fit continued near an hour; then in an instant she was quite calm. The next morning she fell into a fit of another kind, — being stretched out, and stiff as a dead carcass: Thus she lay about an hour. In the afternoon she was suddenly seized with violent involuntary laughter; and she had some or other of these fits several times a day, for about a month. In the intervals of them she was in great heaviness of soul, and continually crying for mercy; till one Saturday, as she lay stretched out on the bed, she broke out, "I know that my Redeemer liveth."[185] Her faith and love increased from that time; but so did the violence of her fits also. And often while she was rejoicing and praising God, she would cry out, "O Lord!" and, losing her senses at once, lie as dead, or laugh violently, or rave and blaspheme. In the middle of February, she grew more outrageous than ever. She frequently strove to throw herself into the fire, or out of the window.[186] Often she attempted to tear the Bible, cursing it in the bitterest manner; and many times she uttered oaths and blasphemies, too horrid to be repeated. Next to the Bible, her greatest rage was against the Methodists, — Mr. W.[187] in particular. She frequently told us where he was, and what he was then doing; adding, "He will be here soon;" and at another time, "Now he is galloping down the lane, and two men with him."[188]

In the intervals of her fits she was unusually stupid, and moped, as if void of common understanding; and yet sometimes broke out into vehement prayer, to the amazement of all that heard.[189] Sometimes she would strip herself stark naked, and run up and down the house, screaming and crying, "Save me! Save me! He will tear me in pieces." At other times she cried out, "He is tearing

---

[185] Jo 19:25
[186] Compare Mark 9:22.
[187] That is, John Wesley.
[188] An example of a clairvoyant (psychic) power given by a demon.
[189] Note here that persons who are demon possessed are sometimes given the ability by the demons to appear to possess what appears to be a strong influence of the Holy Spirit residing upon them. Undiscerning persons who had witnessed the strong prayers of this woman, unaware of her other behavior, would be likely to assume that her strength in prayer came from the Holy Spirit—*yet it was all a counterfeit.*

off my breasts; he is pouring melted lead down my throat. Now I suffer what the Martyrs suffered; but I have not the Martyrs' faith." She frequently spoke as if she was another person, saying to her father, "This girl is not thine, but mine. I have got possession of her, and I will keep her;" with many expressions of the same kind. She often seemed to be in a trance, and said she saw many visions; sometimes of heaven or hell, or judgment; sometimes of things which she said would shortly come to pass.[190]

In the beginning of March, Mrs. G. came over to Rotherham, who herself gave me the following account: — "Soon after I came in, she fell into a raging fit, blaspheming and cursing her father and me. She added, 'It was I that made Green's horse so bad the other day: (Which had been taken ill in a most unaccountable manner, as soon as he was put into the stable:) I did it that thou mightest have the preaching no more; and I had almost persuaded thee to it. It was I that made thee bad last night.' I was then taken in an unusual way. All the time she spoke she was violently convulsed, and appeared to be in strong agony. After about a quarter of an hour she brake out into prayer, and then came to herself; only still dull and heavy."

John Thorpe, of Rotherham, had often a desire to pray for her in the congregation; but he was as often hindered, by a strong and sudden impression on his mind that she was dead. When he came to Woodseats, and began to mention what a desire he had had, the girl, being then in a raging fit, cried out, "I have made a fool of Thorpe!" and burst out into a loud laughter.[191] In the beginning of May all these symptoms ceased; and she continues in health both of soul and body. (*Journal of John Wesley,* entry for *June 5, 1753*)

I was sent for to one in Bristol, who was taken ill the

---

[190] Note again that an undiscerning person could be easily swayed to believe that this person was operating under the influence of the Holy Spirit when all along she was not. Note also that demons will inspire people through visions and trances to speak of hell and judgment. Speaking out against sin under the influence of what appears to be the Holy Spirit is not a sure guarantee that the spirit motivating a person is indeed holy.

[191] Note the ability of demons to give impressions to the mind, even on professing believers. A believer must be careful in allowing their feelings or impressions that come to their mind to motivate and control them because these feelings may be coming from the outside influence of demonic spirits.

evening before. (This fact too I will simply relate, so far as I was an ear or eye witness of it.) She lay on the ground, furiously gnashing her teeth, and after a while roared aloud. It was not easy for three or four persons to hold her, especially when the name of Jesus was named. We prayed; the violence of her symptoms ceased, though without a complete deliverance.

In the evening, being sent for to her again, I was unwilling, indeed, afraid, to go: Thinking it would not avail, unless some who were strong in faith were to wrestle with God for her. I opened my Testament on those words, "I was afraid, and went and hid thy talent in the earth."[192] I stood reproved, and went immediately. She began screaming before I came into the room; then broke out into a horrid laughter, mixed with blasphemy, grievous to hear.

One who from many circumstances apprehended a preternatural agent to be concerned in this, asking, "How didst thou dare to enter into a Christian?" was answered, "She is not a Christian. She is mine." Q. "Dost thou not tremble at the name of Jesus?" No words followed, but she shrunk back and trembled exceedingly. Q. "Art thou not increasing thy own damnation?" It was faintly answered, "Ay, ay:" Which was followed by fresh cursing and blaspheming.

My brother coming in, she cried out, "Preacher! Field preacher! I don't love field-preaching." This was repeated two hours together, with spitting, and all the expressions of strong aversion. We left her at twelve, but called again about noon on Friday, 26. And now it was that God showed He heareth the prayer. All her pangs ceased in a moment: She was filled with peace, and knew that the son of wickedness was departed from her. (*Journal of John Wesley,* entry for *October 25, 1739*)

I was sent for to Kingswood again, to one of those who had been so ill before. A violent rain began just as I set out, so that I was thoroughly wet in a few minutes. Just at that time, the woman (then three miles off) cried out, "Yonder comes Wesley, galloping as fast as he can."[193] When I was come, I was quite cold and dead, and fitter for sleep than prayer. She burst out into a horrid laughter, and said, "No power, no power; no faith, no faith. She is mine; her soul is mine. I have her, and will not let her go." We begged of God to

---

[192] Mt 25:25
[193] An example of psychic (clairvoyant) powers given through a demon.

increase our faith. Meanwhile her pangs increased more and more; so that one would have imagined, by the violence of the throes, her body must have been shattered to pieces. One who was clearly convinced this was no natural disorder, said, "I think Satan is let loose. I fear he will not stop here." And added, "I command thee, in the name of the Lord Jesus, to tell if thou hast commission to torment any other soul?" It was immediately answered, "I have. L——y C——r, and S——h J——s." (Two who lived at some distance, and were then in perfect health.) We betook ourselves to prayer again; and ceased not, till she began, about six o'clock, with a clear voice, and composed, cheerful look, — *Praise God, from whom all blessings flow.* (*Journal of John Wesley,* entry for *October 27, 1739*)[194]

Charles Wesley

BIO: [1707-1788] *The brother of John Wesley and a well known hymnist who authored thousands of hymns.*

I came in the coach to Wycombe. I lodged at Mr. Hollis's, who entertained me with his French Prophets, equal, in his account, if not superior, to the Old-Testament ones.[195] While we were undressing, he fell into violent agitations, and gobbled like a turkey-cock. I was frightened, and began exorcising him with, "Thou deaf and dumb devil,"[196] &c. He soon recovered out of his fit of inspiration. I prayed, and went to bed, not half liking my bedfellow. I did not

---

[194] For these and some thirteen other cases of spiritual warfare reported by Wesley as well as his experiences with other supernatural phenomena the reader is referred to my previous work *The Supernatural Occurrences Of John Wesley* (SEAN Multimedia: Oklahoma City, OK, 2005).

[195] The French Prophets were a group of French Protestants known as the Camisards, some of whom had settled in England. They were known for their emphasis upon the gift of prophecy. Most other Protestants considered them to have been deceived by the Devil.

[196] Mk 9:25

sleep very sound with Satan so near me. I got to London by one the next day. (*Journal Of Charles Wesley,* entry for *December 11, 1738*)

Joseph Easterbrook

BIO: [ca.1750-1791] *The Vicar of Temple Church in Bristol, England whose ministry included serving as the chaplain of Newgate Prison and teaching at Trevecca College during which time he was known to preach up to nine times a week.*

On Saturday May 31st, 1788, Mrs. Sarah Baber called on me, acquainting me that she had just returned from a visit to Yatton, in the county of Somerset, where she had found a poor man afflicted with a most extraordinary malady. She said his name was George Lukins; that he had fits daily during her stay in Yatton, in which he sang and screemed in various sounds, some of which did not resemble the modifications of a human voice; that he cursed and swore in a most tremendous manner, while in his fits, and declared that doctors could do him no service. Some time ago she resided at Yatton several years together, her husband being a native of that part of the country; both of them well knew George Lukins and his relations, and were throughly acquainted with the opinion of the neighborhood concerning them: she from this acquaintance said she could with confidence declare, that George Lukins bore an extraordinary good character from his childhood, and had constantly attended the church and sacrament. Of her own knowledge she likewise said, that she could take upon her to affirm, that he had been subject to fits of a very uncommon nature, for the last eighteen years, for the cure of which he had been placed for a considerable time under the care of Mr. Smith, an eminent surgeon of Wrington, who administered all the assistance in his power, without effect: many other medical gentlemen she said had in like manner tried to help him, but in vain. Many of the people about Yatton then conceived him to be bewitched; but latterly he had himself declared that he was possessed of seven devils, and that nothing would avail but the united prayers of seven clergymen, who could ask deliverance for him in faith; but seven could not be procured in that neighbourhood to meet his ideas, and try the experiment: she therefore earnestly requested me to go to Yatton to see him…

It was through the influence of that direction of St. Paul, *As we have opportunity let us do good unto all men*,[197] that I consented for George Lukins to be brought to me; little expecting that an attention to his pitiable case, would have produced such a torrent of opposition, and illiberal abuse upon the parties concerned in his relief.

A few days after, on Saturday the 7th of June, George Lukins came to Mr. Westcote's, in Redclift-street, where he was seen for some days in his fits, by many of our respectable inhabitants; all of whom as with one voice declared, that they were struck with horror and amazement, at the sounds and expressions which they heard, and the unaccountable agitations and convulsions which they beheld.

In compliance with my promise to Mrs. Baber, I applied to such of the clergy of the established church…as I conceived to be most cordial in the belief of supernatural influences…requesting that these Gentlemen would with me attend a meeting for prayer in behalf of this object of commiserations; but though they acknowledged it as their opinion, that his was a supernatural affliction, I could not prevail upon them to join with me, in this attempt to relieve him…The more I saw and heard of the misery which George Lukins experienced, the more I pitied him, and being unwilling to dismiss him from Bristol till some effort had been made for his recovery, I next desired certain persons in connection with the Rev. Mr. Wesley to attend a prayer meeting on his account; to which request they readily acceded. Accordingly a meeting was appointed Friday morning the 13th of June, at eleven o'clock. And as the most horrible noises usually proceeded from him in his fits, it was suggested that the vestry room of Temple church, which is bounded by the church-yard, was the most retired place that could be found in Temple parish; and for that reason that situation was preferred to any other, it being our design to conduct this business with as much secrecy as possible. But we soon found that our design in this respect was rendered abortive…it having by some means or other been made known, contrary to our desire, that a prayer meeting on Friday morning was to be held in the vestry-room of Temple church, for the man…a considerable number of people (who had met with this information) planted themselves

---

[197] Ga 6:10

upon the walls of the vestry-room, and heard part of the prayers, the singing, the conversation and the wonderful sounds which proceeded from George Lukins...They began [by] singing an hymn, on which the man was immediately thrown into strange agitations, (very different from his usual seizures) his face was variously distorted, and his whole body convulsed. His right hand and arm then began to shake with violence, and after some violent throes, he spake in a deep, hoarse, hollow voice, *personating an invisible agent*, calling the man to an account, and upbraiding him as a fool for bringing that silly company together: said it was to no purpose, and swore "by his infernal den," that he would never quit his hold of him, but would torment him a thousand times worse for making this vain attempt...

He then began to sing in his usual manner, (*still personating some invisible agent*) horribly blaspheming, boasted of his power, and vowed eternal vengeance on the miserable object, and on those present for daring to oppose him; and commanded his "faithful and obedient servants" to appear, and take their stations...

He then spake in a female voice, very expressive of scorn and derision, and demanded to know why the fool had brought such a company there? And swore "by the devil" that he would not quit his hold of him, and bid defiance to and cursed all, who should attempt to rescue the miserable object from them. He then sung, in the same female voice, a kind of love song, at the conclusion of which he was violently tortured, and repeated most horrible imprecations...

Another invisible agent came forth, assuming a different voice, but his manner much the same as the preceding one. A kind of dialogue was, then sung in a hoarse and soft voice alternately; at the conclusion of which, as before, the man was thrown into violent agonies, and blasphemed in a manner too dreadful to be expressed...

He then personated, and said, "I am the great Devil;" and after much boasting of his power, and bidding defiance to all his opposers, sung a kind of hunting song; at the conclusion of which he was most violently tortured, so that it was with difficulty that two strong men could hold him (though he is but a small man, and very weak in constitution); sometimes he would set up a hideous laugh, and at other times bark in a manner indiscribably horrid...

After this he summoned all the infernals to appear, and

drive the company away. And while the ministers were engaged in fervent prayer, he sung a Te Deum[198] to the devil, in different voices, —saying, "We praise thee, O devil; we acknowledge thee to be the supreme governor," &c. &c...[199]

When the noise was so great as to obstruct the company proceeding in prayer, they sang together an hymn suitable to the occasion. Whilst they were in prayer, the voice which personated the great Devil bid them defiance, cursing and vowing dreadful vengeance on all present. One in the company commanded him in the name of the great Jehovah to declare his name? To which he replied, "I am the Devil." The same person then charged him in the name of Jehovah to declare why he tormented the man? To which he made answer, "That I may shew my power amongst men"...

The poor man still remained in great agonies and torture, and prayer was continued for his deliverance. A clergyman present desired him to endeavour to speak the name of "Jesus," and several times repeated it to him, at all of which he replied "Devil." — During this attempt a small faint voice was heard saying, "Why don't you adjure?" On which the clergyman commanded, in the name of Jesus, and in the name of the Father, the Son, and the Holy Ghost, the evil spirit to depart from the man; which he repeated several times:—when a voice was heard to say, "Must I give up my power?" and this was followed by dreadful howlings. Soon after another voice, as with astonishment, said, "Our master has deceived us." —The clergyman still continuing to repeat the adjuration, a voice was heard to say, "Where shall we go?" and the reply was, "To hell, thine own infernal den, and return no more to torment this man." — On this the man's agitations and distortions were stronger than ever, attended with the most dreadful howling that can be conceived. But as soon as this conflict was over, he said, in his own natural voice, "Blessed Jesus!" — became quite serene, immediately praised God for his deliverance, and kneeling down said the Lord's prayer and returned his most devout thanks to all who were present.

---

[198] A hymn of joy and thanksgiving, the Christian version of which is traditionally sang at the conclusion of the Office of the Readings for the Liturgy of the Hours on Sundays outside Lent, daily during the Octaves of Christmas and Easter, and on Solemnities and Feast Days.
[199] The correct lyrics of the Te Deum begin with "O God, we praise Thee: we acknowledge Thee to be the Lord."

The meeting broke up a little before one o'clock, having lasted near two hours, and the man went away entirely delivered, and has had no return of the disorder since.[200] (*An Appeal To The Public Respecting George Lukins (Called the Yatton Demoniac,) Containing An Account Of His Affliction And Deliverance; Together With A Variety Of Circumstances Which Tend To Exculpate Him From The Charge Of Imposture*)

---

[200] Six months later George Lukins was reported as living in Bristol, perfectly clear of any return of his affliction, and regarded as "a well-disposed, sensible, moral good Christian and member of society" (Proceedings Of The Wesley Historical Society, 1899, Vol 2, Part 2, *Bristol Methodist Collectanea,* p.39).

Temple Church, The Site Of George Lukins' Exorcism, Lies In Ruins Today, Though Its 114 Feet (35 Meter) High Tower Still Stands

107

Accounts From The Industrial
Age & The Age Of Missions (19ᵗʰ Century)

Charles G. Finney

BIO: [1792-1875] *An American lawyer turned preacher who was one of the leading figures in the second Great Awakening. He is considered to be an expert on revival.*

Soon after the adjournment of the convention, on the Sabbath, as I came out of the pulpit, a young lady...from Stephentown, was introduced to me. She asked me if I could not go up to their town and preach...Afterward I made inquiry about Stephentown...Many years before...a chaplain in the Revolutionary army, was settled there as pastor of the [only] church. He remained until the church ran down, and he finally became an open infidel...He remained among them, openly hostile to the Christian religion.

After he had ceased to be pastor of the church, they had had one or two ministers settled. Nevertheless, the church declined, and the state of religion grew worse and worse; until, finally, they had left their meeting house, as so few attended meeting, and held their services on the Sabbath, in a small schoolhouse...

The last minister they had...stayed until not more than half-a-dozen people in the town would attend on the Sabbath...No other denomination had taken possession of the field, so as to excite any public interest, and the whole town was a complete moral waste...

Accordingly the next Sabbath, after preaching the second time, one of the young converts at New Lebanon offered to take me up to Stephentown in his carriage. When he came in his buggy to take me, I asked him, "Have you a steady horse?" "O yes!" he replied, "perfectly so;" and smiling, asked, "What made you ask the question?" "Because," I replied, "if the Lord wants me to go to Stephentown, the devil will prevent it if he can; and if you have not a steady horse, he will try to make him kill me." He smiled, and we rode on; and, strange to tell, before we got there, that horse ran away twice, and came near killing us. His owner expressed the greatest astonishment, and said he had never known such a thing before.[201] (*Charles G. Finney, An Autobiography, Ch. 17*)

As I went into [the church] meeting in the afternoon of one Sabbath, I saw several ladies sitting in a pew, with a woman dressed in black who seemed to be in great distress of mind; and they were partly holding her, and preventing her from going out. As I came in, one of the ladies came to me and told me that she was an insane woman; that she had been a Methodist, but had, as she supposed, fallen from grace; which had led to despair, and finally to insanity. Her husband was an intemperate man, and lived several miles from the village; and he had brought her down and left her at meeting, and had himself gone to the tavern. I said a few words to her; but she replied that she must go; that she could not hear any praying, or preaching, or singing; that hell was her portion, and she could not endure anything that made her think of heaven.

I cautioned the ladies, privately, to keep her in her seat, if they could, without her disturbing the meeting. I then went into the pulpit and read a hymn. As soon as the singing began, she struggled hard to get out. But the ladies obstructed her passage; and kindly but persistently prevented her escape. After a few moments she became quiet; but seemed to avoid hearing or attending at all to the singing. I then prayed. For some little time I heard her struggling to get out; but before I had done she became quiet, and the congregation was still. The Lord gave me a great spirit of prayer, and a text; for I had no text settled upon before. I took my text from Hebrews: "Let us come boldly unto the throne of grace, that we may obtain mercy and find grace to help in time of need."[202]

---

[201] Was the horse's strange behavior a Satanic hindrance to Finney's ministry (1Th 2:17-18) or merely a coincidence? Whatever the case, Finney's faith was able to quench the fiery darts of the wicked (Ep 6:16) in Stephentown and see God's grace work in such a way that "nearly all the principal inhabitants of the town were gathered into the church, and the town was morally renovated (*Autobiography, Ch 17*)."

[202] He 4:16

My object was to encourage faith, in ourselves, and in her; and in ourselves for her. When I began to pray, she at first made quite an effort to get out. But the ladies kindly resisted, and she finally sat still, but held her head very low, and seemed determined not to attend to what I said. But as I proceeded she began gradually to raise her head, and to look at me from within her long black bonnet. She looked up more and more until she sat upright, and looked me in the face with intense earnestness. As I proceeded to urge the people to be bold in their faith, to launch out, and commit themselves with the utmost confidence to God, through the atoning sacrifice of our great High Priest, all at once she startled the congregation by uttering a loud shriek. She then cast herself almost from her seat, held her head very low, and I could see that she "trembled very exceedingly."[203] The ladies in the pew with her, partly supported her, and watched her with manifest prayerful interest and sympathy. As I proceeded she began to look up again, and soon sat upright, with face wonderfully changed, indicating triumphant joy and peace. There was such a glow upon her countenance as I have seldom seen in any human face. Her joy was so great that she could scarcely contain herself till meeting was over; and then she soon made everybody understand around her, that she was set at liberty. She glorified God, and rejoiced with amazing triumph. About two years after, I met with her, and found her still full of joy and peace.[204] (*Charles G. Finney, An Autobiography, Ch. 8*)

Robert Baxter

BIO: [ca.1802-1889] *Baxter was a lawyer who became involved with a group of Christians in the Church of Scotland that had begun to experience unusual phenomena wherein a power would*

---

[203] Ge 27:33

[204] I have wondered if this was really a case of demon possession that was never realized as such. It involved a woman who had become insane and showed a strong aversion to prayer, preaching and singing. When the congregational singing began she "struggled hard" to get out of the service. At one point she yelled out a "loud shriek" a little bit after which she began to function as mentally normal. This behavior is reminiscent of the way that demoniacs sometimes act during their deliverance sessions. Compare this with persons in the New Testament whose demon possession resulted in insanity (Mt 17:15) and the deliverance of which resulted in the persons shrieking loudly (Mk 1:26, 9:26, Ac 8:7).

come upon individuals in the church and inspire them to prophesy or speak in previously unlearned languages. Everyone in the group, Baxter included, assumed that this power was the Holy Spirit but eventually Baxter began to have doubts and upon "testing the spirits" he realized that they had been deceived by a counterfeit spirit. The group eventually came to refer to themselves as the Catholic Apostolic Church but was publicly nicknamed the Irvingites after their founder, Edward Irving (1792-1834).

Before we read Baxter's own words we will sum up his description of his experiences.[205] Baxter was a conservative, Bible believing Christian who ministered to the poor in his area (p.4). At the time of his experience, as well as after realizing it was counterfeit, he believed that the gifts of the Spirit were for all times, so he had no theological bias against modern day demonstrations of the Spirit (p.3). While attending a prayer meeting, Baxter felt a power come upon him that convicted him of not sharing enough about the Second Coming to the point that he began to cry over this, felt inspired to deliver a message out loud to those present, and caused his body to experience uncontrollable trembling. After this he began a time of prayer and fasting to seek the Lord on what had happened and while praying verses popped into his head about Elijah accompanied by a message declaring that the Lord was pouring out upon the church the spirit and power of Elijah to prepare it for the return of Christ. This persuaded him that the manifestation was from God (pp.4-7, 147-148). To Baxter, the power was clearly external (i.e. something outside of the person touching and influencing them) and it so focused on pointing people to Christ and encouraging those who listened to it to cultivate the fruits of the Spirit that it seemed that it could only be the Holy Spirit (pp.21-22). The author felt the conviction mentally and his own spirit seemed to bear witness that this was indeed the Holy Spirit (pp. 147, 149). Christ and the need for repentance were preached so strongly under the power that it was hard for Baxter to see it as anything other than a fresh move of God (p.44).

---

[205] Baxter did not divide his book into chapters, so I have included the page numbers to help readers find the referenced sections. The page numbers refer to the James Nisbet publishers' 1833 edition.

This began a regular occurrence of this power coming upon Baxter during which times he would be led to make declarations to others (pp.5, 13, 68-70), be given knowledge about others that he would not normally be able to know (pp.71-72, 86-88), read others' minds (pp.69-70, 87-88), tell people supposedly what God's will was (pp.14, 23), speak in languages that he had not previously studied (pp.68, 133-135), pray in public with power (p.12) and preach with impact (pp.5, 15-16). Eventually the power began to lead Baxter to tell people that they were going to become prophets, apostles or involved in some other kind of special ministry (pp.63, 68-70). One of the characteristics of the power was that it would lead those influenced by it to deliver strong rebukes to people (pp.15, 19-20, 68, 128) and encourage those listening to it to examine themselves spiritually (pp.86-87). This power would also lead people to do bizarre things such as leading Baxter to get up unexpectedly and leave a Sunday School class (p.10), feel compelled to go to a government office with the intent of interrupting the operations to deliver a prophecy (pp.23-25), feel compelled to leave a home meeting because of something unclean being in the house (pp.35-36), and make him feel that he had been called to leave his wife and that this was going to be used by God as a discipline against her for not believing that the power was the Holy Spirit (pp.38-41, 49-51, 90). When Baxter's wife had doubts about the power being from God, she herself began to have mystical experiences that seemed to confirm it (pp.18, 88-89). This power warned the people many times about being diligent to not be deceived by Satan, reminding them that he came as an angel of light (p.62). However, the power said that it would never allow Satan to speak through one of the prophets (p.117) and its followers used the phrase "Satan cannot cast out Satan" to justify their utterances as real (i.e. why would Satan criticize Satan?) (p.136).

The manifestations would travel from one congregation to another when someone with the power would visit that congregation (p.141). The experiences were so awe-inspiring that Baxter was left in amazement at what would happen to him when the spirit would come upon him (p.152).

The power wanted those who followed it to separate from mainstream Christianity, which it described as backslidden and worldly (pp.54-57, 62-63, 87, 128-129, 150, 153). The power indicated that the established church would essentially no longer be used by God but only the new movement that was associated with the gifts of the Spirit (pp.28, 32-33). This ultimately had the effect of distancing the followers of the spirit from any Christians who would challenge them to reconsider whether they were following the right Spirit (p.128). Those who followed the spirit were led to appear as possessing holiness and zeal surpassing that of the Christians of other denominations (p.128) and this naturally inclined them to believe that God was going to use them rather than other denominations.

The spirit claimed to be and declared what was "truth" (pp.104-105) and sought total trust and submission by trying to get people to give up their understanding and just submit to it without judging anything it said. If contradictions appeared, they were told to wait and trust that the power would explain these away (p.127). Baxter noted that it just kind of became natural for those who followed the spirit to rationalize and explain away in their minds the contradictions that they began to notice in the prophecies (p.51). The spirit encouraged the people to trust in those whom it empowered (i.e. the prophets and prophetesses) as they were seen as mouthpieces for the spirit (p.20).

The power would gain people's trust by flattering them with prophecies that indicated that they were extra spiritual or had been chosen by God to be a prophet or apostle, etc. and that only those who were a part of the spirit's movement were the true church (pp.66, 128). This naturally endeared the people to the spirit because it made them to feel important. The power emphasized that the more people would follow it, the more powerful they would become and encouraged them to believe (expect) that greater miracle working power was coming. This made it even more appealing for the people to continue following it and had the effect of creating a rising expectation that they were on the verge of an incredible new era of miracles (p.88).

The power heavily emphasized the Second Coming of Christ (p.142) and rebuked those who did not faithfully declare the near coming of the Lord (p.147). This contributed to the hype and feel of the movement that they were on the verge of a new era about to be ushered in.

The power also encouraged the people to stop practicing baptism and communion, encouraging them instead to see them as no longer necessary as they had been spiritually fulfilled (pp.77-80). This was naturally more acceptable in light of the fact that they were about to enter into a new era.

The power encouraged people that they should seek the baptism of the Holy Ghost and fire and that this would lead to the receiving of the gifts of the Spirit, including expecting teleportation like Philip experienced (pp.63-65, 77-78, 85, 90-91, 100, 106-108, 154). The power would frequently lead people to use the expression "fire" (p.64).

The spirit also used fear to control people. It told them that mocking the new movement would make them guilty of blaspheming the Holy Spirit (p.37) and doubts were seen as temptations rather than using common sense (pp.75, 96). Thus, those who followed the spirit felt compelled to reject any doubts, for fear that by entertaining them they would be falling into sin (p.130). At one point, Baxter said that he trembled at the thought of entertaining doubts (p.117). If a person did have doubts, they would be inclined to focus it on their individual gift (i.e. I experienced a false spirit) rather than seeing the whole movement as erroneous (p.27). When errors did show up the people felt compelled to accept responsibility for them themselves (i.e. they had spoken in the flesh, of their own will, etc.) (p.130).

The spirit noticeably had a tendency to display itself more around people who believed in it, but to be more restrained around those who did not (pp.47-48, 83-84).

The spiritual and mental effects that this spirit had upon those who embraced it were amazing. It could bring strong conviction over sins to the point that people would feel openly and personally rebuked in the public meetings (pp.5, 7, 9, 147), even bringing them to tears (p.147). The power could also bring peace of mind as well as faith (trust and expectation) that God was going to answer the person's prayers (p.151), great joy and thankfulness (pp.10-11, 90). It truly seemed that those who embraced this power would have the love of God impressed upon them (p.152).

The power would give new insights into the Scriptures that Baxter had never thought of before (pp. 55-56, 59-62) and these insights were both beautiful and comforting (p.86). Indeed, the work of the spirit was interwoven with Scripture (p.117). This experience, as Baxter described it, felt like a powerful in-working of the Spirit that led him up into communion in Christ, making him feel that he had a special fellowship with the mind of Christ. This was combined with an internal compulsion to share with others what the Lord had shown him (p.151). Baxter noticed, however, that these new insights had the tendency to become an over focus of the person who received them to the point that the person developed an unbalanced emphasis upon them (pp.140-141).

As the people had these experiences, the natural response was to be led into a more fervent and devoted Christian life (pp.8, 45, 96, 148, 152) and the spirit encouraged those who listened to it to ask for more of God, but Baxter realized that what this really was, was encouraging them to seek more of the power rather than actually God (pp.65-66).

Baxter noticed that if he had apprehensions over following what the spirit said that he would feel relief and peace from these apprehensions when he resigned to do the will of God as it was dictated by the power (p.46).

Despite all of the encouraging feelings that the power instilled into those who embraced it, there was also a dark side to it. Baxter expressed how a darkness would come over his mind when the prophecies given under the power would not come to pass (pp.85-86, 88) and he would sometimes feel disturbed in his mind when speaking under the power (p.120). Although he felt uncomfortable at times in the things that he was led to say, he would reason this away by thinking that if God was saying it, how could it be bad (p.21).

The author also noticed that the more one listened to the spirit, the more it made one naïve and trusting, even in the face of seeming contradictions (p.28). The frequent supernatural impulses that embracing this power caused seemed to weaken the mind to the point that it could be easily changed from one impulse to the next (pp.137-138).

A series of events eventually played a part in Baxter realizing that he had been deceived. These included prophecies that did not come to pass as prophesied or expected (pp.41-42, 52-53, 82-83), conflicting utterances (pp.92-95), a situation where a man whom the power led Baxter to recognize as specially called by God was discovered to be speaking under the power of a demon (pp.91-92, 106), and an instance in which the power could not cast out a demon from a man (pp.72-74).

Baxter eventually came to the conclusion that he had been given over to a seducing spirit as a discipline for his own sins (pp.8, 47-48, 50-51, 83-84, 117-118). But when he tried to share this, he realized that the very thing which had brought the discipline on some people (i.e. the sin of pride) was keeping them from being able to admit that they had been deceived (p.118). After he left the movement, the spirit warned those who were still in it to not associate with Baxter anymore (p.124).

19ᵗʰ Century Illustration Of Edward Irving

What follows is Baxter's personal experience, observation and ultimate realization that he had been deceived into accepting a counterfeit.

Baxter First Experiences The Power

At this period I was, by professional arrangements, called up to London, and had a strong desire to attend at the prayer-meetings which were then privately held by those who spoke in the power, and those who sought for the gifts...After one or two brethren had read and prayed, Mr. T—[206] was made to speak two or three words very distinctly, and with an energy and depth of tone which seemed to me extraordinary, and it fell upon me as a supernatural utterance, which I ascribed to the power of God; the words were in a tongue that I did not understand. In a few minutes Miss E. C.[207] broke out in an utterance in English, which, as to matter and manner, and the influence it had upon me, I at once bowed to as the utterance of the Spirit of God. Those who have heard the powerful and commanding utterance need no description; but they who have not may conceive what an unnatural and unaccustomed tone of voice, an intense and rivetting power of expression—with the declaration of a cutting rebuke to all who were present, and applicable to my own state of mind in particular—would effect upon me, and upon the others who were come together, expecting to hear the voice of the Spirit of God. In the midst of the feeling of awe and reverence which was produced, I was myself seized upon by the power; and in much struggling against it, was made to cry out, and myself to give forth a confession of my own sin in the matter, for which we were rebuked; and afterwards to utter a prophecy that the messengers of the Lord should go forth, publishing to the ends of the earth in the mighty power of God, the testimony of the near coming of the Lord Jesus. The rebuke had been for not declaring the near coming of Jesus, and I was smitten in conscience, having many times refrained from speaking of it to the people, under a fear they might stumble over it, and be offended.

I was overwhelmed by this occurrence. The attainment of the gift of prophecy, which this supernatural utterance was deemed to be, was, with myself and many others, a great object of desire. I could not, therefore, but rejoice at having been made the subject of it; but there were so many difficulties attaching to the circumstances under which the power came upon me, and I was so anxious and distressed lest I should mistake the mind of God in the matter, that I continued many weeks weighed down in spirit and overwhelmed. There was in me, at the time of the utterance, very great excitement; and yet I was distinctly conscious of a power acting upon me beyond the mere power of excitement. So distinct

---

[206] That is, Edward Taplin, considered to be one of the prophets of the movement.

[207] That is, Emily Cardale, considered to be one of the prophetesses of the movement.

was this power from the excitement, that in all my trouble and doubt about it, I never could attribute the whole [experience] to [just] excitement. (*Narrative Of Facts, pp.4-6*)

Baxter Experiences The Power
Giving Him Supernatural Knowledge

The power which then rested on me was far more mighty than before, laying down my mind and body in perfect obedience, and carrying me on without confusion or excitement...Every former visitation of the power had been very brief; but now it continued, and seemed to rest upon me all the evening. The things I was made to utter, flashed in upon my mind without forethought, without expectation, and without any plan or arrangement: all was the work of the moment, and I was as the passive instrument of the power which used me...I was made [by the power] to bid those present ask instruction upon any subject on which they sought to be taught by God; and, to several questions which were asked, answers were give by me in the power. One in particular was so answered, with such reference to the circumstances of the case of which in myself, I was wholly ignorant, as to convince the person who asked it that the spirit speaking in me knew those circumstances, and alluded to them in the answer. (*Narrative Of Facts, pp.13-14*)

On the morrow, at the morning prayer-meeting, nothing peculiar occurred. At breakfast [afterwards], several strangers to me were present, and having been made to give forth what seemed a most glorious prophecy...it was distinctly shown me in the power, before any one had spoken, that some one person in the room had a mind which utterly repudiated what was so prophesied. It was not shown me which of the parties present it applied to, but the power was so impressive, that I said openly, "The Lord shows me that there is one person here whose heart is hardened against the truth; let him speak, for the Lord has a purpose of mercy towards him." For a little time no one spoke...[eventually] a voice at the top of the room struck me, and it was shown me he was the man. I said so to him, and requested him to speak. He did speak out, and showed very strikingly, how exactly his state of mind had been opened to me...I know I had never seen the man, nor to my knowledge, heard the sound of his voice, before I told out the state of his mind; and as soon as I heard the sound of his voice, I recognized him as the person referred to. (*Narrative Of Facts, pp.69-70*)

On the Saturday morning, at Mr. Irving's, another extraordinary incident occurred, showing to me, the discerning of the Spirit which spake in me. In the midst of breakfast, Mr. Irving said, "Our brother – (pointing to a person sitting by him), wishes to ask counsel of the Lord by you." The gentleman, who was a perfect stranger to me, then said, that he had purposed to do something, which he explained, and wished to know if it was the Lord's will he should do it? The power came upon me, giving him an answer, and in it referred to the proceedings of Mr. B—, of Oxford; declared how much he was grieving the Lord by his rashness, and warned us against following his course. There was nothing in the question, or in the gentleman, or in the previous conversation, to lead to Mr. B—; and as I was made to utter it, I wondered why he was referred to; but on inquiring afterwards, I found Mr. B— was a particular friend of the gentleman's, and had been instrumental in leading him into the difficulties about which he asked counsel. (*Narrative Of Facts, pp.71-72*)

One day, in the Scotch Church, when I was meditating as to the propriety of yielding my tongue, and was in prayer to God for teaching on it, an utterance broke from Miss E. C.—"Yield your tongues to Jesus;" and going on exhorting to an entire resignation of ourselves to the Spirit of Jesus speaking and dwelling in us. The instances of such obvious discernment of thoughts are so numerous as to take away the possibility of their being accidental coincidences. In the case of one individual, when praying in silence in her own room, in three or four distinct instances, answers were given, in the power, by a gifted person sitting in the adjoining room. And in almost all the persons with whom I have conversed, who were brought into a belief of the power, instances of obvious discernment of their thoughts, or references to their particular state of mind, have been so striking, as to conduce to their recognition of the power. (*Narrative Of Facts, p.135*)

At breakfast, at Mr. Irving's, the closing scene of my unhappy ministration among them was no less remarkable than mysterious. Very great utterance had, for several mornings, been given me at family prayers there, and particularly beautiful and comforting expositions of Scripture were given from the power. This morning, a clergyman, (who, I have since understood, was from Ireland, and had come expressly to inquire, favourably disposed towards the work, but startled at the doctrines,) was present. He was talking to Mr. Irving, but I did not hear his observations. Presently the sister of Miss E. C., who sat by me, said, "That gentleman is grieving the Spirit." I looked, and saw a power resting upon Miss E. C., and presently she spoke in rebuke; but I did not gather more from it than that the clergyman had been advancing something erroneous. Mr. Irving then began, as usual, to read a chapter, to which I had been made, in power, to direct him; but instead of my expounding as before, the power resting upon me, revealed there were those in the room who must depart. Utterance came from me, that we were assembled at an holy ordinance to partake of the body and blood of Christ, and it behoved all to examine themselves that they might not partake unworthily. None going out, I was made again and again, more and more peremptorily, to warn, until the clergyman in question and an aged man, a stranger, had gone out, when Mr. Irving proceeded in reading the chapter. (*Narrative Of Facts, pp.86-87*)

Baxter Is Given The Ability To
Speak In Tongues Under The Power

I have inadvertently omitted, in the course of the narrative, the mention of my utterances in other languages. As considerable stress has occasionally been laid upon this form of utterance, in support of the work: I will here allude to it.

A few days before the prophecy of my call to the apostolic office, whilst sitting at home, a mighty power came upon me, but for a considerable time no impulse to utterance; presently a sentence in French was vividly set before my mind, and, under an impulse to utterance, was spoken. Then in a little time, sentences in Latin were in like manner uttered, and, with short intervals, sentences in many other languages, judging from the sound, and the different exercise of the enunciating organs. My wife, who was with me, declared some of them to be Italian and Spanish; the first she can read and translate, the second she knows but little of. In this case, she was not able to interpret or retain the words as they were uttered. All the time of these utterances, I was greatly tried in mind. After the first sentence, an impulse to utterance continued on me, and most painfully I restrained it, my conviction being that until something was set before me to utter, I ought not to yield my tongue to utterance. Yet I was troubled by the doubt what could the impulse mean, if I were not to yield to it. Under the trial I did yield my tongue for a few moments, but the utterance that broke from me seemed so discordant, that I concluded the impulse, without words given, was a temptation; and I restrained it, except as words were given me, and then I yielded. Sometimes single words were given me, and sometimes sentences, though I could neither recognize the words nor sentences as any language I knew, except those which were French or Latin. What strengthened me, upon after consideration, in the opinion that I ought not to yield my tongue, was, the remembrance that I had heard Mr. Irving say, when explaining how the utterance in tongues first came upon Mr. T., that he had words and sentences set before him. Immediately following this exercise, there came an utterance in English, declaring that the gift of tongues, which was manifest in London, was nothing more than that of the "the tongue" needing interpretation, manifested formerly in the Corinthian church; but that shortly the Lord would bestow the Pentecostal gift, enabling those who received it to preach in all languages to the nations of the earth. I was on several other occasions exercised in the same way, speaking detached words and sentences, but never a connected discourse.

When I went to London after this, I questioned those who spoke in the tongues, whether they had the words and sentences given, or yielded their tongues to the impulse of utterance, without having them. They answered almost entirely the latter, though sometimes also the former. I was also, in London, made to confirm, in utterance, before Mr. Irving, what had been spoken here concerning the Pentecostal gift of tongues for preaching; and, such was the readiness with which he yielded to the utterances, that though he had both written and published that the Pentecostal gift was not for preaching, he at once yielded, and confessed his error, giving thanks for the correction. (*Narrative Of Facts, pp.133-134*)

Baxter Experiences Supernatural
Gifting In Preaching Under The Power

On the following morning, I attended the early prayer-meeting; and the pastor calling me up to pray, I had a distinct direction from the power to read the eleventh chapter of the book of Revelations. I read it in the power altogether, and as I went on I was made in the power to expound it...In the evening I attended at the pastor's house, where were assembled the young men, who, during the week, taught in schools, and private houses, in different parts of London. Here, again, the power was most abundant upon me; and I was, for the space of near two hours, made to give forth to them what was called by the Spirit, "preaching in the Spirit"—a sermon setting forth the course of the church from the apostles' days; — declaring, amongst other things, that in the apostolic days, the church was as Samson in his strength; that when the church began to commit fornication with the kings of the earth, the world was as Delilah, and seduced the church to surrender its secret source of strength, (which was said to be the teaching of the Spirit;) and, in the stead of it, to seek the applause, and opinion, and learning, of the world... (*Narrative Of Facts, pp.15-16*)

On the morning following the day of my arrival, I was called upon again, and opening upon the prophet Malachi, I read the fourth chapter; as I read, the power came upon me, and I was made to read in the power. My voice raised far beyond its natural pitch, with constrained repetitions of parts, and with the same inward uplifting which at the presence of the power I had always before experienced. When I knelt down to pray, I was carried out to praying in the power for the presence and blessing of God in the midst of the church; in all this I had great joy and peace, without any of the strugglings which had attended my former utterances in power. (*Narrative Of Facts, p.12*)

Baxter Begins To Realize That He
Has Been Deceived By A Lying Spirit

On this evening a circumstance occurred in the midst of my utterance, which, though it made little impression on me at the time, has since seemed to me as ordained of God for a witness to us, that we were deceived. Capt. G., who sat near me when it was said, "Count the days, one thousand and three score and two hundred," repeated the words after me, in order to remember them, and saying the words, "two hundred," louder than the rest, the sound caught my ears, as though he had said, "wonderful;" this conveyed to me the impression, that he thought it wonderful I should be made to speak such things: I turned to him, and was made in the power to rebuke him for thinking it wonderful, and bid him search his own heart, for if he was looking after wonders he would fall into the snare of the enemy. He did not correct the mistake at the time, but after...Capt. G. mentioned the mistake, and said, he had thought not to mention it now, but to tell me in private. (*Narrative Of Facts, p.19*)

Throughout the same day, much utterance was given to me, and a visitation of what seemed to me, upon proof, a mimicry by Satan, of the spirit of revelation. A power came upon me after the manner of revelation, communicating in an indistinct manner, that I should be called to bear witness at Cambridge and in the House of commons; and that for this purpose I should be caught away by the Spirit, as Philip was, (Acts viii.) and it seemed to convey, that it would be done that very day. No sign in proof was given me, and I could not yield full credence to it; but fearing to tempt or grieve the Spirit of God by any despite of such communication I walked out, and giving myself into the hand of God, I waited to see whether the communication was of him. Nothing following upon it, and I judged therefore it was of Satan... (*Narrative Of Facts, pp.41-42*)

A few days after I left him, Mr. Irving forwarding me a letter, added a few lines of his own, telling me how greatly they were encouraged and strengthened in London by my last visit, and stating how they looked forward to my return with the full powers of an apostle; but at the same time adding, that Mr. F., who had spoken in power amongst us, had been found to speak by an evil spirit, Mrs. C.[208] and Miss E. C. having been made so to declare. This troubled me greatly, for I had been made in power to declare to him his call to the spiritual ministry. He had also been present, and spoke in power on the last morning of my presence, at Mr. Irving's, when two persons were sent out; and when it was declared in the power that the Lord would not suffer an unbeliever or unclean person to be present at that holy ordinance, as it was called. Here were contradictions I could not explain away... (*Narrative Of Facts, pp.91-92*)

---

[208] That is, Mary Campbell Caird, one of the prophetesses.

Subsequently to this came utterances, preparing us for some great favour and grace which, it was said, the Lord had ordained for us...At the interval of a day or two, there followed an appalling utterance—that the Lord had set me apart for himself—that, from the day I was called to the spiritual ministry, I must count 40 days—that this was now well nigh expired—that for those 40 days was it appointed I should be tried—that the Lord had tried me and found me faithful, and having now proved in me the first sign of an apostle, "patience," (referring to 2 Cor. xii. 12.) he would give to me the fullness of them, in the gifts of "signs, and wonders, and mighty deeds;"—that the Lord had called me to be an apostle...I was commanded to go back to the church, where my mouth was opened, and, on the fortieth day, power should be given, the sick should be healed, the deaf should hear, the dead should be restored, and all the mighty signs and wonders should appear...The [40th] day, however, passed over without any manifestation of the power which had been foretold...I was weighed down under the delay of the fulfillment of the prophecy concerning the apostolic endowments on the fortieth day...To add to my distress, I heard from my friend in the country, who had spoken in power, and received directions to go and perform a miracle of healing—stating, that in fasting and prayer he had gone up on the errand, but had failed to perform any miracle—that he concluded he had spoken by a lying spirit, and could no longer believe we were speaking by the Spirit of God. My prophecy concerning the fortieth day, had been bruited about in my own neighbourhood, and its failure, together, with that of my friend, had had such an effect, that my wife and greater part of the believers in the country abandoned it as a delusion. (*Narrative Of Facts, pp.65-66, 70, 82-83*)

...I was, as may be supposed, engaged in consideration of the subject; and the whole train of circumstances, from the beginning; with the successive failures of prophecy and contradictions of utterances, when calmly reviewed and compared with the present fact of the support of false doctrine[209] were so strongly affirmative

---

[209] Baxter is here referring to a theological disagreement that he had with Irving's understanding of the human nature of Jesus. At the time of writing this I have not studied Irving's position enough to comment on it. Irving published his

of the evil origin of the work, that, however supernatural I had found it, and still knew it to be, I was convinced it must be a work of Satan, who, as an angel of light, was permitted for a time to deceive us...Being anxious to communicate with Mr. Irving, I travelled on to London, and reached him on the morning of his appearance before the presbytery of London. Calling him and Mr. J. C.[210] apart, I told them my conviction that we had all been speaking by a lying spirit, and not by the Spirit of the Lord. He said it was impossible God could have sent us strong delusions, for that was his final judgment upon the wicked, and we, at least, thought ourselves seeking after the Lord, and desiring his glory. I answered, I believed God had sent it as a chastisement for pride and lofty imaginations; that we had been lifted up in our own hearts, and God would humble us...I saw him again in the evening, and on the succeeding morning I endeavoured to convince him of his error of doctrine, and of our delusions concerning the work of the Spirit, but he was so shut up, he could not see either. (*Narrative Of Facts, pp.118-119*)

Long after I gave up the work as a delusion, the power so continued with me, that I was obliged to resist it continually: when in prayer, the power would come and carry out my utterance in power, and I was obliged to stop to resist it. This was very distressing for a long time, joined as it was to the darkness and deadness of a mind, so long swayed by such delusions; but, under such circumstances, all we can do is to hold fast our confidence, that God will not abandon us; and to watch against every spirit of repining or complaint against God, humbling ourselves, and pleading the blood of sprinkling of the Lamb of God, who taketh away the sins of the world: His mercies fail not, but are new every morning. (*Narrative Of Facts, p.145*)

John L. Nevius

BIO: [1829-1893] *A missionary to China for forty years who was associated with the American Presbyterian Mission. He is best known for his research on demonology that he conducted while in China and his development of a technique for encouraging converted natives to form their own self supporting churches.*

views on this in a work entitled *The Orthodox and Catholic Doctrine of Our Lord's Human Nature* (London: Baldwin & Cradock, 1830).

In the summer of 1861, we removed from Ningpo to the province of Shantung in Northern China. There again I met with many evidences of this same popular belief [in an invisible, supernatural world], which constantly confronted us in the prosecution of our missionary work.

The first event in connection with this subject in Shantung, which I recall to mind, occurred in a country station of one of my colleagues, about the year 1868. This colleague was desirous of renting a native house to be used as a chapel in the market town of Changkia chwang, about thirty miles from Chefoo.[211] After many fruitless attempts to secure such a place, he was surprised by the unexpected offer of an excellent building in a very desirable location, and on very reasonable terms. Fearing that delay might give rise to difficulties and obstructions he concluded the bargain at once. The articles of agreement were drawn up, and native Christians in his employ were immediately assigned to occupy and take charge of the premises. The next morning the new occupants found a crowd of curious neighbors awaiting their first appearance on the street, and were asked with an air of mysterious interest how they had slept, and if they had passed a comfortable night. It soon transpired that the Christians had been sleeping in a "haunted house." No one in the village had for some years dared to use the building for any purpose, which fact accounted for its having been so readily obtained.

So far there was nothing very remarkable in our having come into possession of a house supposed to be haunted, but the matter did not end here. Before night the occupants of a neighboring compound came to see the Christians, informing them that the spirit had taken possession of one of the women in their family, and insisted upon taking up its abode with them, as it had been driven away from its former dwelling place by the presence of Christians, with whom it could not live. The family seemed to

---

[210] That is, John Bate Cardale, one of the apostles of the movement.
[211] Modern day Yantai.

126

think they had a right to complain of this unwelcome visitor having been thus foisted upon them. The native Christians replied that they would do what they could to rid the complainants of the spirit, and returned with them to their home taking with them a New Testament, and a Prayer printed in large characters as a placard. After they had prayed and read the Scriptures the woman supposed to be possessed, was restored to her normal condition. The Prayer was posted on the walls, and the frightened inmates of the house were exhorted to withstand and drive out the spirit in the name of Jesus. They were not troubled afterward, though the spirit was heard of trying to gain an entrance into other families in the neighborhood.

In the above statement the villagers generally, and the native preacher, and the persons principally concerned (some of whom have since become Christians) all concur. (*Demon Possession And Allied Themes, Ch. 1*)

In the year 1871, or 1872, the following experiences were met with in the village of Chumao in the district of Ping-tu. There was a native school there in which was a boy named Liu, about twelve years of age, who was supposed to be at times possessed by an evil spirit. When the attacks occurred he would start and cry out with fear, as if conscious of some unseen presence, and then fall down insensible. On these occasions a woman in the village who was believed to be a spirit-medium, or exorcist, was immediately sent for. On the recurrence of one of these attacks another of the pupils[212] ran to call the exorcist. On his way he met a man named Liu Chong-ho, who had recently been to Teng-chow fu, as an "enquirer," and had, after studying the Scriptures there for a month or more, been baptized. On learning the boy's errand he told him not to summon the exorcist, and at once returned with him to the school. Requiring all the pupils to kneel with him, he earnestly called on Jesus for help. Then turning to the prostrate boy he said in almost Scriptural words "I command you in the name of Jesus Christ to come out of him!"[213] The boy uttered a piercing cry, was at once restored to consciousness. I can say from personal knowledge that he never had another of those attacks from that day to this. Some years since he graduated from the high-school at

[212] From the above mentioned school in Chumao.
[213] Ac 16:18

Teng-chow fu; and is now a useful and efficient man. Both his parents have become Christians...The teacher of the school, Li-Ching pu, who afterward became a Christian, fully corroborated the story...When the boy above referred to was interrogated as to the reason for his crying out, he said it was because the spirit in leaving him hurt him; and he showed the place on his side where he was injured. Those present at the time still declare that they saw the spot, and believed that it originated as represented. (*Demon Possession And Allied Themes, Ch. 1*)

Missionaries To Asia Were Amazed To Experience Demon Possession Exactly As It Was Described In The New Testament. Above Is The Gate Of The Capital Of Shan-Si, China, Where Nearly Fifty Missionaries And Their Children Were Put To Death By Orders Of The Governor.

During the summer of 1878 I received a letter from a native assistant, Mr. Leng, relating some experiences which he had met with in the mountainous district of Ling-ku; his account of which, in his own words, is as follows:

"While visiting the enquirers at 'Twin-Mountain Stream' I was told of a young man, of the family name Kwo, living in the village of Hing-kia, who was suffering all sorts of inflictions from an evil spirit. I desired to see the man, and it was arranged that we should pay him a visit. We found Mr. Kwo at work in the

128

fields, where I had a conversation with him, which was as follows:

'I have heard that you are troubled by an evil spirit.'

He replied: 'It is true, and most humiliating. That I, a man in the full vigor of health, should be a slave to this demon, is the trial of my life; there is no help for it.'

I said: 'I assure you there is help.'

'What do you mean?' he asked.

I replied: 'I will tell you. I am associated with a foreign teacher of Christianity, who often visits the region east of you. His object is to urge all men to worship the one true God, and to believe in Jesus Christ, the only heaven-appointed Saviour. Jesus Christ is all-merciful and all-powerful. It is His purpose to deliver us from the dominion of evil spirits; and they flee before Him.'

'But,' said Kwo, 'I have tried every thing, and in vain.'

I said: 'You have not tried believing and trusting Jesus, and I assure you that if you will do this, and take Jesus to be your Saviour, the demon will leave you.'

He replied: 'If what you say is true then I will believe in Jesus.'

Seeing that he was sincere, I further exhorted and encouraged him. In the meantime we had reached his house, and he pointed out to me the shrine where he worshiped the demon. I then told him that the first thing to do was to tear away this shrine. To this he readily consented. After this we all knelt down praying the Saviour to protect and save him. I then gave Mr. Kwo directions how to acquire further knowledge of Christianity; and leaving with him a few Christian books I took leave. As we separated he thanked us warmly for our visit."

After receiving this account from my native helper, I looked forward with no little interest to seeing this man.

In the month of March, 1879, on my way to the village of the "Twin-Mountain Stream," Mr. Kwo, hearing of my approach, came out some distance on the road to meet me, and invited me to his house. Leaving my conveyance and luggage to go on to the inn by the main road, I accompanied him across the hills to his mountain home. In my way I learned further particulars of his previous life. He had never attended school, and until recently had been unable to read. Moreover, (and this is very unusual in China,) not a person in his village could read. He was a hardy mountaineer, thirty-eight years of age, bright and entertaining, with nothing in his appearance which could be regarded as unhealthy, or abnormal.

It was late in the afternoon when I reached his home. I was at once introduced into the reception-room, which was the place where the evil spirit had formerly been worshiped.

I had scarcely seated myself when he called his little daughter, about ten years of age, to recite to me what she had learned. This bright child, who had never seen a foreigner, stood before me without the slightest appearance of shyness, and repeated page after page of a catechism specially prepared for Chinese inquirers, both question and answer, as fast as her tongue could go, evidently understanding what she said, on, on, half through the book, including the Ten Commandments, and the Lord's Prayer. There she repeated selected passages of Scripture, and various forms of prayer, and also a number of hymns. When she could go no farther she stopped suddenly, saying: "That is as far as I have got!" When she had finished her recitation, her mother, a pleasant intelligent woman with a child in her arms, came in, and she in turn went over the same lessons, and with the same correctness. On examining Mr. Kwo himself, I found that he had got on further still in these same studies.

This was only six months after Mr. Kwo had first heard of the religion of Jesus. Remembering his ignorance of the written language, and also that no one in his village could read, I enquired how it was possible for him to learn all this. The reply was: "On Sundays I go to worship with the Christians at Shen-jen kwo (House of the Genii) or at the 'Twin-Mountain Stream,' and sometimes one of the Christians comes to spend a day or two with me. Whenever I meet those who can teach me, I learn a little; and what I learn I teach my wife and daughter." He then went on to say: "I told my wife and daughter that I intended to ask you for baptism on this visit. They said: 'But you must not leave us behind. We too wish to be baptized.' Now we are all here before you, and we request baptism." Having said this, he anxiously waited my decision. The answer immediately suggested to my mind was: "Can any man forbid water that these should not be baptized?"[214] And with no hesitation, though with some anxiety, I baptized the father, mother, little girl, and infant. The reception to the church of this family, under these novel circumstances, was an event of great interest to me. As the sun was setting I wended my way across the

---

[214] Ac 10:47

130

hills to the village of the "Twin-Mountain Stream," Kwo accompanying me as my guide.

After the services of the next day, which was Sunday, I requested Mr. Kwo to accompany me to the next preaching place; and then drew from him a fuller history of his experiences from the time when he first came under the control, as he supposed, of the evil spirit. I afterward had long conversations with his wife, and also conversed on the same subject at length with his father. All the different accounts supplement and confirm his own, and agree in every important particular. I give these statements as I received them. I offer no opinion of my own respecting the phenomena presented. Of course Mr. Kwo's statements respecting what he said and did when he was in a state of unconsciousness depend on the testimony of those about him. The story in his own words, is as follows:

"Near the close of year before last (1877) I bought a number of pictures, including one of Wang Mu-niang, the wife of Yu-hwang, (the chief divinity of China). For the goddess Wang Mu-niang I selected the most honorable position in the house; the others I pasted on the walls here and there, as ornaments. On the second day of the first month I proposed worshiping the goddess; but my wife objected. The next night a spirit came, apparently in a dream, and said to me: 'I am Wang Mu-niang, of Yuin-men san, (the name of a neighboring mountain). I have taken up abode in your house.' It said this repeatedly. I had awakened and was conscious of the presence of the spirit. I knew it was a *shie-kwei*, (evil spirit), and as such I resisted it, and cursed it, saying: 'I will have nothing to do with you.' This my wife heard, and begged to know what it meant, and I told her. After this all was quiet, and I was not disturbed for some days. About a week afterward a feeling of uneasiness and restlessness came over me, which I could not control. At night I went to bed as usual, but grew more and more restless. At last, seized by an irresistible impulse, I arose from my bed and went straight to a gambler's den in Kao-kia, where I lost at once 16,000 cash, (sixteen dollars, a large sum for a peasant Chinaman).[215] I started for home, and lost my way. But when it grew light I got back to my house. At that time I was conscious of what I was doing and saying, but I did things mechanically, and

---

[215] Roughly $434.00US in 2016 taking inflation into account.

131

soon forgot what I had said. I did not care to eat, and only did so when urged to. After some days a gambler from Kao-kia came and asked me to go with him, which I did; and this time I lost 25,000 cash.[216] On the fifteenth and sixteenth of the first month, I went to Pe-ta where there was a theatre. The same night I again lost 13,000 cash in gambling.[217] The next morning I returned home, and just as I was entering my village I fell down frothing at the mouth and unconscious; and was carried to my house. Medicine was given me which partially restored me to consciousness. The next day I dressed myself and attempted to run away from home, but I soon found myself staggering; everything grew dark, and I rushed back to my room. I soon became violent, attacking all who ventured near me. My father hearing the state of things came from his home to see me. As he entered I seized a fowling-piece, which I had secreted under my bed, and fired it at him. Fortunately the charge went over his head into the ceiling. With the help of the neighbors my father bound me with chains, and took me to his home in Chang-yiu. A doctor was called who, after giving me large doses of medicine without effect, left, refusing to have anything more to do with me. For five or six days I raved wildly, and my friends were in great distress. They proposed giving me more medicine, but the demon, speaking through me, replied: 'Any amount of medicine will be of no use.' My mother then asked: 'If medicine is of no use, what shall we do?' The demon replied: 'Burn incense to me, and submit yourself to me, and all will be well.' My parents promised to do this, and knelt down and worshiped the demon, begging it to torment me no longer.[218] Thus the matter was arranged, I all the time remaining in a state of unconsciousness. About midnight I attempted to leave the house. The attendants followed me, brought me back, and bound me again. Then my parents a second time worshiped the demon, begging it to relieve me from my suffering, and renewing their promise that I myself should hereafter worship and serve it. I then recovered consciousness, and my mother told me all that had happened, and of the promise they had made for me. On my refusing consent to this, I again lost all consciousness.[219] My mother besought the

---

[216] Roughly $677.00US in 2016.
[217] Roughly $352.00US in 2016.
[218] The reader will see in this an example of how demons start and propagate false religions.

favor of the demon, renewing her promise to insist upon my obedience, and I again recovered consciousness. In their great distress my father and mother implored me to fulfill their promise, and worship the evil spirit; and at last I reluctantly consented. The demon had directed that we should call a certain woman in Kao-chao who was a spirit-medium, to give us directions in putting in order our place for worship. So all was arranged, and on the first and fifteenth of each month we burnt incense, offered food, and made the required prostrations before the shrine on which the picture of the goddess was placed. The spirit came at intervals, sometimes every few days, and sometimes after a period of a month or more. At these times I felt a fluttering of the heart, and a sense of fear and inability to control myself, and was obliged to sit or lie down. I would tell my wife when these symptoms came on, and she would run for a neighboring woman less timid than herself, and they two burned incense to the demon in my stead, and received its directions, which they afterward communicated to me, for though spoken by my lips I had been entirely unconscious of them. The demon often bade us not to be afraid of it, saying it would not injure us, but that, on the contrary, it would help us in various ways; that it would instruct me in the healing art, so that people would flock to me to be cured of their diseases. This proved to be true; and soon from my own village the people came bringing their children to be healed by the aid of the demon. Sometimes it would cure the sick instantaneously, and without the use of medicine. Sometimes it would not respond when first summoned, and when it did appear would say it had been absent in such and such places; but it never said on what business. Many diseases were not under its control, and it seemed as if it could perfectly cure only such as were inflicted by spirits. My own child had long been ill, and I invoked the demon, but it did not come. The child died.[220]

"The demon said he had many inferior spirits subject to him. He also frequently indicated his plan for my future life and employment. It was that through his assistance I should grow more and more skilled in healing diseases. The people would soon be

---

[219] Note the inability of the unbeliever to resist the attack of a demon.

[220] This seems to indicate that demons cannot heal diseases, unless they are the result of a previous demonic attack. Notice that this narrative demonstrates that demons can give people the gift of healing, at least the appearance of it.

willing to make a return for my services. In time of harvest I should go about from family to family getting contributions of grain, and these contributions as they accumulated should be applied to the support of the neighboring temple."

I would remark that Mr. Kwo's own account of Leng's visit exactly corresponded with that given above. Mr. Kwo, however, added the following. Said he: "The death of our child occurred a few days after we had torn down the spirit's shrine. My wife was much distressed, believing it was in consequence of my having offended the demon. She urged me to restore the shrine and resume the worship. I told her that whatever might happen I would not break my vow to worship and trust in Jesus. A few days after that the demon returned and, speaking through me, of course, a conversation ensued between it and my wife, which was as follows:

'We understood that you were not to return. How is it that you have come back again?'

The demon replied: 'I have returned but for one visit. If your husband is determined to be a Christian this is no place for me. But I wish to tell you I had nothing to do with the death of your child.'

'What do you know of Jesus Christ?' they asked.

The answer was: 'Jesus Christ is the great Lord over all; and now I am going away and you will not see me again.'

'This', said Mr. Kwo, 'was actually the last visit; and we have not been troubled since."[221] (*Demon Possession And Allied Themes, Ch. 2*)

On the eleventh of October, 1879, at Shin-tsai, in the district of Ling-ku, I was conversing with a simple-minded countryman who was an applicant for baptism, when the subject of demoniacal possessions was brought up very incidentally and unexpectedly. I asked the enquirer: "Have you met any opposition in your family in consequence of your desire to be a Christian?" He replied: "I have from one source; my sister-in-law has for many years been possessed by a demon, and the demon objects to my being a Christian, and so my sister-in-law is afraid, and advises me

---

[221] Nevius continues his account showing that Mr. Kwo was still active in the sharing of his faith and free from demonic activity over ten years later and that the experience had led to numerous other conversions of local Chinese.

against it." "What does the demon say?" I asked. He replied: "It said: 'If you believe in, and worship Jesus, there is no place for me. I must leave.' I said to it: 'I was not aware that I was interfering with you, or your interests. I believe Christianity to be the true doctrine; and I trust in Christ for salvation and eternal life; and I do not want to give up Christianity.' The demon replied: 'It may be very good for you; but it is very bad for us!'"

Then I went on to question the man; "How do you know that it was a *demon*?" "Why," he replied, "it spoke!" "Was it not your sister-in-law who spoke?" "No, my sister-in-law knew nothing about it; she was unconscious. She was frightened when she heard of it." "Had not the demon been in the habit of speaking?" I asked. He replied: "Only once-years ago. Then it told her that when she arrived at the age of thirty-six, it wanted her to heal diseases."[222] I asked again: "If she did not speak when the demon came to her, what did she do?" He answered: "She only breathed hard, and was unconscious."

The narrator of this incident was a few months later baptized. Some years after the sister-in-law and her husband were also admitted to church-membership. There has been no return of the malady-whatever it was. Though extremely poor, they are intelligent and sincere Christians. (*Demon Possession And Allied Themes, Ch. 3*)

Two cases…occurred in connection with our mission station in Chimi, Shan-tung, China. They were described to me in detail by a theological student whose home was in that neighborhood, and who was familiarly acquainted with the subjects of both cases, one being a near relative. Both of them were well-known as sincere and consistent Christians until their deaths. They declared that for many years, before they became Christians, they submitted to, and obeyed the behests of the possessing demons from necessity, being constrained and intimidated by severe physical and mental inflictions and torments; that they believed that the actions purporting to be performed by the demons through them as their agents or instruments were in fact so performed; that they had no means to rid themselves of the dominion of the demons until they heard of Christianity. One of these persons, an aunt of the

---

[222] Note how that demons seem very eager to "gift" people with the ability to heal.

theological student, is said to have had, when in the abnormal state, remarkable clairvoyant powers. (In Nevius' *Demon Possession And Allied Themes, Ch. 11*)

Native Chinese Converts Took The Stories Of Demon Possession In The New Testament At Face Value And Incorporated Spiritual Warfare Into Their Ministries

In the spring of 1883 or 1884, a girl of fifteen of the family Chang, living in the village of Chang kiachwang in southern Shiu Kwang, was supposed to be possessed by an evil spirit. While thus affected and having lost entirely her consciousness, she went to another village where lived her future mother-in-law of the Sen family, going directly to the door without a guide, though she had never been there before, and could not have known the way. A young girl going to the house of her future mother-in-law is entirely contrary to Chinese etiquette, and the last thing a betrothed girl in her sane mind could be induced to do. Her future father-in-law and mother-in-law were averse to receiving her, but were almost obliged to do so in order to avoid scandal. They were sure by her appearance that she was possessed by an evil spirit, and applied to two Christians, Changho-yi and Chaoyu-yieh, living in the same village, to come and cast it out. It was from them that I heard the story. When they went with Mr. Sen to try to cast out the demon it boldly defied them, saying, "I will not go. I once found a home in a family named Mu which spent 60,000 cash (about $50.[223]), in their

---

[223] Roughly $1354.00US in 2016. How many people have wasted money on

attempt to drive me away, but without avail; and do you think you can cast me out?" While the two Christians were offering a prayer for help the girl came to herself at once and immediately returned to her own home as anxious to be there as they were to have her. (In Nevius' *Demon Possession And Allied Themes, Appendix I.f*)

In the year 1885 in visiting the mission station in Kin-tswen in south-eastern En Chiu, a family consisting of a man and his wife and five children, together asked for admission to the church. This is the story as given by the eldest son who acted as spokesman for the family. It was concurred in by the Christians in the village and neighborhood.

"For several months my mother was sorely afflicted by an evil spirit. The attacks were frequent and violent. She pined away until she was a mere skeleton. You see how thin and pale she is now, but she is well compared to what she was, and is constantly growing stronger. We applied to the Christians here to cast out the demon, which they did, but it as often returned. Then we following our Christian neighbors' advice determined as a family to believe on and trust in Christ. These attacks are now less and less frequent. Whenever they come on some one of us kneels down and prays to Jesus, and my mother is at once restored. Some days since she had an attack when no one was in the house except my little sister, (pointing to a little girl present about five years old), who immediately knelt down and commenced 'Our Father who are in Heaven, hallowed be thy name,' etc., when my mother darted towards her as if she would tear her to pieces, saying, 'You little wretch,' but she fell down insensible before she got to her; and very soon rose up well."[224] (In Nevius' *Demon Possession And*

---

modern secular psychologists who refuse to see the possibility of a spiritual cause for some mental illness? Many mental illnesses are the result of physical causes (injury, infection, etc.) but surely some are the result of demon possession and the refusal to accept the possibility of a spiritual cause has played a part in many going to their graves after decades of suffering without having ever found real and lasting mental healing.

[224] The members of the family were all eventually baptized. This example brings out the need to understand that freeing individuals from demon possession may take a considerable amount of time. Christians need to be willing to meet to pray with demon possessed/oppressed individuals for weeks, months or even longer gradually bringing the individual into more and more freedom. In cases of this nature it is my belief that these individuals may be possessed by multiple

Leng Shien-chin

BIO: *A native Chinese assistant to Dr. John L. Nevius known for being very kind and warmhearted. The name Shien-chin means "first entered" and is probably a reference to his being the first child to be born into his family.*

This spring when I was at Tse-kia chwang, in the district of Shiu-kwang, I was giving the Christians there an account of the case of Mr. Kwo at Hing-kia, when an enquirer present said: 'We have a similar case here.' It was that of a woman, also named Kwo. She was thirty-two years of age, and had suffered from this infliction eight years. It happened that at the time of my visit the woman was suffering more than usual. Her husband, in the hope that the demon would not disturb his wife in the house of a Christian, had brought her to the home of his brother-in-law, Mr. Sen, who had lately professed Christianity.[225] On my arrival they said to me: 'She is here, on the opposite side of the court,' and they begged me to cast out the spirit; as they had tried every method they knew of without effect. Then without waiting for my assent, they brought the woman into the room where I was. I said: 'I have no power to do anything of myself. We must ask God to help us.' While we knelt in prayer the woman was lying on the *k'ang*,[226] apparently unconscious. When the prayer was finished she was sitting up, her eyes closed, with a fluttering motion of the eyelids, her countenance like one weeping, and the fingers of both hands tightly clenched. She would allow no one to straighten her closed fingers. I then, hardly expecting an answer, as the woman had hitherto been speechless, said to the demon: 'Have you no fear of God? Why do you come here to afflict this woman?' To this I received instantly the following reply:[227]

---

demons and that each deliverance prayer session may be freeing them from more and more of their demons. The deliverance prayer sessions should be conducted until the individual is completely free and may need to be continued on an ongoing basis until the individual appears to be rooted in the Christian faith in order to prevent a return of the demons (Lk 11:24-26).

[225] Note the impact that a believer who exercises power over demons can have in encouraging unbelievers to trust in the message of Christ.

[226] A bed made of earth and brick, very common in North China at the time the above book was written.

'God and Christ will not interfere. I have been here seven or eight years; and I claim this as my resting-place. You cannot get rid of me.'

She continued for some time uttering a succession of rhymes similar to the above, without the slightest pause; the purport of them all being: 'I want a resting-place, and I'll not leave this one.'[228] The utterances were so rapid that the verse given above was the only one I could remember perfectly. I can recall another line: 'You are men, but I am *shien*,' (i.e. one of the genii). After repeating these verses, evidently extemporized for the occasion, a person present dragged her back to her apartments-the demon not having been exorcised.

I was attending service one Sunday at a village called Wu-kia-miao-ts, two miles from Tse-kia chwang, and Mr. Sen from the latter village was present. Noticing in Mr. Sen's hand a paper parcel I enquired what it contained, and was told that it contained cinnabar. This is a medicine which is much used for the purpose of expelling evil spirits. Mr. Sen said he had procured it to administer to the possessed woman, Mrs. Kwo, who was suffering from her malady very severely. I then spoke to the Christians present as follows: 'We ought not to use the world's methods for exorcising demons, but rather appeal to God only. The reason why we did not succeed before was our want of faith. This is our sin.' I went on to tell them how willing God is to answer prayer, referring to my own experience in the famine region, when, reduced almost to starvation, I prayed to God for help, and was heard and rescued. I asked those present if they would join me in prayer for Mrs. Kwo, and they all did so. After this I set out for Tse-kia chwang in company with two other Christians.

While this was transpiring at Wu-kia-miao-ts the Christians at Tse-kia chwang were attempting to hold their customary Sunday service; but Mrs. Kwo (or the demon possessing her) was determined to prevent it. She raved wildly, and springing upon the table threw the Bibles and hymn-books on the floor. The wife of a younger Mr. Sen, who was a Christian, then became similarly affected; and the two women were raving together. They were heard saying to each other: 'Those three men are coming here, and have got as far as the stream.' Some one asked: 'Who are coming?'

---

[227] I omitted the original Chinese from this transcription of the text.
[228] Compare Matthew 12:43.

The woman replied with great emphasis: 'One of them is that man Leng.' As I was not expected to visit that place until a few days later, a daughter of the family said: 'He will not be here to-day.' To which the demon replied: 'If he does not come here to-day, then I am no *shien*. They are now crossing the stream, and will reach here when the sun is about so high,' and she pointed to the west. No one could have known, in the ordinary way, that we were coming, as our visit was not thought of until just before starting. Moreover the two men who went with me were from different villages, at a considerable distance in opposite directions, and had had no previous intention of accompanying me. When we arrived at the village a large company were assembled at Mr. Sen's house, attracted by the disturbance, and curious to see the result of it. After a time I went into the north building where the two raving women were sitting together on the *k'ang*. I addressed the demon possessing them as follows: 'Do you not know that the members of this family are believers in the true God, and that this is a place used for his worship? You are not only disturbing the peace of this house, but are fighting against God. If you do not leave, we will immediately call upon God to drive you out.' The younger of the two women then said to the other: 'Let us go-let us go!' The other drew back on the *k'ang* angrily saying: 'I'll not go! I'll stay and be the death of this woman!' I then said with great vehemence: 'You evil, malignant spirit! You have not the power of life and death; and you cannot intimidate us by your vain threats. We will now call upon God to drive you out.' So the Christians all knelt to pray. The bystanders say that during the prayer the two possessed persons, awakening as if from sleep, looked about, and seeing us kneeling, quietly got down from the *k'ang* and knelt beside us. When we rose from prayer we saw the women still kneeling; and soon after Mrs. Kwo arose and came forward greeting us naturally and politely, evidently quite restored.[229] (In Nevius' *Demon Possession And Allied Themes, Ch. 3*)

---

[229] Mrs. Kwo was baptized about two months later and maintained a consistent Christian walk. For two years following her baptism Mrs. Kwo said that she was frequently conscious of the presence of the evil spirit seeking to gain control over her again and felt almost powerless to resist it. At these times she would at once fall upon her knees and appeal to Christ for help, which she would always receive. She said that these returns of the demon became less and less frequent and persistent, and after a time ceased altogether. It is interesting to note that in her normal state Mrs. Kwo never showed any aptitude for devising poetical

Native Chinese Christian Leader (Seated) In Peking, Circa 1900

Lichung-pu

BIO: *A native Chinese preacher associated with the Christians in Ping-tu and Chu-Mao, China.*

In the spring of 1874 I went to a 'hwei'[230] east of Len-ko to preach. I saw there a company of twenty or thirty women who came to worship at the temple of Lai shan shing mu,[231] the most of

rhymes as she did when she would come under the influence of the demon.

[230] A market or large gathering of people for the purpose of trade and idolatrous worship. These large gatherings were held annually, or semi-annually, generally in connection with a temple, and continued for several days.

[231] "Holy Mother of the Great Mountain." The name of the goddess of the sacred mountain Tai Shan situated in the western part of the province of Shantung.

whom I personally knew. While there a relative of mine pointed to a woman standing by, belonging to the Sie family, and said: 'That woman suffers fearfully from a demon which gives her no rest; and in obedience to whose command she has come here to worship.' The woman hearing the remark hung her head in shame. I addressed the group of women, assuring them that they need not fear evil spirits, as such spirits can not harm any one who believes in God and Jesus Christ.

On hearing this another woman, Mrs. Ku, from a place six *Li*[232] (two miles) distant addressed me as follows: 'Do you say that there is no reason for fearing spirits, I am a *hiang-to*[233] of twenty year's standing, and am in communication with three spirits. I have at home a beautiful picture of Kwan-yin (the goddess of mercy). If my spirits are afraid of you and your doctrines I will have nothing more to do with them, and will give my painting of Kwan-yin to you and become a Christian myself. If you like to come to my house we will see whether my spirits are afraid of you or not.' I could not decline this challenge, and an arrangement was made that I should visit her that same afternoon. I went accompanied by a Christian Liu Chung-ho[234] to the house of a relative of mine who lives in Mrs. Ku's village. In this family are two Christians, and there was also stopping there at the time a pupil from the girl's boarding school at Teng Chow-fu. After conversing with these persons for awhile Mrs. Ku entered. She said that of her three 'familiars,' she would summon the one which was the most powerful, and who manifested herself, in the character of a girl named Tse-hwa. I then told the crowd that I had been challenged to meet this woman to see whether her spirits were afraid of the true God or not; that we would now pray to God; and if they did not wish to engage in this act of worship they might withdraw. Apparently from fear they all left. I read a chapter of the Bible and prayed. Mrs. Ku then burned incense, and prayed to the demon Tse-hwa. In a few moments Mrs. Ku sank down on her *kang*, her frame rigid, her hands clenched and cold, and her lips and face purple. A few moments later she sat up again. Looking around her she saw her child standing by, and without any provocation struck

---

[232] A *Li* is a Chinese mile, which is about a third of an English mile.

[233] A medium. Literally, a leader of incense burners.

[234] The same person referred to in a previous narrative, spelled there as Liu Chong-ho.

her a severe blow. I said to the spirit, 'The religion of Jesus Christ which has now been brought to this village is opposed to you and all your ways. You are an enemy of the truth and a disturber of man's peace, and as Christ's religion has come here and must prevail you must leave.' The reply was 'I know that wherever the Christian religion is there is no place left for me. I know too that this religion is good and true, and if my *hiang-to* wishes to become a Christian I must leave her.' After a considerable conversation all of this same tenor the demon said, 'I will go'. Mrs. Ku then returned to consciousness with the air of one disappointed and frightened, and soon after took her leave saying, 'I must certainly suffer for this.'

From this place I went to the village where Mrs. Sie lives. Her husband received me very kindly, saying, however, that his wife during the intervals of her attacks appeared as other people, and at this time she was quite well. But it happened that a few moments later a child came running in saying, 'Mrs. Sie has another seizure, and is under the influence of the demon.' I went immediately in to the part of the dwelling where she was. When she heard us coming she rolled herself up in a mat on her *kang* where she kept up an incessant laughing and tittering. I said to her: 'What is your name?' She replied: 'I will not tell you. Tse-hwa gave you her name and you have sent her away. She has just been here to tell me of it. There are eight of us, and I am employed in finding a place for the rest.' After prayer a conversation followed similar to the one described in the visit to Mrs. Ku and with a like result. The woman on returning to consciousness rose from the *kang* and entertained her guests with much politeness. Pointing to a recess in the wall covered by a curtain, where was an image and an incense urn, she told us that the demon exacted worship of her three times a day before that shrine. I tore away the curtain, removed the articles used in worship, and exhorted Mrs. Sie never again to believe in or fear these beings, but to trust only in Christ. It being almost dark I left promising to come back the next day, and then returned to the village of Mrs. Ku the medium.

The next morning Mrs. Ku came in with one cheek swollen and red. The 'familiar' Tse-hwa (so she said) had beaten her the previous evening and upbraided her as follows: 'Why do you requite me thus? After helping you these twenty years to make money and get a living, why do you call in these Christians who

143

would drive me away?' while Mrs. Ku was thus speaking her appearance changed and she seemed to be under the influence of the demon again. I then addressed the demon as follows: 'After having promised yesterday that you would leave, why have you come back again?' The answer was 'I have something to say. If my *hiang-to* wishes to be a Christian I cannot prevent it, and in that case I will never visit her again. But I will tell you something about her. She is a bad woman; if she enters your religion you will have to look after her carefully. I advise you to have nothing to do with her.'

...Mrs. Ku after recovering consciousness asked what Tse-hwa had said. I informed her, and begged her to sever at once her connection with evil spirits, and be a disciple of Christ. I have since heard that after our interview the villagers, unwilling that the spirit Tse-hwa should leave them, because they were in the habit of consulting her through Mrs. Ku for healing their diseases, besought Mrs. Ku to pay homage to the demon and induce her to remain, which she did. I have met Mrs. Ku several times since, but she always hangs her head and turns away from me, and will not speak to me.

Early the same forenoon agreeably to my promise I started out to visit Mrs. Sie again. When I had gone half way to the village I met an old woman who begged me to hurry on saying: 'The demon has taken possession of Mrs. Sie, and she is to-day very violent. She attacks everyone who comes near her, and none of the family or the villagers dare enter her room. She is breaking utensils, scattering about the grain, and threatens to kill anyone who dares come to call you.' I said, 'How then did you dare to come?' She replied: 'I am more than sixty years old, I care little for life, and I determined that I would come.' I found Mrs. Sie's husband outside of the house with the rest, none daring to go in where his wife was. She had bolted the door of her room, but when she heard me outside she unbolted it, and ran into another room, and rolled herself up in a mat as she had done the day before, saying: 'I am not afraid, I am not afraid.' After we had prayed the demon said: 'I will go as I promised yesterday, but I have first a few words to say.' Then addressing a certain member of the family it said; 'I must be revenged on you. You have brandished swords at me, and fired fire-crackers before me, thinking to frighten me and drive me away. If it were not for the restraint I am under I would tear you to pieces.' I commanded the demon to leave Mrs. Sie and never to return, and thereupon Mrs. Sie was restored to consciousness, and spoke to us in a most pathetic way of herself. At this time she was reduced to a mere skeleton, and was so weak that she could hardly speak, though when in her abnormal state she had almost superhuman strength.[235] She told us that she had not eaten food for three days. I urged her to trust wholly in Christ, and told her that if she did so she need not fear for the future. As far as I have been able to learn she has not been troubled since, and is, as she was before she was possessed of the demon, a strong, well woman. She is not a professing Christian. (In Nevius' *Demon Possession And Allied Themes, Appendix I.a*)

Missionary Sponsored Discipleship Group At Hwochow

Chen Sin Ling

BIO: *A native Chinese Christian who aided various missionary organizations in 19th century China working as a scribe.*

In my native district, Chang-lo, there is a man who was formerly possessed by a demon. He believed in Christ, and entered the Christian religion, and was entirely relieved from the control of the demon. He afterwards turned aside from the truth, gave up his Christian profession, and the demon returned and tormented him

---

[235] Compare Mark 5:4.

until his death.[236] (In Nevius' *Demon Possession And Allied Themes, Ch 4*)

Wang Wu-Fang

BIO: *A well known and greatly respected 19th century native helper connected with the English Baptist Mission of Shan-tung, China.*

I was formerly accustomed to drive out demons by means of needles. At that time cases of possession by evil-spirits were very common in our village, and my services were in frequent demand. After I became a Christian these cases rapidly diminished, and finally almost disappeared. When persons from adjacent villages called upon me as before to cast out spirits, it was difficult to know what I ought to do. I could not, as a Christian, follow the former method, so I declined to go. But the elders of the villages would not let me off. On one occasion I told them the demon might perhaps be cast out merely by prayer for God's help. They replied that they were quite willing I should use whatever method I preferred. I was not sure that I should be successful, but I determined to try. When I arrived at the man's house I commenced singing a hymn; and the person possessed immediately cried out, and covered his head. Before the close of the prayer which followed he had recovered. (In Nevius' *Demon Possession And Allied Themes, Ch 4*)

There was another case which I met with on the twenty-fifth day of the first month of the present year (1880). The subject, who was twenty-three years old, was the wife of the second son of Li Mao-lin. When under the influence of the demon she was wild and unmanageable. This continued six days without intermission. The family applied to "*Wu-po*" (mediums, literally female magicians,) and persons who effected cures by needles; but without success. They were at their wits' end, and, all other means having failed, a person named Li Tso-yuen came and applied to me. I declined going, but he urged me at least to go and look at her, which I consented to do. When we entered the house, she was

---

[236] Compare again Luke 11:24-26 and note the need for believers to maintain a consistent lifestyle of repentance in order to effectively keep the door closed to demonic infestation.

surrounded by a crowd of people and her noisy demonstrations had not ceased. When they learned that we were approaching, the people present opened a way for us, and the possessed woman at once took a seat, began adjusting her hair and wonderingly asked: "Why are there so many people here?" Her husband told her what she had been doing for several days past. She exclaimed in a surprised way: "I know nothing about it." The people thought it very remarkable that she should be restored as soon as I entered the house; and I, of course, was very thankful for the result. From this time the fame of Christianity rapidly spread, and there were many accessions to the church.

More than ten days after this, the woman had another attack; and they again sent for me. I went to the place accompanied by another Christian. As we entered, she recovered as before, and sat up; to all appearances quite well. We availed ourselves of this opportunity to preach to the family for a long time. On our way home my friend delightedly exclaimed: "Even the devils are subject to us!"[237]

Ten days afterward, during the night, we heard a loud knocking at the door. It was a messenger from Li Tso-yuen, who informed us that the possessed woman was worse than ever; that her face was purple, her body rigid, her skin cold, her respiration difficult, and her life almost extinct. I called a Bible student who was near to accompany me. He was an earnest Christian, and I supposed that on our arrival at the house the demon would leave as before. To our surprise the woman remained rigid and motionless, as dead. The sight frightened us, and we betook ourselves to prayer. Presently she turned her head away from us, seeing which, the family were delighted, and cried out together: "She has come to life again!" We then sang a hymn. When we had finished, the woman drew a long breath, and was soon restored. Her sister-in-law asked her many questions. She had no recollection of what had occurred. The sister-in-law said to me: "The demon knew your name,[238] and said, the previous time, that when you came it would leave; and when you should return home, it would come back again: How is this?" I replied: "Believers in Christ can cast out devils. If you should believe, the demon would be afraid of you."[239]

---

[237] Lk 10:17
[238] Ac 19:15
[239] Compare Acts 19:13-16.

The family then asked for Christian books, which I promised, and afterward sent them. After this time the demon did not return. (In Nevius' *Demon Possession And Allied Themes, Ch 4*)

Chang Ah-liang

BIO: *A 19th century native Christian helper associated with the China Inland Mission.*

At Yang-fu-Miao, forty li[240] S. E. of Tai-chao, is a family consisting of an elderly woman, two sons, and the elder son's wife; all of whom live together. The eldest son was a zealous Buddhist, and leader in the idolatrous ceremonies in the neighboring temple; the younger a Christian, and a member of the Tai-chao church.

In June 1876 the son's wife was seized with violent pain in the chest. The Christian brother went to a place seven miles distant, to get advice about it. After his departure she swooned for an hour, then revived and said her husband's first wife (long since dead) had come to take her and her husband away. The friends present were much alarmed, and promised the demon that if it would leave the woman they would call six priests to chant the classics for three days. The answer was: 'Not sufficient.' They then said they would burn a quantity of paper, over which the name of Buddha had been repeated many times. The answer as before was: 'Not sufficient.' The husband brought the classics, chanted several, and placed the book on her heart, hoping by this means to get rid of the demon. She said: 'You can't get rid of me by this means.' Then a fishing net was spread over the woman, and she said: 'You can't catch me with this.' After several methods had been tried the Christian brother returned, to whom they related all that had passed. He said to her: 'Why do you talk in this foolish, confused manner.' She replied: 'I am not confused; I am your deceased sister-in-law.' He said: 'you are an evil spirit; leave her!' He read the New Testament to her, but she turned away, and did not want to hear. After two or three verses had been read, she said: 'Your reading pains me to death. Don't read! Don't read. I will go.' The woman then got up and attended to her duties; and until the time I left Tai-chao, at the end of 1878 was well in body and mind. The husband was convinced of the power of God, and professed to

---

[240] About 13 miles.

believe in Christianity. The neighbors were greatly astonished, and one young man present also believed. (In Nevius' *Demon Possession And Allied Themes, Ch. 6*)

Henry V. Noyes

BIO: [1836-1914] *A missionary to China who was associated with the American Presbyterian Mission. He is remembered for taking a handful of street boys and teaching them reading, writing and arithmetic in Canton, China, which led to the formation of seven schools in China and Hong Kong.*

Some time in the year 1868, in the fourth month of the Chinese year, Ho-kao, a preacher of the London Mission, was preaching in Fatshan, and a portion of his discourse referred to Jesus casting out devils. After the service a man came and asked Ho-kao if he could cast out devils, stating that he had a son thus possessed; and if Ho-kao could give him relief he would be very grateful. Ho-kao replied that he could not; but Jesus did of old, and could now if He chose to do so. All that he himself could do would be to pray to Jesus; and that he would be very willing to do. Ho-kao then went with the man to his home in a village not far from Fatshan, and found that his son, a grown up man, had been disordered for ten or more days, attacking people with knives, and making attempts to set fire to the house; so that he had been chained to a tree, with a little mat-shed near him to protect him when it rained. The people were afraid of him. Ho-kao asked the family and friends all to kneel down; and some one forced the man himself down on his knees. Ho-kao then prayed. As soon as the prayer was finished the chained man gave one or two leaps as high as he could, and then Ho-kao said: 'Take off the chains!' They were all afraid to do this, so Ho-kao himself took them off, and led the man into the house. He was quiet and seemed much exhausted, and soon fell asleep. The family wished to burn incense, etc., etc., but were told to do nothing of the kind. The father of the demoniac tore down everything pertaining to idol-worship in his house, and would have nothing more to do with it thereafter. He soon joined the church, and has been in connection with it ever since. The demoniac has never had any return of his trouble...the effect seemed to be good in drawing favorable attention to the work going on in connection with the chapel there. (In Nevius' *Demon Possession And Allied Themes, Ch. 6*)

I know of another instance which occurred early in the autumn of 1872. A native assistant, of the English Wesleyan Mission, was passing along one of the streets of his native village, when he saw a small company making sport of a man, who they said, was possessed of a devil. They called to the native assistant and challenged him to come and cast out the demon; as he claimed that the God of the Christians had such power. He went and prayed with the man, who then became much more quiet. The assistant visited him for two or three days, when he appeared to be perfectly well and, seemed to form an exceedingly strong attachment for the native assistant who had prayed for him. The circumstances led to the formation of a class which met every evening for the study of the Bible, and some were converted. (In Nevius' *Demon Possession And Allied Themes, Ch. 6*)

Ho Yuing-she

BIO: *A 19th century native Chinese preacher associated with the London Mission.*

I was stationed in the city of Fu-san, and engaged in chapel preaching, when I was visited by a man from the neighborhood of Shin-Tsuen, about twenty *li* distant.[241] He said that his elder brother Tsai Se-hiang had been for several months afflicted by an evil spirit; and they had made use of every kind of magic for expelling demons, and had exhausted all the forms of idol-worship without the slightest result. He said that night and day they were borne down by this calamity, and found themselves absolutely powerless; that they had heard that Jesus was the Saviour of the world, and that by His name evil spirits might be cast out; and therefore they had come to beg the disciples of Jesus to visit them, and in the name of Jesus cast out the demon. I said: 'Your

---

[241] About seven miles.

determining to come and invite a disciple of Jesus to your home to cast out the devil by prayer, is certainly an excellent thing; but it is not certain that the members of your family will be willing to trust and follow us. Please enquire particularly whether his wife, children, and brothers are willing to give up all idolatrous practices, and reverence the true God. If they are willing to do this, bring me word again, and I will gladly go.' The next day the man came again, and said all were willing to comply with the Christian customs, and begged me to come. I then with a companion went back with him to his home. Arriving at his house I saw Tsai Se-hiang's wife, children and relatives all very sad and distressed. I asked the wife about her husband's malady. She said: 'My husband has been afflicted for a long time; we have wasted our substance on physicians; but without avail. All the day long he moans and mutters; he has almost ceased to be a man. In the night his malady is still more severe. In our extremity we have besought you two gentlemen to visit our humble home, and pray for him; and in the name of Christ cast out the evil spirit. It depends on you to bring back peace and happiness to our family; and our grateful remembrance of you shall have no end.' I said to the woman: 'Do you believe in Christ?' She replied: 'I believe.' I said: 'If you believe kneel with me and pray.' After prayer we looked at Tsai Se-hiang and saw that his countenance was peaceful and natural. All the family were wild with delight, and their astonishment knew no bounds. Very strangely and unexpectedly about ten days afterwards Mrs. Tsai Se-hiang again worshiped idols; and from that time her husband's malady returned. She immediately sent her brother-in-law to inform me of what had happened. He told me that his sister-in-law had not kept her promise, that she had disobeyed the commands of our religion, and gone to the temple to worship idols; and the evil spirit had returned. 'So,' said he, 'we are obliged to come and trouble you again, and if you will come and pray for him our gratitude will be more than we can express.' This time we ourselves did not go, but told the messenger to return and tell his sister-in-law that she herself ought in sincere repentance and reformation to trust in the power of Jesus, and in simple faith pray without ceasing; and she might hope that her husband would again be restored to health. The wife followed my direction, and continued in earnest prayer night and day; and the evil spirit was driven away and entirely left her husband.[242] From that time he was completely cured. In the eighth month he came to the chapel with gifts and offerings to express his gratitude. I very gladly accepted his thanks, and acknowledgments, but declined his gifts.[243] (In Nevius' *Demon Possession And Allied Themes, Ch. 6*)

John Innocent

BIO: [1829-1904] *An English missionary to China associated with the New Connection Methodist Missionary Society.*

I have obtained the enclosed account from one of our catechists who was stationed at the place where, and at the time when, the event narrated took place...In the province of Shantung, Wu-ting fu, Shang-ho-hien, in the village of Yang-kia lo, there is a family named Yang, in which a woman was grievously tormented by evil spirits, and had been for fifteen years. She frequently appeared on the streets declaring to the people that the teachings of the Christian religion came from heaven; and that men ought to believe and reverence this religion.[244] She was asked: 'Has not the Mi-mi religion (a local sect) power to cast you out?' She replied: 'The Mi-mi kiao is a religion of demons; how could it cast me out? I am also a demon (mo-kwei).' Some of the native Christians heard this and said: 'When Jesus was in the world He healed diseases, and cast out demons. Why cannot we who believe in Christ do the same?'[245] Whereupon those present, Yang Ching-tsue, Yang Shing-kung, and Yang Shiu-ching[246] earnestly prayed for God's help in casting out this demon. After prayer they proceeded to the afflicted woman's house. Before they reached it the woman said: 'There are three believers in the

---

[242] Note the importance of much prayer when it comes to performing spiritual warfare.
[243] Reminiscent of the woman with the incurable issue of blood who had spent all that she had on physicians and cures to no avail only to find complete healing in Jesus Christ (Mk 5:25-34).
[244] Compare Acts 16:16-18.
[245] Compare Hebrews 13:8.
[246] In Chinese the last name is usually given first. Thus, in this instance Yang is the last name, not a shared first name.

heavenly doctrine coming.'[247] On their arrival she called each one by name, and asked them to be seated. She then said: 'You are the disciples and servants of the God whom I greatly fear.' They then asked: 'What is your name?' The answer was: 'My name is Kyuin (Legion).' The three men then charged the demon to leave the woman's body. The demon replied: 'I have helped this woman fifteen years. She has not an ornament on her head or her feet which she has not obtained by my assistance.' After a violent fit of weeping[248] the demon promised to leave the woman on the tenth day of the first month. And on that day agreeably to its promise, it left. (In Nevius' *Demon Possession And Allied Themes, Ch. 6*)

Mrs. Liu

BIO: *An elderly Chinese native who lived in Shin-tsai, about 230 miles west of Yantai. She was known for being a warm and energetic convert to Christianity who was chiefly responsible for more than twenty of her friends and neighbors accepting Christ.*

In the village of Chang-Chwang Tien-ts, lives a Mr. Chang, about fifty-seven years of age, who is a literary graduate of some wealth. His home is six miles from Shin-tsai. His family is related to ours by marriage, and I have been for years familiarly acquainted with the members of it.

In 1883 this family was afflicted by a demon or demons. It appears (or they appeared) as possessing different women of the family, and occasionally two at the same time. It demanded that worship should be paid to it, that a special shrine should be erected to it in the house; and public services performed in the temple; and that its commands in general should be implicitly obeyed. The women at first complied, and spent a considerable amount of money in paying homage to it. When these proceedings came to the knowledge of Mr. Chang, the head of the family, he felt indignant, and determined to oppose the whole thing, ordering the women to disregard and defy the spirit. The spirit then took possession of one of the women and repeated its demand. Mr. Chang refused. The spirit threatened revenge and commenced executing it immediately by attempting to burn the house; by stealing and wasting the substance of the family, and by making

---

[247] Another example of clairvoyant powers exhibited.
[248] Notice that demons can move people to tears.

153

trouble generally. Food, clothing, and valuables were stolen from the house in the most mysterious way, even when they were secured by lock and key; furniture and dishes shook and rattled without any perceptible cause; and three women in the family were, at different times, possessed. Fires broke out without apparent cause, and, on one occasion, destroyed a number of buildings.[249]

In the summer of 1884 Mrs. Chang, having heard that the Christian religion gives to its adherents immunity from the inflictions of evil spirits, came to Shin tsai to see and consult with me. She related to me her trouble, and said that she had come to seek help, through me, from the God I worship. She arrived at my house physically weak and emaciated, reporting that the demon had not allowed her to eat anything for a long time;— that when her food was prepared and brought to her, before she could take it, she was seized with an irrepressible aversion to it and obliged to turn away from it: After staying a few days with me Mrs. Chang's health was restored. She requested me to go home with her but as this was impracticable at the time, Mrs. Fung, (another Christian) went in my stead, and remained with the Chang family some days. She exhorted the women to worship the true God, and trust in Christ as their Saviour, and taught them also, elementary and easily understood truths of Christianity. In a short time comparative quiet was restored in the family, and Mrs. Fung returned home.

Before many days had passed a messenger came to me from the Chang family, informing me that their troubles had increased, and begging me to come to their help. They told me that two women in the family had been possessed by demons for several days, and were still in a state of unconsciousness. Mrs. Fung and I returned with the messenger. Arriving about noon, we found all in great confusion. Buckets and jars of water were set in different places about the house to put out fire whenever it might appear on the thatched roof, and men were constantly on the watch, prepared with water and step-ladders for mounting the house if necessary. They informed us that fire frequently broke out where it was least expected. We were first shown to the room of Mrs. Chang's eldest daughter-in-law, a person of about forty years of age. She was under the influence of the demon and demanded

---

[249] Compare Job 1:12, 16.

wine, which she drank in large quantities, though ordinarily she would not touch it.[250] Followed by some servants and attendants we entered the apartment where she was lying, and stood observing and talking about her for a time, she the meanwhile reclining on the bed, tossing her arms, and staring wildly and unnaturally. We then requested most of those present to withdraw, so as to leave the place as quiet as possible, that we might read the Scriptures and pray. The demon seemed aware of our purpose and turning to us said: 'You profess to be Christians do you? And you read the book from Heaven, and think you are going to Heaven yourselves; and you have come here from Shin tsai to cast me out; you need not flatter yourself with any such expectation. I have been here thirty years and I am not cast out so easily.' We replied: 'We have no strength to cast you out, but we have come to do it in the name and by the power of Jesus.' The demon replied: 'I acknowledge the power of Jesus but I am not afraid of you. You have not faith enough to cast me out. You have not faith as much as a mustard seed.' We replied: 'We came trusting in Christ and in his name we will cast you out.' The possessed person replied by a contemptuous smile followed by a fit of weeping. We then proceeded to hold a religious service. We first sang the hymn 'The judgment day will surely come,' and read the 10th chapter of Matthew. Then each of us in succession prayed, after which we sang. When we had finished the service the woman was lying perfectly quiet, apparently unconscious or asleep.

We then went to the apartment where the other woman was lying. She is a widow. When under the influence of the demon she was constantly watched by her only daughter, as she had a fixed propensity to commit suicide by jumping into a well or pond, or by hanging herself. We held a similar service with this woman, and left her in a state of insensibility.

As we were leaving the room of the second woman, the one first visited came to find us, greeted us very cordially, and said she had just awakened from a long sleep, and had heard from others of our arrival, and all that had followed. Her manner was perfectly natural; she was her old self again. She had no idea whatever of what happened during the abnormal state from which she had recovered.

---

[250] This would seem to indicate that abuse of alcohol can be a sign of demon possession.

About this time, just before dark an extraordinary commotion occurred among the fowls,[251] which rushed and flew about in great consternation without any apparent cause, the family and servants having difficulty in quieting them, and restraining them from running away. After awhile they cowered up in the corner of the yard in a state of fright. The swine also belonging to the family, more than a dozen in number, occupying a large pen or walled inclosure near by, were put into a singular state of agitation rushing about the inclosure, running over each other and trying to scramble up the walls. The swine would not eat, and this state of disquiet continued until they were exhausted. These manifestations naturally excited a great deal of interest and remark, and were accounted for by the supposition that the demons had taken possession of the fowls and swine.[252]

The next morning the second woman also made her appearance. She seemed perfectly well and natural. We remained in the Chang family several days instructing the women in the truths of Christianity, I have visited them frequently since at their request. The women have made very encouraging progress in the knowledge of Christianity. Five in the family regard themselves as Christians, are continuing the study of the Scripture, and meet for a religious service on Sunday, even when we are not with them.[253] (In Nevius' *Demon Possession And Allied Themes, Appendix I.b*)

Chu wen yuen

BIO: *A 19th century Chinese Christian from Sa-wo.*

In the village of Sa-wo, there is a woman of the family Chu, who has two sons Wen-hen, and Wen-fa. The mother obtained a wife for Wen-fa from the family Li, and while she was very young took her into their own family to bring her up. The girl was harshly treated by her future mother-in-law, and drowned herself. Some years after another daughter-in-law was secured from a family named Yang, and it was agreed that she should remain in her own home until the time for her marriage. A few

---

[251] That is, domesticated chickens, etc.

[252] Compare Mark 5:12-13.

[253] Dr. Nevius relates that upon follow-up after nearly six years the people involved reported that the manifestations had entirely ended and the family had lived in peace since embracing Christianity.

156

days before the marriage she was taken ill with what seemed to be possession by an evil spirit.

On the night of the wedding and after the wedding ceremony, when most of the guests had left the house, the bridal pair were conducted to their apartments, and left to drink wine together, as is the custom with us in our neighborhood. At this time the bride, changing to an unnatural appearance, and with the voice and manner of the deceased daughter-in-law Lo, and a strength almost superhuman flew upon the unfortunate bride-groom in a fury of passion, and seized him by the throat, exclaiming, 'You never treated me in this fashion; you never gave me wine to drink. My life in this family was a very wretched one.' Wen-fa cried out for help, and other members of his family ran to his assistance, and with difficulty extricated him from the relentless grasp of the young woman who seemed transformed into a fiend.

After this the wife of the elder brother Wen-heng was similarly affected. In the transition into this abnormal state she was at first rigid and insensible, and then she would regain consciousness and laugh, and cry, and talk, always assuming, like her sister-in-law, the voice and manner of the deceased sister-in-law Li, recounting the bitter trials which had driven her to commit suicide.

Her husband Wen-heng, came to me, and begged me to go and cast out the demon in the name of Christ. I could not well refuse. My brothers, (I have five brothers, none of them Christians) remonstrated. They said: 'Why should you meddle with such matters and disgrace yourself and us? The whole thing is disreputable; besides you will certainly fail and make yourself ridiculous.' I said: 'I cannot fail for the promise of Christ is sure.'[254] One of them replied: 'If you succeed in casting out this spirit we will all be Christians.'

I arrived at the house in company with several other Christians, about the middle of the afternoon. A large crowd had collected to see the result of the matter, most of them entirely out of sympathy with us, and openly expressing their opinion that we should fail. I addressed the spirit in this language. 'You have no right to come here to trouble this family, and we have come to insist on your leaving.' The reply was: 'I will leave, I will leave,'

---

[254] Most likely a reference to the promise embodied in either Mark 16:17 and/or Luke 10:17-20.

but it did not leave. We then knelt down and invoked God's help, and when we arose from our knees both women seemed perfectly well and normal. The people generally were favorably impressed, others said that it was certainly a very happy coincidence, and still others that the women would probably have recovered just the same if we had not been called. Wen-fa said: 'This spirit-business is all a delusion. You women are a weak set specially given to this sort of thing. Let the spirits take possession of *me* and I will believe in them.' The crowd then dispersed. Wen-fa went to his own room, and the other Christians returned home. I stayed sometime to converse with those who had not dispersed. In a few minutes Wen-heng came running in to inform us that Wen-fa was really possessed of a demon, and had entirely lost consciousness. He urged me to go to him and cast the demon out. I declined on the ground that I was alone, the other Christians having gone to their homes, or their fields, and besides, Wen-fa was an unbeliever and opposer, and if we should succeed in casting out the demon it would probably return. After I went home Weng-heng came to me again urging me to go home with him, as he and the other members of the family believed in the power of Christ, and he had no resource but to come to me. I told him to return home and if Wen-fa should be very bad in the evening to come again, and I would try to gather a few Christians and go back with him.

After dark, and just after several of us Christians had had prayers in the chapel, Wen-heng appeared, saying that his brother was very violent, and it required several men to hold him. We were told that a great crowd had gathered at the house, and that they had interrogated the demon, and had long conversations with it. Among others these questions and answers were reported, 'Who are you?' 'I am a friend of Wen-fa and have come to see him.' 'Where do you come from?' 'My home is south-west of here,' 'It seems that you are a friend of Wen-fa, how do you like these Christians? Are they your friends, too?' 'No, they are far from being my friends,' 'We propose to send for them to drive you out.' 'I am not afraid of them.' Wen-fa's mother asked: 'Why do you not take possession of me instead of Wen-fa?' The reply was: 'Oh, every one has his affinities and preferences; we do as we please in this matter.'

Arriving at the house we made our way through the crowd into the inner court with difficulty. To our distress we found the two women apparently again possessed and they and Wen-fa were all together in the same abnormal state. Wen-fa was more violently affected than the others and I directed my attention particularly to him. When I entered he seemed very restless and uneasy. He said to me: 'Why do you trouble yourself to come here to see me? I do not need your services.' I replied: 'Our friends have come, why should I not come also.' He said he wished to leave the house for awhile, and I requested those who were restraining him to release him, and he tried to run through the crowd. His brother followed him and with the help of several others brought him back. We then engaged in prayer, invoking the presence and power of Christ to cast out the evil spirit. During prayer he was rolling and tossing himself about on the *kang* (earth-bed), his mother removing everything from the *kang* for fear he would injure himself. When we rose from prayer all the persons affected seemed perfectly restored, and in their natural state. The villagers present asked Wen-fa a great many questions to satisfy themselves that he was quite himself again. It was evident to all that when he came under the influence of this spell he was not himself, and when restored he had no recollection of anything he had said or done. A large proportion of the villagers were now won to our side. There was still, however, a company of unbelievers and opposers, one of the most prominent of whom was the employer of Wen-fa, a man who kept a *tanfang,* an establishment for beating and cleaning cotton. The Chu family was delighted with having found a way in which they could rid themselves of their unseen and unwelcome visitors. They urged me to remain after the other villagers had returned. While they were preparing food, (as most of the family had hardly eaten anything for the last twenty-four hours), they asked me a great many questions about Christianity. They said they all wanted to learn, and requested me to come in any time I could and teach them. I remained there teaching them the Lord's prayer until a late hour. Wen-fa did not oppose his wife and the rest of the family in their wish to learn the new doctrine, but he evidently had no heart in the matter.

The next day Wen-fa went to the *Tan-fang* to work, and there was naturally a great deal of conversation about what had happened the night before, most of the workmen having been at Wen-fa's house. They said: 'You stay here among us, no demons will dare to come here.' (It is believed that an influence emanates from the bodies of strong men in active exercise which resists and drives away evil spirits.) There was one person present who was favorably disposed to Christianity, who demurred to their speaking so lightly of the subject, and being so self-confident. A warm discussion arose in which Christianity was denounced. Before this controversy was closed Wen-fa fell down in a fit. He was perfectly rigid and breathless, apparently dead. His companions at once ran for guns and swords, especially an executioner's sword which spirits are supposed to be particularly afraid of, and shouted and brandished their weapons to intimidate the demon, but all without effect. Wen-fa still remained ghastly and insensible. Fearing that he would die on the premises the head of the establishment ordered his men to carry him out. About this time his muscles relaxed and he became limp, though still motionless and insensible. When they reached the street a great crowd gathered, which was soon joined by Wen-fa's mother. Some one raised the cry, 'take him to the chapel.' his mother and others cordially assented, and the men who carried him directed their steps that way. As they turned from the main road to enter the chapel Wen-fa commenced resisting, and it required the men in charge to use their utmost strength to prevent him from breaking away from them. By dint of great effort they dragged him into the chapel. Arriving there he fell down apparently exhausted and insensible. He soon got up, however, perfectly himself again, and asked, 'What are you all here for? What are you about? What does this mean?' He had no idea of what had happened.

After this all the villagers, including Wen-fa, acknowledged the power of Christianity to cast out evil spirits. They said if this had only happened once we might have thought it a mere coincidence, but the connection to Christianity with these cures was too evident to be doubted. To this day all the villagers take this view of the matter. Wen-heng, his mother, wife, and sister-in-law all commenced studying Christian books, and seemed very much interested, and made remarkable progress. The new year, however, came on in the course of a few weeks with its many idolatrous ceremonies and offerings. They agreed together to do away with the usual ceremonies, and pass the new year as Christians, but a wealthy and influential uncle opposed and over-ruled them. Having yielded to his commands to pass the new year in accordance with Chinese customs, they gradually gave up the

160

study of Christianity, and have had but little intercourse with us since. They, however, seem very kindly disposed to us, and grateful for what we did to them. They have had no further trouble from evil spirits. Cases of this kind were very frequent in our village some years ago, but since the introduction of Christianity we hardly ever hear of them. (In Nevius' *Demon Possession And Allied Themes, Appendix I.c*)

Chiu chi-Ching

BIO: *A prominent and highly esteemed 19th century native Christian from eastern En Chiu, China who was largely responsible for the founding of several mission stations.*

I was applied to one day by a man of a very respectable family to go to see his mother who was possessed by a demon which they could not by any means rid themselves of. When possessed she insisted on being provided with wine and meat which she took in inordinate quantities, though in her normal condition she never took wine at all. I went to the place in company with a few other Christians. Arrived at the house, we found a large number of relations and neighbors assembled, and the woman wild and unmanageable, and several strong men with difficulty kept her under control. It was with fear and trembling that I commenced the work before me. When I addressed the demon demanding that it should leave, the woman flew at me like a fury, exclaiming, 'Who are you?' I knelt down in prayer, the sweat streaming from every pore, and oppressed with an awful sense of personal weakness and responsibility. The woman was at once restored, and with unaffected surprise and chagrin apologized for the condition in which her visitors had found her and her house. She was convinced of the truth and importance of Christianity and commenced studying Christian books, but was afterwards restrained from continuing their study by the influence of the male members of the family. Her malady did not return. (In Nevius' *Demon Possession And Allied Themes, Appendix I.g*)

Baptist Missionary To India William Carey Regretted That Ministers Would Not Take The Gospel Stories Of Demon Possession Literally

Xi Shengmo

BIO: [1835-1896] *A Confucian scholar who converted to Christianity and afterwards became an energetic and successful soul-winner. Given the name Liaozhi, after his conversion he changed his name to Shengmo which translates to "conqueror of demons" and he is remembered for being very effective in the area of spiritual warfare. He became affectionately known to westerners as Pastor Hsi (pronounced Shi).*

I had not at first the courage to confess Christ before others. But soon after this new experience I destroyed all the idols in my house, fitted up a room for Christian worship, had family prayers every day with my mother and my wife, and public worship every seventh day. One day my wife was very suddenly possessed by a demon. Assuming a violent and threatening manner, she attacked me, endeavoring to stop the worship. At first I was put to my wit's end and knew not what to do. Suddenly I bethought myself of the words of Scripture in which our Lord gave to his disciples power to heal diseases and cast out devils, and in Christ's name, and with the laying on of my hands, I commanded the demon to depart. My wife awoke as from a sleep, and was immediately well, and joined us in worshiping and praising God for his goodness. The faith of all my family was much strengthened.[255] (In Nevius' *Demon Possession And Allied Themes, Appendix I.i*)

XI Shengmo, Seated In Center, With Other Christians

In the village of Hu-tsai, less than a mile from my own home, lives a relative of mine named Han Yang-lin. A servant of his Hieh Pei-Chwang believed and received baptism. Suddenly his young son was possessed by a demon, writhed in agony, foamed at the mouth and with a loud cry fell down insensible. The family were in great consternation. I was not at home at the time, but my wife hearing of the event, after prayer for help and guidance, went to the house and in the name of Christ prayed, with the laying on of hands. The child awoke perfectly well. Afterwards Han Yang-lin's own little boy was seized by a demon, and afflicted in the same manner. His mother immediately got into her cart with the boy in her arms, and came to my house to ask my wife to pray over him. My wife first exhorted her to believe in Christ and then prayed for the child

---

[255] For a more in-depth account of this case of possession the reader is referred to Geraldine Taylor's biographical account of Shengmo entitled *Pastor Hsi (of North China) One Of China's Christians*, chapter 2.

when it immediately recovered.[256] (In Nevius' *Demon Possession And Allied Themes, Appendix I.i*)

During the eighth month of the present year a man named Heo Tai-ts, living in the village of Hu-kia, was possessed by a demon which came and went. When it left him he was extremely weak owing in part probably to the fact that he was an opium-smoker.[257] When the demon possessed him the strength of three or four men was not sufficient to control him. His mother applied to 'Wu-po' (exorcist) to expel the demon, but it answered them in a loud voice, 'I am not afraid of you. I am only afraid of the one great God,'[258] Their village was only about a mile from the village of Keo-si where lives a Christian named Liang Tao-yuen. He hearing of the matter exhorted Heo Tai-ts to believe in God and pray for succor. When he had recovered he started to go to my house. On the way while he was passing the home of Liang Tao-yuen, the demon took possession of him again in a most violent manner, and called on several members of his family to take him back to his home. Liang Tao-yuen followed him, and spent the night in praying over him. He was restored to his normal consciousness. The following day Liang Tao-yuen assisted him to mount a donkey to come to my house. I was absent in the city of Ho Chiu. My wife was at home, and exhorted him to depend on God rather than man, saying our Christian teachers cannot be always present with us, but our Lord is. A Christian, Jen San-yiu, went with him to his house and cast away his idols, and his mother and wife joined in prayer for his recovery.

When Heo Tai-ts was at my house, the demon came and insisted on his returning home, but my wife prayed for him, in the name of the Lord, and the demon left him. She urged Jen San-yiu

---

[256] Compare Mark 9:17-29.

[257] Does this show us that there is a connection between drug addiction and demonic activity? Drug abuse counseling has suffered greatly in its effectiveness by ignoring the influence and working of demons in leading persons to turn to drugs as a solution to their problems. Not only should spiritual warfare be considered when dealing with persons involved in the abuse of stronger drugs (crack, cocaine, etc.) but it should also be considered when dealing with weaker drug addictions such as marijuana, alcohol and the smoking of cigarettes. A person may not be possessed who turns to these drugs but anyone who turns to illicit drugs or alcohol for help rather that God is certainly being led by Satan.

[258] Compare James 2:19.

to pray with him, with laying on of hands and fasting, so that the demon would not dare to return any more. He soon recovered entirely, and also broke off the opium habit. He changed his name from Tai-ts, to Su-sing, (restored to life) in attestation of the Lord's having given him back to life again. The disciples brought to Christ from the region south-east of us have come from this beginning. Five families were freed from the opium habit, cured of their diseases, cast away their idols, and gave themselves to the Lord. (In Nevius' *Demon Possession And Allied Themes, Appendix I.i*)

Warren Robert Stuart

BIO: [1850-1895] *A Chinese missionary associated with the English Church Missionary Society. He died as a martyr in the Kucheng Massacre.*[259]

One Sunday morning, about a year ago, a woman with her husband and four children came to my house here, and asked to be taken in and taught 'the doctrine.' We replied that we had no place where they could reside, and no means whereby to support them. The poor people fell down before us, knocking their heads on the ground, beseeching that we would have pity on them, and teach them the doctrine, (i.e. Christianity) for that the woman was possessed by an evil spirit, and had come a very long way at considerable expense, in obedience to a dream commanding her, if she would get rid of the evil spirit, to go to Foochow, and learn the doctrine of Jesus. Still we replied that it was quite impossible that we should take them in. However, just at that time the students of our Theological college were in need of a cook, and hearing of this family they sent over word that they themselves would take the man as their cook, and subscribe among themselves sufficient to support the family for a while; allowing them to occupy an empty room underneath the college. To this we agreed; the entire expense being borne by the students.

Some few days afterwards I was suddenly summoned by a message that the woman was in one of her fits, and I immediately went down with Dr. Taylor.[260] We found her sitting on her bed,

---

[259] In some sources his name seems to have been spelled R. W. Stewart.
[260] Probably, Dr. Howard Taylor, son of Hudson Taylor who was the founder of the China Inland Mission.

waving her arms about, and talking in an excited manner. She evidently had no control over herself, and was not conscious of what she was saying. Dr. Taylor, in order to ascertain whether it was merely a hysterical fit, or some thing over which she had no control, called for a large dinner knife, and baring her arm laid the edge against the skin, as though he intended to cut; but the woman seemed to take no heed whatever. He then threw a cupful of water in her face; but she seemed to mind this as little as the knife; never for a moment stopping in her loud talk; and strange to say, as far as I could follow it, it was entirely about God and Christ and the Holy Spirit; and that she believed in the Son of God.

This was the more strange, seeing that, as far as we could reason, the woman never had any opportunity whatever of learning the doctrine. Holding her hand I induced her to stop for one moment, and said: 'Who is this Son of God; do you know?' She replied at once in the same wild way as before: 'Yes, I know, He is Jesus: Jesus is the Son of God.'

A few moments afterwards she shivered all over three times in a strange way. I caught her hands thinking she was about to fall. But she seemed to get better, and lay quietly down on the bed. The next day or two she remained in bed, and on Saturday night following she again had a dream. The evil spirit seemed to seize her by the neck, commanding her to leave Foo-chow at once, and return to her home, or it would kill her. However, instead of obeying she ran by herself Sunday morning to the church, and while there the pain which she had been feeling all the morning in her neck left her, and she experienced a strangely happy sensation; and since that day she has had no return of those attacks which she had been subject to continually for three years previously, and to obtain a cure for which she, poor woman, had presented many costly offerings to the idols. Now for a year she has been working with Mrs. Stuart, and nothing could exceed her diligence and earnest desire to learn the way of God more perfectly. Just lately she has returned home well able to read the New Testament, and parts of the Old Testament, burning with a desire to teach her relations and friends at Chia-Sioh, none of whom, as yet, know anything of the truth. (In Nevius' *Demon Possession And Allied Themes, Ch. 7*)[261]

---

[261] This was from an article originally titled "A Chinese Demon-Possessed Woman Becoming A Bible-Woman", published in *Christian Herald and Signs*

**Warren Robert Stuart And Wife With Mrs.
Ahok (Seated), A Wealthy Native Chinese Convert**

of the Times, August 4, 1880. According to Nevius, further details relating to this case were published in the May 1880 issue of *Woman's Work* by Rev. Stuart's wife.

Adele Marion Fielde
BIO: [1839-1916] *A Baptist missionary to Siam and China.*

I have among my personal acquaintances several women who have been or are spirit-mediums. One of these resides at Cannon Stand, on the Kit-ie river. The account which she gave of herself was, that for twenty years she had been a spirit-medium, but now she believed that Jesus could and would save her from the powers of darkness. When she was first attacked by the spirits, she had convulsions, and was as one delirious, and while in this state she announced that she would the next morning walk over a bed of burning coals. When she came to herself she trembled and wept, because she thought she should be burnt to death; but, as the people were accustomed to such manifestations, they prepared the bed of coals, thirty-five feet long, and at the appointed time she again became frenzied, and walked over it unharmed. Since then, every year when there was to be a pestilence or when cholera was to prevail, she went into this frenzy and cut her tongue with a knife, letting some drops of the blood fall into a hogshead of water.[262] This water the people drank as a specific against contagion.[263] With the rest of the blood she wrote charms which the people pasted upon their door-posts or wore upon their persons, as preventatives of evil. Sometimes she predicted that two little girls of the same height would walk the burning road with her, and when she was ready to start, a pair of the girls of the village were impelled to come out of the crowd of spectators, and in spite of themselves to follow her over the fiery path.[264] She also took off her head-cloth dipped it into a pot of

---

[262] Compare the prophets of Baal in 1Kings 18:28, who are believed to have cut themselves under the influence of demons as a part of their religious worship.
[263] A violation of Acts 15:29.

168

boiling oil, and washed herself with it unscathed; but _ scattered any of it on other people it blistered them. While in this condition, she was possessed by the spirit of a female demon, and did its will, not her own. She says that the sensations of being possessed are worse than sea-sickness, which was probably a new and impressive experience to her when she came to my house by boat. She held communication with this spirit at any time, and people came constantly for consultation with it through her. She received no money for her services as interpreter, but told what offerings were to be brought to propitiate the spirit, and she kept the food which remained after the ceremonies of worship were completed.

Soon after she met the Bible-women and heard the gospel from them, a man came to get, from the spirit, advice concerning a sick child; but she took the incense-pot used in her practices, and threw it with all its belongings into the river. Her adherents said she had gone crazy, but she told them she had only just become sane. *(Pagoda Shadows, Ch. 9)*

Tolerance Yong

BIO: *A native Chinese convert to Christianity.*

When I was fifteen, my mother was attacked by a demon, and she could not drive it away. Christians have only to resist the devil, and he flees from them;[265] but people who know nothing about God have only their own strength with which to meet demons, and they have to succumb to them. My mother had violent palpitation of the heart, spasmodic contractions of the muscles, and foaming at the mouth.[266] Then she would speak whatever the demon told her to say, and would do whatever he impelled. My father told her that it was very bad to be a spirit-medium; but, if she was going to be one, she must be an honest one, and never give other than good advice, nor take more than fair pay for her services. She never took more than a penny or three-halfpence from any one who came to her for a consultation with her demon...There was a dark hole in the river near our village, where

---

[264] Note how that those empowered by demons can manipulate people in a crowd.

[265] Ja 4:7

[266] Compare the demoniac in Luke 9:38-39.

two boys and a man had at different times been drawn in and drowned, and it was supposed that an evil spirit lived down there and devoured human beings. My mother, in one of her frenzies, plunged into the hole, dived down out of sight, and brought up a soft white animal, with four legs, and a head like a cat's. It was put under an inverted rice-box, and for a long time nobody dared lift the cover off the captive. When the cover was lifted, the creature was gone...The report of my mother's having dragged the evil spirit from its den spread far and wide, and brought many to her for advice...When I was twenty-two, my father died, and shortly after, the two young women that my mother had taken as wives for two of my brothers, both died within twenty days. My brothers then said that the familiar spirit was a harmful one, and that they would no longer live in the house with it. The two elder boys went away and became the sons of a wealthy kinsman, the third set up housekeeping apart from us, and the youngest hired himself out to a petty official. My mother was greatly distressed by all this, and thought she would try to rid herself of her possessor; but the demon told her that, if she tried to evict him, she would be the worse for it, and she then dared do nothing for her own salvation...Three years ago, a friend of mine came from Kui Su, twenty-four miles away, to visit me. She told me that she had heard from some Bible-women at Kui Su a new doctrine that was very strange and interesting. She expounded it to me, and it seemed to me that what she said was true. I had before heard that there were missionaries at Swatow, who taught people not to worship idols, and I had considered such teaching very reprehensible. My eldest brother, Po Heng, happened to come home while my friend was with me, and he also heard what she said. I told him that, as his feet were strong and large, while mine were bound and weak, he must go to Kui Su for me, and find out all he could about this true God, and then come back and tell me. He went and found the chapel, and stayed there several days with the preacher, Hong An. Hong An taught him, but did not know whether he was a sincere inquirer, or whether he had some sinister object in coming so far and staying at the chapel. He told Po Heng when the next communion gathering would be at Swatow, and that he would do well to go then and meet the assembled brethren. Po Heng came home and told me what he had learned, and the next month he and I came. I got my mother-in-law to come with me, so that she might have her prejudices removed, and not thwart me if in the future I should wish to become a Christian. I went home after a few days, convinced that the doctrines of Jesus were true. I taught my mother, and she gradually believed. As the Holy Spirit came in, the demon went out. When she knew about the true God and trusted in Jesus, she no longer feared the demon; and when he came and agitated her heart and twisted her muscles, she prayed to God till the demon left her. The idols were all put out of the house, and the other members of the family began to believe...All the neighbors protested against my mother's ceasing to interpret the will of the gods to them. When they saw that Po Heng and I were determined to be Christians, they urged my mother to separate herself from us, and continue her old occupation. But we held to our mother, and finally brought her, heart and all, with us...The familiar spirit troubles my mother no more. Every member of our household is a believer, and several of our neighbors come to our house for Sunday worship. (*Pagoda Shadows, Ch. 31*)

Francis Mason

BIO: [1799-1874] *A missionary to the Karen ethnic group in Burma who was associated with the American Baptist Missionary Union.*

Having often heard of the wonderful effects produced in that American institution, the camp-meeting, I availed myself the opportunity to see one that was held in the vicinity of Lexington.[267] It was said that hardened opposers were often "struck down," and converted on the spot...At one of the services I attended, I saw a young lady "struck down," and I saw her carried out of the assembly and laid on a couch in a state of exhaustion...while preaching to a Karen congregation in the Mergui district[268] in a grove of trees, many

---

[267] In the U.S. state of Kentucky.
[268] Of Burma.

years ago, I was forcibly reminded of the young lady that I saw "struck down" in Kentucky. A young man in the congregation fell down, and was carried off in an insensible state. He was more like a person in an epileptic fit than anything else, yet it was not epilepsy. He muttered, and it was said that a spirit speaking in him forbade the people listening to the religion of Christ.

The next day he was rational again, and a few months after I returned to Tavoy, he walked into the house one day with his wife, professing himself a believer in Christ. I questioned him closely on his former "possession," and he said he felt as if something impelled him to speak and do as he did, but that the impelling power had left him…He entered school, learned to read, and was afterwards baptized, but not by me. He appeared like a sincere believer, was intelligent, talented, and became a teacher. In process of time he was sent off with others to a missionary in Mergui, who was so pleased with him, that after employing him for years, he finally ordained him to the ministry.

He did well so long as there were missionaries in Mergui, but soon after the station was abandoned, he completely apostatized, and went back to his old profession of being possessed by a spirit. Yet, it is said, he often expresses his regret that he ever administered the Lord's Supper. (*The Story Of A Working Man's Life: With Sketches Of Travel In Europe, Asia, Africa, And America, As Related By Himself, Ch. 14: Lexington And President Monroe*)

Geraldine Taylor

BIO: [1865-1949] *A British missionary to China and the daughter-in-law of J. Hudson Taylor, founder of the China Inland Mission.*

Another of our earliest friends in C'en-cheo has also been much used in spreading a knowledge of the truth. His conversion was even more sudden than Mrs. Uen's, and his case more touchingly sad.

It was one day when my husband was seeing patients in the men's guest hall, that this young fellow came in. We used to see patients every day, excepting Sundays; men on the even days of the month, and women on the odd ones. In this way people could be sure of coming at the right time. Among all the crowds of patients, sometimes as many as sixty or eighty in one afternoon, few ever impressed us as that man did. He was a young country farmer, a big, powerful, well-built fellow, but worn and emaciated, with a wild, haunted look in his eyes, disordered dress, and strange excited manner. My husband, after a very few questions, felt sure as to the nature of his case, which the young man shortly explained.

Let me say, before proceeding with this story, that I know it cannot but be received with a measure of hesitation by most at any rate who are present. We have not seen or heard of such things in England, and are accustomed to suppose that they are entirely phenomena of the past. But it is well to regard the subject with an open mind, for there exists abundant proof that, in China at any rate, the power of evil spirits is just as great in these days as in the time of Christ.

The young man who sat beside my husband in that little guest hall at Ch'en-cheo was literally possessed by evil spirits, and he knew it. For many months he had been in that condition, and was rapidly sinking into depths of degradation. Night and day he could get no rest. He could not eat, or work, or sleep. Strange perversity characterized him; and he would pick up the vilest refuse in the street and keep it for food. Restless, haunted, miserable, it was as though some awful nightmare was always upon him, overshadowing him with terror and oppression. At times, paroxysms came on of fearful violence, in which he was possessed of superhuman strength. And when these passed away, he was left in a state of utter exhaustion. He saw and knew the spirits that were haunting him, and sometimes heard their voices urging him to end his miserable life by suicide.[269]

After listening to all he had to say, my husband answered sadly and impressively: "My poor fellow, do you not know? There is no medicine in the world that can do you any good."

"Ah, sir, that was what I feared," responded the young man. "I have been to many of the local (Chinese) doctors, and they all say they can do nothing for me. I only thought that perhaps you,

---

[269] Note that spirits can be seen and heard at times.

173

sir, being a foreigner, might have some skill that could relieve me."

"No," said my husband again, "I can do nothing for you." And then, seeing by his despondent face that the poor fellow had quite taken that in, he added slowly: *"But I have a Friend Who can make you perfectly well."*

"What, sir, a friend? Have you really? Where is he? Would he take up my case?"

"Certainly he would. And He is here. There is no reason why you should not be perfectly cured before you leave this house to-day. Just come with me into this inner room, and you shall hear all about it."

Full of eagerness and interest, the young man followed my husband into a tiny chamber partitioned off the guest hall, and used as a spare room for visitors. A dear old Chinese gentleman, an earnest Christian and a great friend of my husband's, was staying with us at the time, and to him the doctor handed over his new patient, with a brief explanation, while he went back to others who were waiting.

Dear old Mr. Ch'en was then quite in his element. There was nothing he loved better than to tell of Jesus. Converted himself only a few years before, he always seemed full of the joy and wonder of life in Christ. The Bible was his great delight, and all his leisure time was given to preaching. In early life he had been a wealthy mandarin in connection with the salt trade, and though retired from office, he was still a man of means and distinction. Having plenty of leisure, he spent a great deal of time with us, giving invaluable help in all branches of our new work. It was wonderful to hear that dear old gentleman preach! Such eloquence; such power! He never seemed to tire of telling the old, old story; and people would gladly listen to him, any time, by the hour.

Well, dear old Mr. Ch'en sat down with the young man, whose name was also Ch'en as it happened, and began to tell him all about our Divine Friend, Who was just the Physician for his case. With deepest interest the young man listened; and soon it was evident that he was one whose heart the Lord was opening to receive the truth.

"Sir," he said to the old man, after hours of conversation, "all that you tell me I believe. I intend henceforward to follow the teachings of Jesus, and will now go home and take down my false gods, and rid the house of every trace of idolatry. Do you think, sir, that the Lord Jesus would save me from the power of these evil spirits, that are wearing out my life?"

"Of course he will, here and now," responded the old man gladly. "Let us kneel down together and ask Him, before you leave the room."

So, together they knelt in prayer; and Mr. Ch'en laid his hand upon the young man's head, and in the name of Jesus commanded the devils to come out of him and return no more. I do not know what happened. I cannot explain the mystery. I only know that the young man came out of the little inner room that day a new creature in Christ Jesus. The restless, troubled look in his eyes was gone. His face was bright and calm. He was rejoicing in a consciousness of freedom and light he had not known for months, in a deep peace and gladness he had never known before. He went home to his little village, took down his idols and burned them, swept out the house and cleaned it thoroughly, told his wife and parents about his new-found Saviour, and from that day to this has gone right on in a bright, useful, Christian career. He soon became a most earnest preacher of the Gospel, and has been the means of leading not a few to Christ. His own father, mother, wife, brothers, and some other relations have become Christians, and all round that district Ch'en himself has gone, preaching Christ. (*In The Far East, Chapter 16: Recent Experiences*)

F. B. Meyer

BIO: [1847-1929] *A Baptist pastor and evangelist who was friends with D. L. Moody.*

I want to narrate the essence of a most interesting conversation at the breakfast-table with Baron von Uexkull[270] and others…The baron also told of a man of his acquaintance who occupied a farm on his estate, and who was under the power of what seemed to be a nervous disease. The baron asked him to kneel in prayer, and repeat the words of petition, after himself, which the young man did, until he came to the name of Jesus—this he refused to repeat. When the baron insisted on his saying it, and with great effort he did so, he fell on the ground with a scream. The baron bade the evil

---

[270] A well-known philanthropist in Estonia.

spirit come forth, which it appeared to do, leaving the man exhausted but well. (*Demon Possession In Russia*)

The Lord Challenged F. B. Meyer To Believe That Spiritual Warfare Could Be A Part Of His Ministry Through The Power Of Jesus' Name

A similar instance was related of an old and wealthy count, who was subject to fits of ungovernable passion, and was the terror of his wife and children. But when, in answer to definite prayer, God gave power to His servant to command the evil spirit to go forth, he became calm and gentle, and afterwards died in the full faith of Christ. (*Demon Possession In Russia*)

On one occasion Count Pashkoff,[271] with some other believers, prayed for four hours for a man who was all the while mocking them and saying that their efforts were useless, that there was not one demon only in possession, but many. Finally, when in despair, the count said, "Lord Jesus, we have no power at all to drive forth this evil spirit, do Thou do it," there was an evident going forth of some evil influence, and the man became subdued and quiet.

Another terrible incident was told me by the count of a man whom he knew in the early days of his religious life, and whom the neighbors had imprisoned in a large iron cage, the bars being of terrific strength. And whenever any were brought in to see him, he held out towards them a silver rouble, saying, "This is my God, this is my God." I confess that these incidents have greatly impressed me. I wonder how far it will be right to deal with certain forms of impurity and drunkenness as being cases of demon-possession. It may be that there is more of this demon work among ourselves than we know, and specially in cases of mania. The baron told me that once, when visiting an asylum there was a great movement among the patients on his entrance of the wards as though they recognized in him the power of the living Savior. (*Demon Possession In Russia*)

In connection with the above, we should like to mention a few cases which have come under our own observation in the past years of our contact with the sick and suffering.

The first case was that of a Christian man, wholly insane, yet whose friends were not willing to send to an asylum, as the family believed in the power of the Lord to heal. Whenever anyone of them would enter his room, he would mock at them with the most satanic leer upon his face, taunting them with the powerlessness of their God to heal him, telling them to call upon their God and let Him heal if He could, followed by mocking laughter. To remain in his presence became unbearable. One day

---

[271] A Russian nobleman who converted to Protestantism from Russian Orthodoxy and suffered persecution by the Czar for doing so.

when we were in his room praying with the family, the Lord said to me *"Go and rebuke that evil spirit in him casting it out."*

"O! I cannot," I said, never having had to deal with such cases of demon-possession before. "I have not the power or the faith to do it." *"Do you believe in the power of My Name? Do you believe it has the same power as when I was on earth?"* He asked. "Yes, Lord," I replied. *"Then go and use it. You do not need to have faith in any power of your own, but in the power of My Name."* I arose, timidly to be sure, but with perfect confidence in the power of the name of Jesus (see Mark 16:17) and commanded the blaspheming spirit to come out, and found it instantly obeyed, for even the countenance altered and the whole sickness changed from that hour. (*Demon Possession In Russia*)

The next case was that of a young lady suffering from melancholia, sent to us by a friend rather than to an asylum which was a last resort. The poor girl could do nothing when awake, but arraign the wisdom and government of God in the affairs of men, by constant questions, till one felt like running from the room. At other times she would lie for days in bed with her face buried in her hands, refusing to reply to anyone addressing her, or to rise. We prayed over her for days with no apparent results, when one day God shewed us that she was possessed with a demon which must be cast out before the healing could come. (There is no healing the devil.) We accordingly went to the bed where she was lying and one of our number in the name of Jesus commanded the evil spirit to come out of her. This was repeated several times, as we felt great resistance, when the demon left, and the girl arose and proved to be entirely delivered from all satanic power. She soon after gave her heart to God, and was admitted to full membership in one our city churches, giving every evidence of a sound mind. (*Demon Possession In Russia*)

Another case was that of a little girl nine years old, who, her mother said, had been always so perverse, stubborn and ugly as to make her friends despair of ever being able to manage her. No discipline seemed to have the slightest effect. There seemed to be an unnatural hartlessness and cruelty about her that no amount of kindness could change.

She had been the subject of most earnest prayers for years and sometimes seemed touched, but only a transient impression was made upon her, which quickly passed away, leaving the old satanic meanness uppermost. The mother was a consecrated woman, but the father, though a professing Christian, was a wicked man. One day as we engaged in prayer with the mother, being in real despair over the child, it was shown us that she had been possessed with a stubborn, obstinate demon from her birth. We at once cried mightily to God for deliverance and in the name of Jesus commanded the spirit to leave her, which it did.[272]

This was sometime ago. The mother informs us that she is a changed child, all cruelty and stubbornness having left her from that hour, making her easy to govern. (*Demon Possession In Russia*)

Amy Carmichael With Indian Children

---

[272] Did the father's wickedness open up the door for his child to become possessed?

Amy Carmichael

BIO: [1867-1951] *A missionary to India, Japan and Sri Lanka whose ministry influenced Jim Elliot.*

Friday night, July 14.—May the Spirit of Truth now hold my pen, as I try to tell you of yesterday's life. A week might have been compressed into those twelve hours, one seems to have lived through so much.

Early in the morning we heard that quite close to us an old man was possessed by "the fox-spirit." Demoniacal possession is much the same here as in Palestine, of old. I had heard about it, but barely believed in it. We listened now while they talked.

It was the old story retold. "Wheresoever it taketh him, it teareth him; and he foameth and gnasheth with his teeth and pineth away."[273]

And as we listened wonderingly, suddenly flashed the question, "Why could not we cast him out?"

Almost stunned with the thought, I went straight to my room, and asked Him. And the answer came, "Because of your unbelief."[274]

Of the next few hours I cannot write.

Then I went to T. San our interpreter, and asked her, did she believe our Lord Jesus was willing to cast the devil out of that man. She was rather startled, but after praying over it, she too believed.

Our first impulse was to go at once, but "this kind goeth not out but by prayer and fasting"[275] caused us to wait; in the meantime we sent a message to the people, asking might we go to see him, and they replied we might, but that he was very wild, "had six foxes," and was tied up.

Then we waited, T. San and I, each alone, before the Lord. I cannot tell you much of these solemn hours, but just this much seems to His glory. Even physical strength and mental power left me, it was in literal utter nothingness we went forth in His Name. What was done, was *all* of God.

---

[273] Mk 9:18
[274] Mt 17:19-20
[275] Mt 17:21

We went, and were taken upstairs. I had been prepared for much, but for nothing so awful as this. Stretched upon the floor, fastened crosswise upon two beams, bound and strapped hand and foot, his body covered with burns and wounds —it was terrible. . . . But nothing to what followed. At the name of Christ a fearful paroxysm came on. It seemed as though the powers of hell were let loose. Blasphemies which even I could recognise as such, were poured forth. A voice not his own spoke, and then *his* voice, dry and cracked, seemed to echo the other. He struggled to get at us, but they held him down, and covered his face. We knelt and prayed, but it seemed as though the devil were mocking us. He grew more violent every moment; it was worse than useless to wait. Can you think how I felt then? His Name dishonoured among the heathen, and *I had done it.* Far, far better never to have come! *This* was the fiery dart which was hurled against me. And yet, surely He had sent us, surely it was no self-movement. "My sheep hear My voice, and I know them, and they follow Me."[276] In the lull which those words brought, I could hear it again. *"All power is given unto Me"*[277] it said. *"These signs shall follow them that believe: in My Name shall they cast out devils.*[278] *Fear thou not,* FOR I AM WITH THEE!"[279]

As the poor wife followed us to the door, with no thought of reproach for what must have seemed to her a cruel intrusion, I could tell her through T. San, what had just been told me, our God would conquer. When the evil spirit was cast out, we asked her to let us know, until then we would pray at home.

And yet, I'm afraid my faith was very weak, for I was almost broken down, and when dear Sarah met us with loving sympathy, and told us she too was praying, it was very comforting.

One hour afterwards the Answer came. The "foxes" had gone, the cords were off, and he was lying, weak indeed, but himself again. At night they sent once more. He was sleeping, very prostrate after all the excitement, but well. We remembered then, how when our Lord cast the "foul spirit" out of the child, he was as one dead, but Jesus took him by the hand, and lifted him up, and he arose.[280] So we asked Him to do it for him.

---

[276] Jn 10:27
[277] Mt 28:18
[278] Mk 16:17
[279] Is 41:10

This morning he asked to see us. I should not have known the man. Only the scars on the "sore vexed"[281] body told of what had been. One could hardly speak for very gladness: it was such a transformation.

He sent for flowers, a lovely spray of scarlet pomegranate blossom, and offered it gracefully to me. Then iced water was brought, the first we had tasted this season, sugared, and served with chopsticks instead of teaspoons. Joy and peace reigned in the selfsame room, the fury had raged in, yesterday.

We talked to him, and his gentle wife, and prayed with them ere we left them. They knelt and joined with "Hai! hai!" Yes, yes! when T. San asked for a saved soul, from Him who had saved the body. Clothed and in his right mind, worshipping the God he had reviled. How glorious it was!

As we came away, a priest passed, and looked at us with no friendly eye. Among them is a sect called "Fox Exorcists." The spirits of evil are supposed to take the form of foxes, one or more take possession of the victim, henceforth he lives a dual or a complex life. There are various medical explanations, which I don't understand. It is mysterious enough to be considered fabulous by those who do not know how true it is.

Certainly we are in a land where the Prince of Darkness has power. The dreaded Fox Spirit is worshipped, shrines are dedicated to him. Little stone foxes are often set side by side with the Buddhas by the wayside. The strangest tales are told and believed, many of course superstitious, but many based on fact. Fox Spirits have been known to lead their prey into deep mountain pools, and there leave them to drown. This poor man, out of whom our God cast six, according to their count, was bent upon destroying himself. "Ofttimes he falleth into the fire, and oft into the water,"[282] it sounds very much like that.

To-day I have been reading an opinion given by a Professor of the Imperial University of Japan, upon the phenomenon, as he calls it, and I see how what seemed serious hindrance, has resulted in glory to His name. The exorcist's first endeavour is to impress upon the patient his own great power, and thereby win his confidence. Had this man or his friends believed in us, had I been

---

280 Mk 9:17-27
281 Mt 17:15
282 Mt 17:15

stronger in the crisis hour, and *seemed* as one empowered, the cure might have been attributed to us. As it was, they all saw clearly enough that we were nothing. There was nothing tangible to lay hold of. All the glory went straight to God. Truly we may trust Him to plan His own means, for us 'tis "work enough to watch the Master work."[283] (*From Sunrise Land: Letters From Japan, Ch. 5*)

John Gualbert Casting Out A Demon

[283] A phrase from Robert Browning's (1812-1889) poem *Rabbi Ben Ezra*.

Accounts From The Modern &
Post-Modern Eras (20th-21st Centuries)

James Lyon

BIO: *A Methodist Episcopal missionary stationed in India. This event was reported around 1901.*

We recently made a preaching tour of several days and while holding service in one of the towns which lay in our route, and where we encamped for a few days, a young man came to me in much distress saying, "My wife is possessed by an evil spirit, can you help?" I replied, "Where is your wife? Can I see her? Do not fear. Our Jesus can cast out a thousand demons. He is the same yesterday, to-day, and forever."[284]

He proceeded to conduct me to his house, but on the way thither word came that she had gone out. Together we began to search for her, and found her sitting in a Gospel service being held by Mrs. Lyon near her house.

The poor demon-possessed woman who had a few minutes before been raving in madness was sitting clothed and in her right mind and quietly listening as if the demon had gone.

She had heard the Gospel songs and had arisen and left her house and become one of the most attentive listeners. We prayed, and made her a special object of our prayers, in simple faith asking Jesus to manifest himself as he did yesterday (two thousand years is just like yesterday to Jesus), when he came down from the Mount of Transfiguration and if the demon had not gone out, just to cast it out. Surely he did.

The woman was comforted, and so was her husband, and they went home together, and nothing has been heard of the demon since. (*Casting Out Demons In India*)

Herr Seitz

BIO: *A distinguished German evangelist.*

...I united with a number of brethren and sisters one whole week every month, in prayer to God to pour out more of His Spirit, gifts and power. After having done this for some time with great

---

[284] He 13:8

earnestness, such powerful and wonderful manifestations of God and His Holy Spirit (apparently) took place, that we no longer doubted God had heard our prayer, and His Spirit had descended into our midst, and on our gathering. Amongst other things this spirit, which we thought to be the Holy Spirit, used a 15-year-old girl as his instrument, through whom everyone belonging to our gathering, and having any sin or burden of conscience, had it revealed to the gathering. Nobody could remain in the meeting with any burden of conscience without it being revealed to the meeting by this spirit. For example: A gentleman of esteem and respect from the neighbourhood came to the meeting, and all his sins were exposed in the presence of the gathering by the 15-year-old girl. Thereupon he took me into an adjoining room, so broken down, and admitted to me, with tears, that he had committed all these sins which the girl had exposed. He confessed this and all other sins known to him. Then he came again into the meeting, but hardly had he entered when the same voice said to him, 'Ha! You have not confessed all yet, you have stolen 10 gulden, that you have not confessed.' In consequence, he took me again into the adjoining room and said, 'It is true, I have also done this...This man had never seen this 15-year-old girl in his life, neither she him.

With such events, was it astonishing that a spirit of holy awe came over all at the meeting, and there was one controlling note which can only be expressed in the words, 'Who among us shall dwell with the devouring fire? Who among us shall dwell with everlasting burnings?' Fearfulness hath surprised the hypocrites.[285] There was a most earnest spirit of adoration, and who could doubt when even the strong were broken down, and nobody dared remain in the meeting if they were a hindrance.

And, yet we had to unmask this spirit which had brought about these things--and which we took to be the Holy Ghost--as a terrible power of darkness. I had such an uneasy feeling of distrust which could not be overcome...As I made this known for the first time to an older brother and friend...he said, 'Brother Seitz, if you continue to foster unbelief, you can commit the sin against the Holy Ghost which will never be forgiven.' These were terrible days and hours for me, because I did not know whether we had to

---

[285] Is 33:14

do with the power of God or a disguised spirit of Satan, and one thing only was clear to me, viz., that I and this meeting should not let ourselves be led by a spirit when we did not have clear light, and confirmation whether this power was from above or below. Thereupon I took the leading brethren and sisters to the uppermost room of the house, and made known to them my position, and said we must all cry and pray that we may be able to prove whether it was a power of light or darkness.

As we came downstairs the voice of this power said, using the 15-year-old girl as his instrument, 'What is this rebellion in your midst? You will be sorely punished for your unbelief.' I told this voice that it was true we did not know with whom we had dealings. But we wanted to be in that attitude, that if it was an angel of God, or the Spirit of God, we would not sin against Him, but if it was a devil we would not be deceived by him. 'If you are the power of God, you will be in accord as we handle the Word of God.' 'Try the spirits whether they be of God.'[286] We all knelt down and cried and prayed to God in such earnestness, that He would have mercy upon us, and reveal to us in some manner, whom we had dealings with. Then the power had to reveal itself on its own accord. Through the person which he had been using as his instrument he made such abominable and terrible grimaces, and shrieked in such a piercing tone, 'Now I am found out, now I am found out...'[287] (In Jessie Penn-Lewis' *War On The Saints, Appendix section entitled "The Working Of Evil Spirits In Christian Gatherings"*)

---

[286] 1Jn 4:1

[287] Satan knows that the greatest lie is the one with the most truth in it. Believers must be aware that things which seem to be good may have evil lurking behind them. This is why Paul entreated his disciples to "Despise not prophesyings (i.e. supernatural utterances as in the case above). Prove all things; hold fast that which is good. (1Th 5:20-21)" and John encouraged his disciples to "believe not every spirit, but try the spirits (1Jn 4:1)". If there were no danger of being deceived, there would have been no reason for the Apostles to caution their disciples. God wants to work in a mighty way in our midst, but the reality is that Satan also does. We must be careful, however, to not let Satan's willingness to deceive us keep us from seeking the Lord to move in mighty ways amongst us. If our hearts are sincere and if we test the spirits as above, God will let us know whether our experiences are from above or from below. Seek God in great ways, but always test when He appears to come to make sure that it really is Him.

Daniel Paul Rader

BIO: [1878-1938] *An influential evangelist in the Chicago area who was the first preacher in the United States to appear nationwide on the radio. From 1914-1921 he pastored the Moody Memorial Church, which had been founded by D. L. Moody.*

God blessed the Moody Church, and 1,800 people were converted in ten days. He cast out demons. He did business.

One night a fellow came down the aisle barking like a dog. "What do you do in a case like this?" I was asked. "Prayer," I answered. "It is the same old dose." That fellow began to praise the Lord. He is a chauffeur for a taxie company now. Every once in a while I hear a whistle, and he goes by with his hand up and a "Hallelujah" on his lips. He was bound by the devil and barked like a dog. He is now filled with the joy of Jesus and has a hallelujah on his lips, living for Jesus, and walking with Jesus. It is Himself that does it. (*At Thy Word-A Farewell Message, The Alliance Weekly, Vol. 54, No. 34, November 20, 1920*)

[Due to copyright laws the following testimonies marked with an * are summaries based upon the original accounts. For those interested in learning more about these individual cases reference information to where the original case can be found is included.]

John A. MacMillan*

BIO: [1873-1956] *A Canadian Presbyterian businessman who served as a missionary in China and the Philippines with The Christian and Missionary Alliance (C&MA).*

A young woman serving as a missionary in China was suddenly seized with an intense depression. The depression became so overpowering that her missionary supervisor contacted the field chairman requesting that she be removed from the station as she was causing harm to the ministry work there. She was then sent to the mission headquarters where much prayer was made for her with the result being that her depression *increased*. When

MacMillan was introduced to her he spoke strongly to her saying "Miss_____, you are doing wrong in keeping up this continued blueness of spirit; I want to tell you that all depression is of the devil."

This kind of treatment, direct and placing the blame for her depression upon herself was in stark contrast to the treatment she had been receiving in which she had been babied and coddled by the other missionaries at the headquarters. She expressed resentment at MacMillan's accusation that she was responsible for not lifting herself out of the depression but MacMillan knew that her resentment was a sign that he was getting through to her. He repeated his words, reminding her that the Lord commands all of His followers to rejoice in Him;[288] something that she was in direct disobedience of. He continued by explaining that her condition had come as a result of her giving in to the lies of the devil and that she must resist him. In a short time she was back at her station, better realizing the tricks of the devil and better prepared to throw them off. (*Encounter With Darkness, Ch 5*)

This event occurred in the early part of 1950. A thirty-five year old woman, in her early childhood, had been cared for by her grandmother, who was a devoted follower of Christian Science as well as being interested in a number of heterodox cults. As the granddaughter learned to read her grandmother used her to read to her literature from the various cultic groups that she was interested in.

The granddaughter was converted at nineteen but did not deeply pursue spiritual things for a number of years until she began to attend Bible school. It was there that she began to seriously follow the Lord and was baptized.

One day, while working in the school kitchen, she fell unconscious to the floor. After a second experience of this she was taken to the hospital room where she was visited by the school doctor. When he noticed that her behavior was somewhat violent he decided that it was in her best interest to commit her to the State Hospital. It was asked if John MacMillan could see her before her committal and this was agreed to.

---

[288] Ph 4:4

When MacMillan entered her room she was partly unconscious and he began to challenge the demonic presence inside of her who answered back from her lips in a direct "No." MacMillan then commanded the demon to give his name, to which he answered "Cults." As MacMillan continued with casting out the spirits, the first group that left her called themselves by well-known cult groups, which surprised some of those present. In all, several groups of demons were expelled, the number of them totaling 171. (*Encounter With Darkness, Ch 7*)

A young man of twenty-two years of age had been very desirous of receiving the gift of tongues. Despite having been warned of the serious danger of focusing on any gift, rather than on the Giver of spiritual gifts, he intensely continued to seek the gift of tongues. Finally, he received the gift and afterwards became so confident that his experience was from the Lord that he came to the conclusion that he had enough light to carry him forward without reading the Word of God—his personal revelation was enough. One day, while at John MacMillan's house he attempted to pray and fell unconscious. When his gift of tongues was tested it was revealed that there were demonic presences, one of whom stated that its name was "False Tongues." After a somewhat protracted struggle he was delivered from the demons and became free in spirit, mind and body. The effect of realizing that his gift of tongues was a counterfeit was a most bitter disappointment for him but after being set free he learned to abide in the Lord, and became useful as a helper for others.[289] (*Encounter With Darkness, Ch 7*)

---

[289] Undoubtedly, some readers will be offended by the inclusion of cases of demon possession occurring in connection with persons seeking the gift of tongues. There is a legitimate gift of tongues mentioned in the Scriptures (Mk 16:17, Ac 2:4), however, the testimony of history indicates that many persons who have sought this gift have received in its place a *counterfeit*. Many have sought this gift under the false impression that it was a gift which could be exercised in such a way as to build them up spiritually—*that it was a gift for personal edification*—based upon a misunderstanding of 1Corinthians 14:4. But nowhere in the Scriptures are persons directly encouraged to seek this gift and both 1Corinthians 12:7 and 1Peter 4:10-11 indicate that *all* spiritual gifts are to be used in such a way as to minister to *others*, not ourselves. This misunderstanding has surely opened a door for many cases of spiritual oppression. I am somewhat surprised that more Christians do not "test the spirits" when they receive what they believe to be the gift of tongues. Thousands (maybe millions) of Christians have sought this gift, received what they believed

Victor H. Ernest[*]

BIO: *A Baptist pastor who, before coming to Christ, was heavily involved in séances and spiritualism.*

One night Ernest attended a séance on the shore of Lake Bemidji, near a place known as Diamond Point. It was autumn and the night seemed ideal for an open-air séance.

With night birds calling, frogs and crickets sounding off in the background the medium place a metal trumpet[290] on the picnic table and very soon entered into a trance. The trumpet eerily levitated off of the table and floated out over the water of the lake, glistening in the moonlight of the twilight night. Periodically the trumpet would float back to the circle of eager spiritualists and finally settled near the hearers who were addressed by the control spirit.

Ernest found himself paying little attention to what the spirit said until his mother gasped out in shock, "But that is not what the Bible says." Ernest's mother did not know much about the Bible but she had a special love for what she did know and could not accept something that the spirit had said. Normally, this kind of behavior would have received a very strong lecture from the spirit but this time the trumpet floated on and the control spirit continued to talk as if nothing had happened.

Ernest often wished that he had asked his mother what the spirit had said to make her respond as she did but he never pursued it with her. As a younger man his mother had taught him about God's existence, creation and power but other than that he knew very little of the Bible. It was this incident which made him begin to wonder just what the Bible did teach, and he made up his mind to purchase a Bible.

Unable to find a Bible in any of his local stores he ended up ordering one from Montgomery Ward, thinking that because of its price it was not the full Bible. It was only later that he realized that he had purchased an entire copy of the King James Version.

---

to be this gift and never obeyed the Scriptural command to "believe not every spirit, but test the spirits to see whether they are of God... (1Jn 4:1)".

[290] A metal trumpet is an object used by spiritualists to communicate with the supposed departed spirits of humans. The spirits, really demons in disguise, supposedly speak through the trumpet.

He began by starting in Genesis but eventually became bored with the extensive genealogies of generations. Assuming that the Bible was like any other book he decided to turn to the end to see how it ended but the symbolism in Revelation seemed to be too much for him. Discouraged, he almost gave up reading the Bible but since he had invested money into it he was reluctant to let his investment lie idle, so he decided to examine the middle, shorter books of the New Testament.

1John was the first book that he read in its entirety and when he arrived at the fourth chapter and read "Beloved, believe not every spirit, but try the spirits…" he was amazed. After reading this he realized that this must mean that there are good spirits and bad spirits. Reading further he read "…whether they are of God: because many false prophets are gone out into the world. Hereby know ye the Spirit of God: every spirit that confesseth that Jesus Christ is come in the flesh is of God; and every spirit that confesseth not that Jesus Christ is come in the flesh is not of God; and this is the spirit of antichrist, whereof ye have heard that it should come; and even now is it in the world."[291]

Ernest came to the conclusion based on this that Jesus had come in the flesh to be a Savior and that if he did not believe this then he was wrong. He decided that at the next séance he attended that he would "try the spirits" although he was not exactly sure how to do this.

To Ernest's amazement at the next séance it was announced that this would be a question and answer séance and the spirit specified that the questions were to be of a spiritual nature. Each person would be allowed three questions. This had never happened at any séance he had attended before.

With fear and trembling he directed his first question to the control spirit asking if he believed that Jesus was the Son of God.

Smoothly, the control spirit answered, "Of course, my child, Jesus is the Son of God. Only believe as the Bible says."

Ernest had never heard a spirit affirm this before. He had often heard in séances that Jesus was a Judean reformer or a great medium, who was now an advanced spirit in one of the higher planes.

---

[291] 1Jn 4:1-3

Soon the trumpet was back at Ernest for his second question. "O thou great and infinite spirit," he asked, "do you believe that Jesus is the Savior of the world?"

Immediately the spirit answered back, "My child, why do you doubt? Why do you not believe? You have been this long with us; why do you continue to doubt?" This was followed by the spirit readily quoting Bible verses about believing.

Ernest, being unfamiliar with the Bible, was not sure if they were really quotes from the Bible but they sounded authentic to him.

As the trumpet returned for his third and final question he phrased his question, "O spirit, you believe that Jesus is the Son of God, that he is the Savior of the world-do you believe that Jesus died on the cross and shed his blood for the remission of sin?"

At this question the medium, who had been deep in a trance, was catapulted off of his chair and fell into the middle of the living room floor where he lay groaning as if in deep pain. The disordered sounds suggested that the spirits had become confused.

Everyone rushed forward to the medium to help him. The control spirit had previously instructed them with how to revive someone in an emergency and they massaged the pulse areas until he came back like a person who had fainted.

Ernest never went to another séance. He had tested the spirits and found that they were not of God. What he had thought was a great power of God, he now realized was only the counterfeit of what God had to offer. From that time he began to search the Scriptures to find the truth. (*I Talked With Spirits, Ch. 4*)

Alien "Abductions" Are Really Demonic Experiences

Carel Luck[*]

BIO: *A Christian wife and mother who experienced what today is referred to as an "alien abduction" encounter only to later realize that it was demonic.*

In 1973 Carel was living in Virginia with her husband and two children. One night she awoke in her bedroom to find herself paralyzed and unable to move anything except her eyes. To the left of the bedroom she could see three figures floating into the room out of the walk-in closet. Her first thought was "How did they get in there?" to which they mentally communicated to her that they had come in through a large, second story window and then floated through the wall into her closet. They then began to share that they were going to levitate her paralyzed body, ram it through the bedroom window and drop her to her death. And they wanted Carel to know that her husband was going to be blamed for the death!

Overwhelmed with terror Carel tried to scream to wake up her husband but was unable to do so—even her vocal cords were paralyzed! But then she began to pray. She tried to call out "JESUS" but nothing would come out. Once again she tried and finally she was able to say the name of "Jesus". At the name of Jesus the strange beings disappeared into the air. Her ability to move returned and she quickly woke up her husband and told him what happened.

Time passed on and over twenty years after this event Carel was given a book on alien abduction, a topic that she did not really know much about. While reading through the book it struck her at how similar the people's experiences were to hers. Then she saw a drawing in the book that one of the abductees had made of his alien abductors. They were the same beings that had come into her room in 1973.[292] (*The Terror That Comes In The Night*)

Similarities Between Alien And Demonic Encounters

	Demonic Encounter	Alien Encounter

---

[292] Joe Jordan is a UFO researcher who has collected over 100 testimonies of "alien abductions" being stopped when the abducted called out to Jesus. These testimonies can be read and listened to online at http://www.alienresistance.org/ce4testimonies.htm.

Abduction	YES	YES
Periods Of Unconsciousness	YES	YES
Appearing In The Form Of Humans	YES	YES
Communicating Mentally	YES	YES
Levitation	YES	YES
Going Into Trances	YES	YES
Endowing With Special Powers	YES	YES
Becoming A Channel Or Mouth-Piece For The Entity	YES	YES
Physical Suffering	YES	YES
Raping/Sexually Molesting	YES	YES
Accompanied By The Smell Of Sulfur	YES	YES
Appearing At Night In Their Bedroom	YES	YES
Submitting To The Name Of Jesus	YES	YES[293]

Kurt Koch*

BIO: [1913-1987] *A German Lutheran pastor who wrote, lectured and counseled extensively on spiritual warfare.*

While on a lecture tour of the Far East Kurt Koch had the opportunity to visit the Bible School of Febias in Manila, Philippines. While there, one of the students who was a professing Christian, went to see the school director. He complained that he was feeling sick and suffering from a terrible headache and wanted to know if the director could pray for him. As the director offered up prayer the student, whose name was Pat Tolosa, suddenly lost

---

[293] For historical sources demonstrating these similarities see my article entitled *Similarities Between UFO Encounters And Demonic Encounters* available online at http://www.danielrjennings.org/SimilaritiesBetweenUFOActivityAndDemonicActivity.html.

consciousness and began to rage in a fury. It took the concerted effort of several men to hold him down. By this time Koch and a few others had been called in to assist with the young man. As they stood there the young man began to speak with strange voices. One of the teachers addressed the voices saying, "In the name of the Lord Jesus, tell us why you have possessed Pat".

"*Because he did not surrender his life completely,*" was the answer.[294]

"How many are you?"

"*Fifty,*" they replied.

The adults continued to counsel the young man. Koch, directly challenging the demonic presences commanded, "In the name of the Lord I command you to come out of him".

"*No, we need somebody to live in,*" was the answer he received back.

"In the name of the Lord you have to go," Koch repeated.

The demons then replied, "*Then we will go into the children of Dr. Hufstetler.*" (Dr. Hufstetler was the director of the school.)

Dr. Hufstetler resisted them telling them directly "You cannot enter my children. Go instead to where Jesus sends you."

The group continued to command them to leave the young man and started singing the hymn 'There is power in the blood of the Lamb' to increase the strength of their prayers. Suddenly, the boy began to scream and his whole body convulsed. Then there was silence as he lay there unconscious. They began to pray again and as they did a new voice spoke from the boy's mouth.

"How many of you are left," Koch asked the voice.

"*Forty nine,*" it answered.

---

[294] This story should serve as a stern warning to any believer who refuses to make an entire consecration of every area of their life to the Lord. By entire consecration is meant two things. First, a turning from all known sin and secondly, approaching God and telling Him with all sincerity that you will go where He wants you to go, do what He wants you to do, and be what He wants you to be with the strength that He gives you. This is really the only way to be saved. Jesus said in Luke 9:23-24 "If any man will come after me, let him deny himself, and take up his cross daily, and follow me. For whoever will save his life shall lose it: but whosoever will lose his life for my sake, the same shall save it." It is one thing to believe in Jesus and all that He did but it takes more than that to be saved. A person must "lose their life" to Him and His will for their lives if they want to be saved. A refusal to surrender your life completely is nothing less than rebellion against God and it opens the door for you to become demon possessed.

By this time an hour had already passed and the group was unsure what would happen next.

In the midst of this counseling session a group of students and teachers had begun to pray and offer praise, in a separate place, for the situation. As the adults continued to command the demons to leave the young boy they found that no single person could endure confronting the demons for more than a short period of time as it was just too strenuous to do so.

At one point a teacher commanded the demons, "In the name of Jesus tell us your name."

The voice answered, "*Rahrek*".

"Where do you come from?"

"*From Manchuria.*"

"In the name of Jesus tell us why you have come to our school!"

"*You have a good school. We have come to bring in modernism and liberalism. You won't be able to stop us. They are our friends.*"

When Koch heard that the voice had come from Manchuria he recited a Russian Bible verse which he knew. Immediately the voice began to speak fluent Russian, despite the fact that the student only knew English and his own Filipino dialect.

The demons were again commanded to leave the young man in the name of the Lord which resulted in the student shrieking and convulsing which was followed by him becoming quiet for a short time.

"How many of you are there now," the adults asked.

"*Forty eight*," it was answered.

At one point one of the demons stated, "*We have come to destroy Pat*" and he immediately began to choke himself. Several men who were present forcibly restrained him. The young man's strength was enormous. At times it took up to nine men to restrain him.

As the deliverance session continued other voices spoke out. One claimed to be from Holland and to have come from an occult group there. Every voice seemed dominated by a fear of the name and the coming of the Lord Jesus Christ.

In the end Pat was freed from his demonic oppression. He regained consciousness after the last demon left and began to cry and then to praise the Lord. The whole session had lasted from 8

196

o'clock Friday morning until 3:30 the following Saturday morning, a total of nineteen and a half hours. (*Demonology Past And Present, Ch. 6*)

Benedict Of Nursia Casting A Demon Out Of A Man

Ray Comfort*

BIO: [b.1949] *Founder of Living Waters Publications and a well-known speaker whose ministry has focused on educating*

197

One day Ray was in the town square and two young women approached him. Neither of them were Christians and they seemed a bit embarrassed. They asked Ray if they could talk to him about something and with a certain amount of hesitation shared with him that they had a question about demons. Ray replied "You don't need to be embarrassed. I believe in demons. I'm a Christian. I understand what you're talking about" and arranged for them to meet with him at his office the following day.

When the young ladies came one of them expressed that she hated her parents and as Ray spent time with them it became obvious to him that there was a demonic problem with this girl and he began to pray for her.

Ray left the room and then one of the girls came running out saying, "Hey! Hey my friend's gone into one of those blackouts. She's fallen on the floor."[295] As Ray returned he found her groveling and making all kinds of noises and it was clear that it was a demonic manifestation. Ray then approached her and offered prayer for her. Some other Christians began to pray for her and as they were doing so Ray noticed a little medallion around her neck that looked like it was in the shape of a fairy or something like that. Ray shared with her, "I don't know what that is but to me it looks kind of like a goddess of fertility and if I were you I'd get rid of that thing and become a committed Christian."

Two weeks later Ray received a phone call from her. She had not become a committed Christian and was still suffering from the blackouts and wanted to know if she could meet with Ray again. Ray told her to come back and see him again.

After arriving she was coming up the stairs and went into a blackout state. She was kind of leaning against the wall and as Ray went down the stairs to help her up she suddenly flung herself out of his arms and ran over and tried to throw herself off of a balcony.[296] Ray grabbed her legs in time to stop her and two other Christians were able to restrain her and help get her into his office.

As they prayed for her Ray noticed that her fist was tightly clenched—so tight that it had cut off all of the blood from going to it. She was holding it there right next to her neck. As she sat there

---

[295] Note that demons can cause people to fall out.
[296] Compare Mark 9:22.

in this blackout state, clutching something, Ray prized open her hand and realized that it was the little fairy medallion. He pulled it out of her hand and went across to the other side of the room. The young woman's eyes were closed, she was in the corner and two Christians were standing in front of her. Ray had his back towards her so there was no way that she could see what he was doing. He took the medallion, placed it on a table and got a hammer. As he hit the medallion, every time that he struck it, the girl screamed out. He struck it five times and five times she screamed out.[297] (*Hell's Best Kept Secret sermon series, Sermon 11: The Occult*)

My Own Observations

I thought it would be good to close by looking at some of the things I have observed which I believe to be examples of demonic activity in the world today. While my experiences will not be as dramatic as some of the ones I have shared, I feel that they will have practical applications.

Case #1

Mary[298] was raised in a liberal Protestant church and was about forty years of age when I first met her. I met her at an interdenominational service that held worship and teaching on Thursday nights. Mary herself suffered from several health

---

[297] Seemingly harmless trinkets that are in some way associated with false religions can be an open door to bringing demonic activity into one's life. In the Old Testament God commanded the Israelites that as they conquered the Promised Land they must "destroy their altars, break their images, and cut down their [worship] groves...destroy all their pictures, and destroy all their molten images, and quite pluck down all their high places...destroy their altars, and break down their images, and cut down their groves, and burn their graven images with fire... (Ex 34:13, Nu 33:52, Dt 7:5)." It is dangerous to play with items from the occult. God's warning that "The graven images of their gods you shall burn with fire: you shall not desire the silver or gold that is on them, nor take it unto yourselves, lest you be snared therein: for it is an abomination to the LORD your God. Neither shall you bring an abomination into your house, lest you be a cursed thing like it: but you shall utterly detest it, and you shall utterly abhor it; for it is a cursed thing (Dt 7:25-26)" is a warning that all need to remember. No Christian should have anything, whether it is toys, movies, games, trinkets, etc., that have anything to do with the promotion of the occult in their homes.

[298] To protect the identity of the woman in my first case I have changed her name.

problems, one of which caused her to have extremely swollen hands and feet. She had a full time job as I recall but also worked at a Christian bookstore part time. The first time I met her she was talking to me after one of the services about wanting to commit suicide and she was rocking back and forth as she sat in such a way that I could only be impressed that there was something demonic in her.

On one occasion Mary was spending the day with myself and a friend. We had picked Mary up and taken her to an apartment that I was house-sitting for the owner. While there we began to pray for Mary but she became extremely upset and ran into the bathroom, closing herself inside. At one point she threatened to just leave if we did not stop praying (which would have put her at a disadvantage because she had rode with us and was at a considerable distance from her home and car). Finally, she said that if we did not stop praying that she was going to call the police and tell them that we had tried to rape her! Eventually she calmed down. She told us that as we were praying it felt as if her body was being pricked with needles.

Several months after this incident myself and some others decided that we needed to have a full intervention prayer meeting to pray with Mary for her deliverance. We picked a date to have the deliverance session and Mary agreed to attend. However, before the meeting Mary became extremely ill and had to be admitted to the hospital. She was not released until after the intended date of the prayer meeting had passed. After this no future date was set but individuals continued to pray for and with Mary.

As time went on, it seemed that Mary was slowly getting better. She became involved in a more conservative church and herself seemed to grow more focused on Jesus. As I watched this change in her, I came to the conclusion that she had been possessed by multiple demons and that as prayers were made for and with her she was gradually being freed from these demons.

I eventually ended up moving from the city and, at the time, I do not believe that Mary was completely delivered from her demons but she was certainly better. I share this to encourage people that sometimes, as noted in section three, deliverance may take time and that one should not give up if results do not occur immediately. Rather than becoming frustrated, our own limitations in dealing with demonic forces should spur us on to seek a greater degree of God's power in our lives (Mk 9:28-29).

Case #2

Our second case begins in the summer of 2002 with the little congregation of *Southside Church of the Nazarene*. Southside was a small church affiliated with the Nazarene denomination. At its peak it had counted 150-200 members but in recent years it had dwindled down to about thirty-five. I am not sure exactly when Satan found an open door into this congregation but things began to flare up around June when the church fired their district appointed pastor (something that neither their denomination nor the Scriptures allow a congregation to do[299]). Instead of leaving he continued to show up on Sunday mornings to preach even though they had stopped paying him a salary. In August the district unexpectedly showed up on a Sunday morning and informed the congregation that this would be their last service and that *Southside* would be closing. The following day the district changed the locks on the building, effectively shutting down the church. When the members, some of whom had attended there for over fifty years, went to check the church's bank account they realized that the district had asked the bank to put a hold on the account because the money was involved in a dispute. When the church members protested over the seizure of their church building and bank account, an amount equaling some $64,000, the district pointed out that according to the denomination's manual when a church closes the district is entitled to all of the property. *Southside Church* members asked the district to allow the Nazarene headquarters in Kansas City, Missouri, to settle the arguments over the money but the district refused. The bank with whom the funds were deposited then filed a lawsuit asking the secular courts to decide who the rightful owner was. *Southside Church* filed a motion asking the courts to allow the denomination's headquarters to settle the matter. The district also filed a motion with the courts, claiming ownership of the money. After review by a judge it was decided that the issue should be relegated to the State Supreme Court where the courts decided in favor of the district over *Southside Church*.

---

[299] He 13:17, 1Ti 5:17, 1Th 5:12-13

For some time the building sat vacant, under the control of the district, until it was decided to reopen it as a mission church in an attempt to reach out to the local immigrant community. An ordained Nazarene was installed as the pastor and the church was renamed in the language of the local immigrant community as *The Good Shepherd Church Of The Nazarene*. Under his leadership a new congregation grew and appeared to be heading towards becoming a healthy and thriving church. The pastor, his wife and three children moved into the church, turning one area into an apartment. At one point the pastor made an agreement with another pastor to allow his congregation to hold services in the basement of the church in a small chapel area.

Things seemed to be going well, although there was something admittedly creepy about the church building. It was an older building and older buildings have a tendency to be creepy but for those attending things began to go beyond just *feeling creepy* to actually *becoming creepy*.

One day, the pastor's wife had come to the church for something and when she was in the basement she kept hearing the voices of children down the basement hallway. Every time she tried to follow the voices they seemed to be moving away from her and she could never find the source of the voices. The pastor himself stated that he felt uncomfortable going down into the basement and when a friend of his came to visit he expressed that he felt that there were demons in the church.

Eventually the pastor and his family moved out and three brothers moved into the church. One day the brothers very excitedly came to the pastor, telling him that they had seen a ghostly man dressed in all white inside of the church. They were convinced that it was an angel but the pastor and his wife had their reservations. On another occasion one of the brothers experienced hearing a mumbling in his ear, as if someone was speaking to him although he couldn't understand what was being said.

The church itself also began to experience strange behavior on the part of its members. Whereas the church at one point had been thriving and growing many members decided to leave for no apparent reason. When asked why they left they expressed that they felt hurt and didn't want to come back anymore, yet the pastor could not understand why they felt hurt. The other pastor's congregation, who had been holding services downstairs, also experienced a strangely similar phenomenon. His membership dwindled down until he finally decided that there was no point in even having services anymore and he closed his church and started attending *The Good Shepherd's* services.

It was around this time that I started attending *The Good Shepherd*. By the time I started attending the church that was meeting in the basement had closed and *The Good Shepherd* had dwindled down to about eight adults and a few children.

When the pastor learned that I had graduated from Bible College he immediately gave me the right hand of fellowship and asked me to come and help him with the ministry of the church. At the time I was serving in the Air Force but I readily joined in as best I could to help them out. My initial impression was that they were just a struggling congregation that needed some encouragement and that with prayer, fasting and hard work God would help us to get on track.

With the pastor's approval I began to develop an evangelism program that would guide the church in how to pray and go out into the community to try and reach new people.

Admittedly, there was a creepiness to the church, especially the basement. It was dark and old and I remember there being all of this old medical equipment (a wheelchair, crutches, etc.) that seemed to give it an even creepier feeling. Once, while exploring in the basement I found a room with a pool table and entering into the room to inspect it my attention was drawn up high to a vent duct that ran across the ceiling where in very large letters (several feet wide) the word "Hello" had been written. The writing was sloppy (which added to its creepiness), and looked as if a child had written it. It was so high, that no child could have reached it and anyone who could have done it would have had to have stood on a chair or a table to reach that high. I found this to be so strange that I came back another time with my camera to take a picture of it but when I went to turn on the light in the basement to go downstairs the light wouldn't come on.

Behind the church was a smaller building that had been built to hold dinners and other fellowship activities. It was basically just a large room with a kitchen area. One morning the pastor's wife came to prepare this building for an activity that was planned and discovered that a homeless woman had been living in there. Without asking for the pastor's permission one of the three brothers who lived there had allowed this woman to sleep in the fellowship building. When the pastor's wife found her the woman was very emotional exclaiming that there were "ghosts" in the church.

Soon after starting the evangelism campaign I was required by the Air Force to go to Saudi Arabia for four months. The pastor and myself had spent quite a bit of time thinking, talking and praying about getting the church back on its feet so this was a great disappointment to both of us that I would have to leave for several months.

Up until this point I really had not made a connection between the things that were going on in the church and the possibility of there being an actual demonic presence that had taken up residence in the building. Prior to leaving for Saudi Arabia I had not been told anything about any of the supernatural occurrences that had occurred nor did I know of any of the troubles that the first church (Southside Church) had experienced in their battle with the district.

By the time I came back from Saudi Arabia things in the church had gotten worse. The praise team leader, a young woman who had lived with the pastor and was going to school to go into full time ministry, had started dating an unbeliever, left the church, turned against the pastor and his wife and would have nothing to do with them. After my return the pastor and his wife began to share the supernatural things that had happened with me. I also did research on the first congregation that had met in the building and I realized that of the three churches that had met in the building (*Southside*, *The Good Shepherd*, and the downstairs congregation) all of them had went through a similar pattern in that they all ended up dwindling down. Two had closed and I knew that if something was not done soon *The Good Shepherd* was fast heading in the same direction.

Much to my discouragement, while I was overseas the pastor had decided to try and find another church to minister in. There had not been the kind of support from the district that he had hoped for and it seemed to him that the best thing was to just uproot and start anew somewhere else.

On a Wednesday night I shared the research that I had done and how that I felt that the church was under a real spiritual attack and that if we did not face the demonic presence attacking the church that it would close like the other two had. It was decided that a special series of prayer meetings would be scheduled during a future week. I had to miss the first meeting but told the pastor that I would be there the next day. However, when I showed up there was no one at the church and the front doors were locked. When I asked the pastor what had happened he said that he had forgotten I was coming and decided to cancel the meeting, which at the time struck me as rather odd.

At a Wednesday night service around this time the service was interrupted by a smoke alarm going off. When the pastor went to investigate he said that he smelled brimstone but could not locate any source for it. He appeared to be shaken up by this experience but he continued with his message.

At one point the pastor explained how we felt to the District Superintendent but he didn't seem to take the idea that the church could be under demonic attack very seriously and just encouraged him that pastoring would have its challenges.

The pastor eventually found an opportunity to move to another city to work with a Nazarene church there. A date was set for his last service, which was strangely decided to be held in the basement chapel rather than the main sanctuary. (Why this was, I was never told but I thought it was strange.) During this service a man dressed like a hippie, whom we had never met before, showed up for church. He smelled like cigarette smoke and said that he was going up north for an intercessory prayer meeting. During the meeting he kept leaving the chapel room, disrupting the service and he made strange noises muttering something during the meeting. A car alarm also noticeably went off causing another disruption to the service. To our surprise the District Superintendent announced that this would be the last service for *The Good Shepherd* and that everyone was encouraged to start attending another Nazarene church on the other side of town.

Now I would encourage everyone reading this to be careful not to be too superstitious. Old buildings have a tendency to be creepy by themselves (with or without demons). Perhaps the mysterious "HELLO" written on the vent duct was some teenager's idea of a practical joke, and the light not working when I came to take a picture was just a burned out bulb. The car alarm may have just been that—a car alarm (which have a tendency to go off at inconvenient times). But the pastor's wife hearing the mysterious voices of children in the basement, the individual who heard an unintelligible mumbling in his ear, the mysterious man in white seen moving through the church, the homeless woman who claimed that there were "ghosts" in the church, the unexplainable smell of brimstone that set off the smoke alarm, the mysterious behavior of the praise team leader and the many members who had left the church for no apparent reason, well, for these I just don't have an answer.

Readers may feel puzzled, wondering how a demonic entity gained access to a church. The Bible indicates that "the devil...walks about, seeking whom he may devour (1Pe 5:8)" and that sin is an open door to the devil (2Co 2:10-11). As an outsider I can see many things that were done by *Southside* which opened the doors for an experience of demonic discipline against them similar to what King Saul experienced (1Sa 16:14). In my research I discovered that the *Southside Church* not only had a problem with their last pastor but were reported as having had a succession of pastors that they had conflicts with. This, I fear, is indicative of an attitude of disrespect towards the office and God-appointed authority of the pastor. Beyond this there is the potential issue of ignoring both Paul's command against going to court with a fellow believer (1Co 6:1-7) and Jesus' command that if someone tries to take something from you, you let them have it rather than fight for it (Mt 5:38-42, Lk 6:29-30). And on top of all of this, both sides seemed to have had very little concern over the effect that their behavior would have on their testimonies. It was as if the reputation of Jesus (for whom they were both ambassadors) was less important than who would get the building and money in the bank account. It is no surprise to me, that with such carnality and backsliddenness, that the Devil was given authority over the building that was at the center of their fight.

As far as I am aware no church ever met in the Southside building again after *The Good Shepherd* closed down. Today a business sits on the spot where God's truths were once proclaimed, silenced by the sinfulness of people who gave a foothold to the Devil (Ep 4:27). Incidentally, things did not fare too well for the pastor of *The Good Shepherd* after he left. After taking another church in a different city, he just became overwhelmed with problems in the church, even being wrongfully accused of stealing from the offering and stepped down from his new pastorate. Only

God knows why this happened to him but perhaps there is a lesson to be learned in that. One can run from the Devil but running is no guarantee that he will not follow you. Sometimes it is best to just plant your feet in the ground and fight.

Conclusion

And so closes our 2000 year investigation into whether Jesus' promise that his followers would exercise power over the demons is true or not. To sum up what we have discovered we note that:

- ➢ When Jesus was on earth he exercised power over all demonic forces
- ➢ He promised his followers that they too would experience this same power
- ➢ In the parts of the world where his followers became prominent the activity of these demons diminished, to the point that many in those parts eventually began to doubt whether it ever had (or still did) occur
- ➢ When his followers expanded into new territories for missions work they found these demons still operating
- ➢ As they were faced with this new challenge to ministry, many of these missionaries accepted Jesus' promise of authority over unclean spirits at face value and began to exercise the same authority over them that the early Christians had

In a court of law one reliable witness can be enough to determine whether a defendant's claims are true or false. I have provided here dozens of witnesses, all defending the claims that Jesus made. We noted at the beginning that the spiritual world is an *invisible* one and many people are of the opinion that unless I can see it, I will not believe it. As I have looked throughout history *I have seen it* and I trust that the stories included here will not only strengthen the faith of those who already believe but also encourage those who are doubtful to reconsider whether there really is an invisible spiritual world that, though not normally seen, is regularly involved in the affairs of men.

> "We have not seen or heard of such things in England, and are accustomed to suppose that they are entirely phenomena of the past. But it is well to regard the subject with an open mind, for there exists abundant proof that…the power of evil spirits is just as great in these days as in the time of Christ." *–Geraldine Taylor*

Works Cited

Anonymous. *The Life And Works Of Our Holy Father, St. Daniel The Stylite.* Original rendition.

Arnobius. *Seven Books Against The Heathen.* In *Ante-Nicene Fathers, Vol. 6* (Albany, OR: Ages Software, 1997)

Athanasius of Alexandria. *On The Incarnation Of The Word.* In *A Select Library of the Nicene and Post-Nicene Fathers of the Christian Church, Series II, Volume 4* (Edinburgh: T& T Clark, 1891)

Athanasius of Alexandria. *Life Of Antony.* In *A Select Library of the Nicene and Post-Nicene Fathers of the Christian Church, Series II, Volume 4* (Edinburgh: T & T Clark, 1891)

Baxter, Robert. *Narrative Of Facts Characterizing The Supernatural Manifestations In Members Of Mr. Irving's Congregation, And Other Individuals, In England And Scotland, Formerly In The Writer Himself* (London: James Nisbet, 1833)

Brainerd, David; Edwards, Jonathan; & Dwight, Sereno Edwards. *Memoirs of the Rev. David Brainerd; Missionary to the Indians on the Borders of New-York, New-Jersey, and Pennsylvania: Chiefly Taken From His Own Diary* (New Haven, CT: S. Converse, 1822)

Browning, Robert. *Rabbi Ben Ezra* (Portland, ME: Thomas B. Mosher, 1909)

Caesar of Heisterbach. *Distinctio.* Cited in English in *Translations and Reprints from the Original Sources of European History, Series 1, Vol. 2* (Philadelphia, PA: University of Pennsylvania Press, n.d.)

Comfort, Ray. *Hell's Best Kept Secret sermon series, Sermon 11: The Occult* (Bellflower, CA: Living Waters Publications)

Cornelius I. *Letter To Fabius of Antioch.* In Eusebius of Caesarea's *Ecclesiastical History.* Itself printed in *A Select Library of the Nicene and Post-Nicene Fathers of the Christian Church, Series II, Volume 1* (Edinburgh: T & T Clark, 1890)

Clarke, Adam. *Memoirs Of The Wesley Family* (New York: Carlton and Porter: n.d.)

Clarke, J.B.B. *An Account of the Infancy, Religious and Literary Life of Adam Clarke* (London: T. S. Clarke, 1833)

Cyprian of Carthage. *An Address To Demetrianus.* In *Ante-Nicene Fathers, Vol. 5* (Albany, OR: Ages Software, 1997)

Cyprian of Carthage. *On The Lapsed.* In *Ante-Nicene Fathers, Vol. 5* (Albany, OR: Ages Software, 1997)

Cyril of Jerusalem. *Catechetical Lecture.* In *A Select Library of the Nicene and Post-Nicene Fathers of the Christian Church, Series II, Volume 7* (Albany, OR: Ages Software, 1997)

Dionysius of Alexandria. *Epistle 11: To Hermammon.* In *Ante-Nicene Fathers, Vol. 6* (Buffalo, NY: The Christian Literature Publishing Company, 1886)

Drake, Samuel. *The Witchcraft Delusion In New England: Its Rise, Progress, And Termination, Vol. 3* (Roxbury, MA: W. Elliot Woodward, 1866)

Drake, Samuel. *The New England Historical and Genealogical Register, Vol. 12.* (Boston, MA: Samuel G. Drake, 1858)

Easterbrook, Joseph. *An Appeal To The Public Respecting George Lukins (Called the Yatton Demoniac,) Containing An Account Of His Affliction And Deliverance; Together With A Variety Of Circumstances Which Tend To Exculpate Him From The Charge Of Imposture* (T. Mills, 1788)

Ernest, Victor. *I Talked With Spirits* (Tyndale House Publishers, 1970)

Eusebius of Caesarea. *Ecclesiastical History.* In *A Select Library of the Nicene and Post-Nicene Fathers of the Christian Church, Series II, Volume 1* (Edinburgh: T & T Clark, 1890)

Eusebius of Caesarea. *Oration In Praise Of Constantine.* In *A Select Library of the Nicene and Post-Nicene Fathers of the Christian Church, Series II, Volume 1* (Edinburgh: T & T Clark, 1890)

Eusebius of Caesarea. *Life of Constantine.* In *A Select Library of the Nicene and Post-Nicene Fathers of the Christian Church, Series II, Volume 1* (Edinburgh: T & T Clark, 1890)

Fielde, Adele. *Pagoda Shadows: Studies From Life In China* (Boston, MA: W. G. Corthell, 1884)

Finney, Charles G. *Charles G. Finney, An Autobiography* (Albany, OR: Ages Software, 1997)

Firmilian. *Letter 74* in *The Epistles Of Cyprian.* In *Ante-Nicene Fathers, Vol. 5* (Albany, OR: Ages Software, 1997)

Foster, H. J. *Bristol Methodist Collectanea.* In *Proceedings Of The Wesley Historical Society, Vol 2, Part 2* (The Wesley Historical Society, 1899)

Guinness (née Taylor), Geraldine. *In The Far East: Letters From Geraldine Guinness. From The Mediterranean To The Po-Yang Lake, China, 1888-1889 And Most Recent Experiences* (London: Morgan & Scott, 1901)

Gregory of Nyssa. *The Great Catechism.* In *A Select Library of the Nicene and Post-Nicene Fathers of the Christian Church, Series II, Volume 4* (Edinburgh: T & T Clark, 1892)

Gregory the Great. *Dialogues* (London: Philip Lee Warner, 1911)

Hippolytus of Rome. *Apostolic Tradition.* Original rendition.

Holy Bible, *King James Version*

Holy Bible, *New American Standard Bible* (La Habra, CA: The Lockman Foundation, 1995)

Holy Bible, *World English Bible* (http://worldenglishbible.org/)

Irenaeus of Lyons. *Against Heresies.* In *Ante-Nicene Fathers* (Buffalo, NY: The Christian Literature Publishing Company, 1885)

Irenaeus of Lyons. *Proof Of The Apostolic Preaching.* J. Armitage Robinson, tr. (London: Society For Promoting Christian Knowledge, 1920)

Irving, Edward. *The Orthodox and Catholic Doctrine of Our Lord's Human Nature* (London: Baldwin & Cradock, 1830)

Jerome. *Life of Saint Hilarion.* In *A Select Library of the Nicene and Post-Nicene Fathers of the Christian Church, Series II, Volume 6* (Edinburgh: T & T Clark, 1892)

Jennings, Daniel R. *Similarities Between UFO Encounters And Demonic Encounters.* Available online at http://www.danielrjennings.org/SimilaritiesBetweenUFOActivityAndD

emonicActivity.html, accessed January 20, 2015

Jennings, Daniel R. *The Supernatural Occurrences Of John Wesley* (SEAN Multimedia: Oklahoma City, OK, 2005)

Jonas of Bobbio. *The Life Of St. Columban* (Philadelphia, PA: Department Of History Of The University Of Pennsylvania, 1895)

Jordan, Joe, ed. *Testimonies.* Available online at http://www.alienresistance.org/ce4testimonies.htm, accessed January 20, 2015

Justin Martyr. *Dialogue With Trypho.* In *Ante-Nicene Fathers* (Buffalo, NY: The Christian Literature Publishing Company, 1885)

Justin Martyr. *Second Apology.* In *Ante-Nicene Fathers* (Buffalo, NY: The Christian Literature Publishing Company, 1885)

Koch, Kurt. *Demonology Past And Present: Identifying And Overcoming Demonic Strongholds* (Grand Rapids, MI: Kregel, 1973)

Lactantius. *The Divine Institutes.* In *Ante-Nicene Fathers, Vol. 7* (Albany, OR: Ages Software, 1997)

Lactantius. *The Epitome Of The Divine Institutes.* In *Ante-Nicene Fathers, Vol. 7* (Albany, OR: Ages Software, 1997)

Lactantius. *Of The Manner In Which The Persecutors Died.* In *Ante-Nicene Fathers, Vol. 7* (Albany, OR: Ages Software, 1997)

Lancelot, Brenton. *The Septuagint Version Of The Old Testament, According To The Vatican Text* (London: Samuel Bagster & Sons, 1844)

Luck, Carel. *The Terror That Comes In The Night.* Available online at http://www.alienresistance.org/17-stop-terror-by-night-alien-abduction/, accessed January 21, 2015

Luther, Martin. *Letter To Katie, from Weimar, July 2, 1540.* In Jaroslav Pelikan's *Luther's Works, Vol. 50: Letters III* (Philadelphia, PA: Fortress Press, 1999)

Luther, Martin. *The Table Talk Of Martin Luther.* William Hazlitt, tr. (London: H. G. Bohn, 1857)

Lyon, James. *Casting Out Demons In India.* In *The Gospel In All Lands* (New York, NY: Methodist Episcopal Church, 1901)

MacMillan, John A. *Encounter With Darkness* (Christian Publications, Inc., 1980)

Mason, Francis. *The Story Of A Working Man's Life: With Sketches Of Travel In Europe, Asia, Africa, And America, As Related By Himself* (New York, NY: Oakley, Mason & Co., 1870)

Mather, Cotton. *Wonders Of The Invisible World* (Boston, MA: Benjamin Harris, 1693)

Mather, Increase. *Cases Of Conscience Concerning Evil Spirits Personating Men* (Boston, MA: Benjamin Harris, 1693)

Mather, Increase. *Remarkable Providences Illustrative Of The Earlier Days Of American Colonisation.* (London: Reeves & Turner, 1890)

Meyer, F. B. *Demon Possession In Russia* in W. B. Godbey's *Demonology* (St. Louis, MO: Pickett Publishing Company, 1902)

Minucius Felix. *The Octavius of Minucius Felix.* In *Ante-Nicene Fathers, Vol. 4* (Albany, OR: Ages Software, 1997)

211

Nevius, John L. *Demon Possession And Allied Themes* (Chicago, IL: Fleming H. Revell, 1896)

Origen. *Against Celsus*. In *Ante-Nicene Fathers, Vol. 4* (Albany, OR: Ages Software, 1997)

Origen. *First Principles*. In *Ante-Nicene Fathers, Vol. 4* (Albany, OR: Ages Software, 1997)

Origen. *Commentary On The Gospel Of Matthew*. In *Ante-Nicene Fathers, Vol. 10* (Albany, OR: Ages Software, 1997)

Palladius. *The Lausiac History Of Palladius*. Clarke, W. K. Lowther, tr. (London: Society For Promoting Christian Knowledge, 1918)

Rader, Daniel Paul. *At Thy Word-A Farewell Message*. In *The Alliance Weekly, Vol. 54, No. 34, November 20, 1920*

Seitz, Herr. *The Working Of Evil Spirits In Christian Gatherings*. Appendix in Jessie Penn-Lewis' *War On The Saints, A Text Book On The Work Of Deceiving Spirits Among The Children Of God, And The Way Of Deliverance* (Overcomer Book Room, 1912)

Sozomen, Hermias. *Church History*. In *A Select Library of the Nicene and Post-Nicene Fathers of the Christian Church, Series II, Volume 2* (Albany, OR: Ages Software, 1997)

Stuart, Warren Robert. *A Chinese Demon-Possessed Woman Becoming A Bible-Woman*. Originally published in *Christian Herald and Signs of the Times, August 4, 1880*. Cited in this work from John L. Nevius' *Demon Possession And Allied Themes* (Chicago, IL: Fleming H. Revell, 1896)

Sulpitus Severus. *On The Life of Saint Martin*. In *A Select Library of the Nicene and Post-Nicene Fathers of the Christian Church, Series II, Volume 11* (New York: The Christian Literature Company, 1894)

Taylor, Geraldine. *Pastor Hsi of North China: One Of China's Christians* (New York: Fleming H. Revell Company, 1906)

Tertullian. *The Shows*. In *Ante-Nicene Fathers, Vol. 3* (Albany, OR: Ages Software, 1997)

Tertullian. *Apology*. In *Ante-Nicene Fathers, Vol. 3* (Albany, OR: Ages Software, 1997)

Tertullian. *To Scapula*. In *Ante-Nicene Fathers, Vol. 3* (Albany, OR: Ages Software, 1997)

Tertullian. *A Treatise On The Soul*. In *Ante-Nicene Fathers, Vol. 3* (Albany, OR: Ages Software, 1997)

Theophilus of Antioch. *The Apology of Theophilus to Autolycus*. In *Ante-Nicene Fathers* (Buffalo, NY: The Christian Literature Publishing Company, 1885)

Wesley, Charles & Jackson, Thomas. *The Journal Of The Rev. Charles Wesley* (London: John Mason, 1849)

Wesley, John. *Journal of John Wesley* in *The Complete Works of John Wesley, Vol. 1* (Albany, OR: Ages Software, 1997)

Wesley, John. *Journal of John Wesley* in *The Complete Works of John Wesley, Vol. 2* (Albany, OR: Ages Software, 1997)

Wesley, John. *An Account Of The Disturbances In My Father's House*. In *The Works Of The Rev. John Wesley, Vol. 13* (London: Wesleyan Conference Office, 1872)

Wesley, Samuel. *Journal Of Samuel Wesley.* Excerpted in Adam Clarke's *Memoirs Of The Wesley Family* (New York: Carlton and Porter: n.d.)

Wilson-Carmichael, Amy. *From Sunrise Land: Letters From Japan* (London: Marshall Brothers, 1895)